In Defence of Populism

In Defence of Populism

FRANK FUREDI

polity

First published in 2026 by Polity Press Ltd.

Polity Press Ltd.
65 Bridge Street
Cambridge CB2 1UR, UK

Polity Press Ltd.
111 River Street
Hoboken, NJ 07030, USA

ISBN-13: 978-1-5095-7167-3

A catalogue record for this book is available from the British Library.

Library of Congress Control Number: 2025947922

Typeset in 11 on 14pt Warnock Pro
by Cheshire Typesetting Ltd, Cuddington, Cheshire
Printed and bound in Great Britain by CPI Group (UK) Ltd, Croydon

For further information on Polity, visit our website:
politybooks.com

Contents

Preface

The idea for this book first began to take shape in February 2024. This was a moment when hundreds of thousands of European farmers launched a protest movement against the attack on their way of life by the technocrats running the European Union. As the Director of a Brussels-based think tank – MCC Brussels – I did what I could to support the movement that erupted in Belgium, France, the Netherlands and Germany.

As I watched their tractors roar into the centre of Brussels, I shared the sense of exhilaration of the protestors who felt that for once their voice was being heard. Tom, a Flemish farmer who drove his tractor to Brussels to protest against the harsh environmental laws that the European Union bureaucracy imposed on his community, told me that the media tried to scare off the public from supporting his cause by calling his movement far right and populist. He was livid. Having been told that he had to cut down the number of livestock he had on his land, he knew that it was only a matter of time before he would have to close down his farm.[1]

Our conversation ended when he smiled and said, 'They call me a populist, fine I'll take that!'.

As soon as Tom said 'I'll take that', I was struck by the defiant countercultural tone of his voice. These days the word populist carries so much negative baggage that you struggle to come across individuals who are prepared to publicly identify themselves as populist. And yet here was someone who enthusiastically embraced a designation that the media used as a term of condemnation.

Tom has never been interested in politics, but like hundreds of thousands of people living in rural Europe, he decided that he wanted his voice to be heard. He was not alone. During the months of 2024, populism demonstrated that it possessed a formidable staying power. Within the nation states of the European Union, the populist parties rattled the political establishment to the point that it is now on the defensive. In the United States, it was not old-fashioned party politics nor the old worn-out Republican establishment that bore responsibility for the victory of Donald Trump but the MAGA movement. Movements that are labelled as populist are visible throughout Europe and by all accounts they are growing from strength to strength. Yet, paradoxically, almost none of these parties or their political leaders refer to themselves as populist.

Populism is surrounded by ceaseless hostility and mystification. Just about everything you are likely to read about populism in the specialist academic literature is motivated by their authors' animosity and contempt. Their sentiments are reproduced in an intensely polemical form by the mainstream media that habitually dismisses populists as far right and even fascists. According to the dominant media narrative, populists are racist xenophobes, homophobes and a variety of other phobes. At times the media hysteria regarding the so-called populist threat echoes the Red Scare of the 1920s and 1950s in the United States.

After my conversation with Tom, I concluded that it was time that the moral panic against populism was demystified and challenged. I was already engaged in a study of the cultural

drivers of twenty-first-century populism and had concluded
that most publications dealing with this topic were simply
not concerned to understand what made this movement tick.
They appeared to be far more interested in pathologizing populism than in serious scholarly exploration. Though there is a
veritable industry of so-called populism experts, their publications reflect a disposition – even an ideological commitment
– towards demonizing this movement.

The term populist is applied to a bewildering variety of
movements that have very little in common. Former Brazilian
President Jair Bolsonaro was regularly characterized as a populist as is his bitter opponent, Lula (Luiz Inácio Lula da Silva),
who replaced him as the leader of Brazil in the election of
2023. That the right-wing conservative Bolsonaro and the
leftish socialist Lula can be ascribed the same political label
speaks to a confusing use of the term populist. The Turkish
President, Recep Tayyip Erdoğan, the Prime Minister of India,
Shri Narendra Modi and Viktor Orbán the Prime Minister of
Hungary are all referred to as populists even though Erdoğan
presents himself as a Turkish Islamist, Modi speaks the language of Hindu nationalism and Orbán claims that his regime
is committed to Christian democratic and bourgeois values.

At present, populism often works as an unhelpful umbrella
term that is used to describe movements displaying an orientation towards activism and to parties that diverge from the
centrist mainstream legacy political institutions. Even governmental policies that seek public popularity are described
as populist. Some commentators attempt to get around the
confused state of affairs by distinguishing between left-wing
and right-wing or democratic and authoritarian populism.[2]

Some commentators have even invented the term technopopulism to characterize the use of populist rhetoric by
politicians associated with the technocratic-managerial elites.[3]
The use of the term populist to characterize movements that
have little in common, beyond that their policies and actions

diverge from those of the legacy political establishment does little to illuminate what is specific and distinct about a phenomenon that represents an increasingly influential force in Western societies.

The focus of this text is national populism, arguably the most distinct and increasingly powerful movement in our times. National populism is often demonized as far-right and even as fascistic. However, as we explain in the chapters that follow, national populist movements such as those supporting Reform in the UK, or Fratelli in Italy, or Rassemblement Nationale in France, have no ideological affinities with the far-right politics of the 1930s far right. It is not ideology that draws sections of the electorate to support these parties but a demand for policies that secure and enhance people's way of life and provides them with a voice and a sense of solidarity.

In Defence of Populism sets out to put the record straight. It explains that the motives that inspire movements that are characterized as populist are positive expressions of the quest for solidarity. The story that unfolds in the following chapters highlights the democratic spirit that drives populism forward. It argues that in the current conjuncture, populism alone is serious about promoting the politics of hope. The impulse that drives populism forward is fuelled by a demand for voice and a determination to uphold the traditional values that are demonized by the political and cultural establishment of Western society.

Populism is not simply committed to the renewal of democracy but also to the advocacy of a system of cultural values that are antithetical to those of the technocratic-managerial classes that rule society. The polarization of values has acquired an intense logic which explains the degree of intolerance that society's elites direct towards populism. *In Defence of Populism* argues that what is important about populism is the spirit of freedom and community that it embodies. We hope that once the democratic spirit that animates populism is understood, readers' attitude towards this subject will become more sympathetic to people's quest for a voice.

During the course of working on this problem I had the good fortune to discuss the issues outlined in this book with representatives from a variety of parties labelled as populist. Members and supporters of the European Parliament political groups Patriots for Europe and ECR kindly shared their thoughts with me, as did some of the activists from Reform UK. My discussion with participants in the patriotic grassroots flaggers movement in August 2025 reinforced my conviction that the quest for a voice is one of the most animating forces in contemporary politics.[4] Paradoxically none of my informants self-consciously identified themselves as populists, but their sympathies were clearly with people like Tom.

I am grateful to my colleagues at the think tank MCC Brussels, where I work alongside a great team of people. In particular, I have drawn on the insights of the formidable Jacob Reynolds, Tony Gilland, John O'Brien and Richard Schenk. Dr Jennie Bristow provided ruthless criticism of the text and saved me from not a few embarrassing faux pas. My editor at Polity Press, George Owers, offered some invaluable advice about how to improve the text. Needless to say, none of them are directly responsible for the views expressed in this text.

The book is dedicated to the memory of Hannah Arendt, whose wonderful reflections on judgement and common sense reinforced my conviction that populism represents democracy in action. If, as Simon and Garfunkel noted, 'silence like a cancer grows', then we urgently need a movement committed to helping people find their voice.

Frank Furedi

Brussels, September 2025

1

Introduction:
A Spectre Haunting . . .

In 1848, Karl Marx and Friedrich Engels opened *The Communist Manifesto* with this warning: 'A spectre is haunting Europe – the spectre of communism.' For much of the twentieth century, that spectre gripped the West, casting a long shadow over both foreign and domestic policy.

Today, that spectre has been replaced by another. Once again, elites speak of contagion, instability, even revolution. Once again, the anxiety centres less on ideas than on the people who might embrace them. But this time, the menace is not called 'communism' – it is called 'populism'.

The language is familiar. The 'spectre' of populism is now a staple of academic conferences, policy briefings and journalistic editorials. But this paranoia stretches back further than most remember. In 1967, a conference at the London School of Economics (LSE) brought together a group of political scientists, historians and sociologists in one of the first serious attempts to define populism as a global phenomenon. Their concern was not with Europe, which they still considered immune, but with Latin America, Africa and post-colonial states in what was then referred to as 'the developing world'. Populism, warned these social scientists, was rising where the liberal order had not yet taken hold – and it was not to be trusted.[1] Looking back, this discussion seems prescient. Reading the contributions at this conference, it is evident that participants were preoccupied principally with the apparent displacement of the fear of communism with a fear of populism.

In wider society, populism was not yet a widely recognized phenomenon. It would take another half a century before it gained recognition as a powerful and growing force. Today, references to populism pepper both specialist and non-academic publications. Indeed, even the metaphor of 'the spectre' is repeated lazily. An essay written for the NATO Association of Canada in 2019, titled 'A spectre is haunting Europe: the rise of populism worldwide and its humanitarian implications' is paradigmatic in this respect. It observed that the 'lingering spectre that now seems to lurk around every corner is no longer communism – but populism'.[2] Numerous case studies, such as 'The spectre of populism in Philippine politics and society' or *Twenty-First Century Populism: the Spectre of Western European Democracy* use the term.[3] Others refer to the spectre of 'heritage populism'.[4]

The *Oxford English Dictionary* refers to a spectre as 'an apparition, phantom, or ghost', one that is 'terrifying'.[5] Certainly, during the past 15 years, populism is frequently framed through a *narrative of fantasy* that communicates alarm and fear. As far as the mainstream cultural and political establishment is concerned, populism is an unwelcome, threatening and unmanageable phenomenon.

There is something truly contrived about the constant promotion of the slogan 'Beware!'. The 'politics of populism' fear has acquired its most systematic form in the European Union, principally driven by an awareness of the EU's legitimacy deficit.

The EU leadership is especially alarmed by the potential for a populist movement. In April 2010, the then president of the European Union Herman Van Rompuy declared that populism was the 'biggest danger to Europe'.[6] Two years later, his successor, José Manuel Barroso, referred to populist movements as his greatest concern. The current holder of this office, Ursula von der Leyen, declared in her acceptance speech at the 2024 European People's Party Congress that 'our peaceful and united Europe is being challenged like never before by populists, nationalists and demagogues'. She added that 'they want to trample on our values, and they want to destroy our Europe'.[7] The values of pluralism and tolerance within the EU's institutions have been forgotten, which is paradoxical since its leaders, like von der Leyen, constantly accuse populists of aspiring to totalitarianism.

Because Europe's political establishment regards populism as an existential threat, it invests heavily in the promotion of anti-populist propaganda. In June 2024, the European Commission's ethics group issued a statement 'Resisting authoritarian populism'.[8] Its purpose was to justify an ideological crusade against populism. Jan Kubik, the principal investigator of one such project on 'Populism's threat to democracy in the EU' stated that 'the threat' of populism 'is deadly'.[9] Kubik even went so far as to argue for restricting the freedom of speech of populists. He wrote: 'I hate to say this, being born under communism, but when the collapse of liberal democracy becomes a real possibility, we may need to censor more radical voices, as happened with Trump in the United States.'

The EU finances numerous academic projects whose aim is to challenge the scourge of populism. One such project aims to challenge 'the rise of euroscepticism and of populist, extreme right parties, threatening with exit from the [European Union]' by 'educating young people about Europe, its common values and active European citizenship'.[10]

The mainstream academic community echoes the appeals to fear of EU leaders and it willingly provides the advocates and politicians with ideological support. Books like

William Galston's *The Populist Threat to Liberal Democracy* amplify the concerns of established politicians. 'There is no threat to Western democracies today comparable to the rise of right-wing populism' notes the introduction to a series of essays on *Populism and the Crisis of Democracy*.[11] As the French philosopher Pierre-André Taguieff noted, 'populism is often denounced as the embodiment of the "European evil"'.[12]

Fascination with this phantom-like, terrifying spectre has led to a flood of publications on this subject. The decade between 1950 and 1960 produced fewer than 200 publications on populism; that number rose to over 1,500 between 1990 and 2000. During each year between 2000 and 2015, an average of 95 academic papers and books included the term 'populism' in their title or abstract, as catalogued by *Web of Science*. Since 2016, that number has exploded. Between 2016 and 2020, more than 31,000 books, studies and articles have been published on populism.[13] The deluge continues, yet despite this, it is far from evident what the term 'populism' actually means.[14]

The populist moment

But whatever dispute exists about its definition, academics agree that populism is not disappearing anytime soon. In 2007, the Bulgarian political scientist Ivan Krastev developed the concept of the *populist moment*. Krastev asserted that populism had become the most significant movement in contemporary politics.[15] In his seminal essay, Krastev anticipated that what might be seen as a moment might turn out to be much more enduring.

It is important to note that in 2007 the political and cultural impact of populism was relatively insignificant compared to the influence it exercises today. At that point, there was no government in Europe that could be described as remotely populist. Populist parties were just about to stir and to gain influence over sections of the electorate. Krastev's comment was written nine years before the people of Britain voted for Brexit and Donald Trump was elected to the American presidency, and 14 years before Trump won a second term. Today, numerous mass parties in Europe, characterized as populist, vie for power.

But although the populist movement is in the ascendancy, its actual definition is still unresolved and remains interpreted though the medium of a modern mythology. Almost everything you are likely to read about contemporary populism bears little relationship to the real impulses that drive this movement forward.

There is a widespread tendency to interpret populism as an intellectually illiterate movement that interprets society simplistically as merely dominated by a conflict of interest between the people and the elites.

Representations of populism as a shallow anti-intellectual movement often bear the hallmark of an academic fantasy. Take the narrative provided by Cas Mudde, the most cited academic commentator on populism and arguably the most influential 'expert' on the subject.[16] His definition of the populist vision as one where society is divided between the 'pure people' and the 'corrupt elite' is repeated *ad nauseum* in academic commentaries.[17] This definition has been repeated so often that it has acquired the status of an incontrovertible truth.

Yet, it is worth noting that the supposed populist attachment to a 'pure people' is an invention of its critics; one will struggle to find references to a pure people in writings authored by populists themselves. Unlike the hundreds of authors who refer to a 'pure people' in their anti-populist polemic, I have not found a single instance of a prominent political leader such as Nigel Farage, Viktor Orbán or Giorgia Meloni referring to a 'pure people'. Mudde's invention of this problematic term appears to be motivated by the impulse to blemish populism through associating it with the discredited politics of racial purity. Moreover, the idea that populism is simply about 'the people against the elites' represents a gross simplification of the issues at stake. Populist activists are often hostile to this or that group of elites. But their hostility is not against elites *per se*. Their animosity is directed against elitist policies that are underpinned by a paternalistic disdain for their culture and the communities that ordinary people inhabit. Supporters of populism have no problem with leaders from an elite background such as Donald Trump or Nigel Farage, whose views appear to converge with theirs.

Mudde also asserts that populism is not only anti-elitist but also anti-pluralist.[18] What this argument suggests is that the supposed aspiration of populism for purity and cultural homogeneity leads it to reject the political rights associated with pluralism. One of Mudde's close intellectual co-thinkers Jan-Werner Müller sums up this approach by asserting that populism is a 'moralized form of antipluralism'.[19] This representation of populism as an inherently anti-pluralist and exclusionary movement was strikingly confirmed by Mudde when he responded to *Cambridge Dictionary*'s declaration that populism was its 2017 word of the year by stating that 'nativism, not populism should be declared word of the year'.[20] The association of populism with nativism and xenophobia is widely circulated by the academic industry dealing with this subject. Supporters of populism are frequently caricatured as racist bigots who represent a threat to minorities. Reading between the lines it is difficult to avoid the conclusion that so-called expert commentators have opted to embrace a classic politics of fear as a substitute for objective analysis.

One reason why academic commentators and their associates in the mainstream media are so hostile to populism is because the values that this movement upholds are often antithetical to theirs. In particular, populism rejects the globalist project of de-nationalizing people's identity and detaching society from its national roots. It also rejects the attempt by the political and cultural establishment to dispossess people of their cultural heritage. Since populism attempts to reconnect with its community's cultural heritage, it possesses a strong commitment to conserve the legacy of the past.

Critics of populism are also frequently wary of democracy, particularly in its majoritarian form. Müller for one regards the ideal of popular sovereignty with contempt and writes that 'populism is something like a permanent shadow of modern representative democracy, and a constant peril'.[21] In his writings Müller and many of his co-thinkers express an ambivalent attitude towards democracy because they fear that populists leaders can use this political system to manipulate and mislead the electorate. Paradoxically, their scepticism towards democracy often coexists with the assertion that it is not them but the populists who are the enemies of democracy. According to one such study, right-wing 'populist attitudes are negatively related to support for democracy'.[22]

The inescapable conclusion that I draw from my reading of the mainstream literature on populism is that its authors possess a deep-seated unease about the electoral reliability of people. This sentiment is most strikingly expressed by Jürgen Habermas – arguably one of the most influential European social theorists, who casually writes of national electorates as 'the preserve of right-wing nationalism'.[23] Habermas's disdain for electorates is based on the presentiment that when confronted with the challenge posed by populist movements, they struggle to match their influence over public opinion.

The demand for populism

The discussion of the populist moment sometimes overlooks one of its most important features, which is the existence of a popular demand for a party or a movement that expresses the many concerns of the people that the legacy parties reject or ignore. That there is a very real demand for movements that are more in tune with the concerns of people who feel that their concerns have been systematically ignored is shown by the speed with which new populist-oriented parties have made electoral headway during the past decade. Almost out of nowhere the Chega (meaning 'Enough') party emerged to become the main opposition party in Portugal. The spectacular rise of Reform in the United Kingdom caught many observers by surprise and its success has exposed the fragile authority of the nation's two main legacy parties. A similar patten is evident in many European societies, such as Austria, France, Germany, Holland and Italy.

There is considerable evidence that the rise of populist movements in the Western world is demand driven. As an analysis of the 2024 European Parliamentary elections noted, it is the voters who demand the kind of answers that populism provides. These are not mindless voters who simply internalize the rhetoric of populist demagogues.[24] Explanations for this demand have focused on economic and cultural grievances.[25] Numerous accounts assert that economic dislocation, deindustrialization, the feeling of being left behind due to the impact of globalization or the disorienting effect of mass migration are the main drivers of the rise of populism. Yet, many of these concerns – particularly the devastating impact of deindustrialization and growing inequality – pre-date the rise of populism.[26] One of the most fascinating features of the demand for populism is that it transcends the peculiar features of different nations and encompasses former electoral constituencies of both the left and the right.

It is important to stress that the demand for populism is chronologically prior to the astonishing rise of movements and parties that have given a voice to this demand. The survey carried out by the *Timbro Authoritarian Index 2024* concludes that 'populist parties have grown in tandem with an increasing demand for their ideas – on immigration, Europe, multicul-turalism, globalization, etc.[27] However, many of these issues were the focus of public anxiety for many decades before the crystallization of the current wave of populism.

In this book I make a distinction between the politi-cal movements that are characterized as populist and the *zeitgeist* that reflects a public mood or a spirit that finds its expression in a populist outlook. One account of contempo-rary populism writes of an 'impulse', an 'impetus, a motivating spirit or drive', one 'that implies ordinary men and women believe that the government ought to serve the people, not just the special interests'.[28] Another article notes that this spirit encourages people to be 'keenly attuned to the distribu-tion not only of resources and opportunities but of honour, respect and recognition, which may be seen as unjustly with-held from "ordinary" people and unjustly accorded to the unworthy and undeserving'.[29] These are people who wish to be taken seriously and not patronized by those who pre-sume to have the moral authority to lecture them about their lives.

So what is the best way of making sense of the spirit of populism? Ever since the nineteenth century when modern populism emerged, it expressed what outwardly appears as a contradictory sensibility: the spirit of loss and of hope. Typically, in the first instance populist movements are defen-sive. They represent people angered by the loss of certain economic or legal rights or violation of their community life and cultural norms. The classical example is offered by the Russian Narodnik Movement (1860s–1880s). This movement sought to defend the communal rights of the peasantry which were systematically violated by the landlords with the back-ing of the Russian state. Throughout history, the theme of protecting long-standing rights that were threatened by pow-erful elites constituted an important theme in the evolution of popular movements.

In the United States, the Greenback Party (1874–89) sought to combat the loss of economic rights due to the gold standard which lowered the real price paid to producers and harmed the standard of living of farmers and workers. Rural populism has always possessed a defensive outlook. Tom, the Flemish farmer whom we met earlier, stands in this long tradition of resisting the violation of a pre-existing right; in his case regarding the ownership and management of his livestock. One interesting analysis of why people voted for Trump in 2016 concluded that their vote represented 'the revenge of those who had been divested of something'.[30] It added that 'all of them, even among the middle and upper classes, feel that they have somehow lost out: whether this means losing their male privilege, part of their income (however high), their social status, recognition of their work, respect for their faith or their country, their place in the world, their power, their hegemony'.

I first became interested in the phenomenon of populism during my doctoral research on the anti-colonial Mau Mau rebellion. As I explained in my book, *The Mau Mau War in Perspective* (1989), this was not simply an anti-colonial revolt but an agrarian movement driven by the impulse of protecting communal rights regarding the possession of livestock.[31] The supporters of Mau Mau were not simply motivated by economic grievances but what they perceived as violations of their cultural norms and practices. They were determined to defend – by any means necessary – their cultural traditions.

The philosopher Roger Scruton stated that since the Enlightenment conservatism 'has been engaged in the work of rescue'.[32] Scruton's reference to rescue referred to ensuring that the legacy of European culture and the values associated with it were protected against the forces that sought to marginalize them and render them redundant. The experience of the post-Second World War era indicates that mainstream conservative parties have often failed to attend to this work of rescue, and it fell to communities and often unorganized people to try to defend the values that defined their way of life. As we argue in the chapters to follow, the commitment to rescue and uphold many of these traditions has played a key motivating force in the rise of contemporary populism.

The spirit of loss exists in an intimate relationship with that of hope. That is why the spirit of populism expresses such a powerful democratic impulse. It understands that it is only through the exercise of democracy that it can make its voice heard and rescue the integrity of its community traditions and way of life.

As noted previously, populism has a history that goes back to the nineteenth century. During the past two centuries, numerous movements have articulated populist concerns. My aim is not to provide a history of this movement nor to discuss every party described as populist throughout the world. I am interested in exploring the populist movements that have emerged in the Western world in the decades following the 1960s cultural revolution. Unlike populist movements in the past and in other parts of the world – the driving forces of which were focused primarily on economic grievances – current Western national populism is principally oriented towards countering threats that are mainly cultural in nature.

Since the historical context and cultural influences that led to the growth of these movements are quite specific, I have resisted the temptation of comparing and contrasting them with different movements from other parts of the world.

The subject matter of my discussion is best described as that of **national populism**. The term was invented by the Italian social scientist Gino Germani. He used this term mainly in his discussion of Latin American populism.[33] Germani framed national populism as a negative phenomenon and thought that, although not totalitarian, it is authoritarian in nature. He never quite explained what was 'national' about his subject matter. In contrast, Matthew Goodwin's excellent *Values, Voice and Virtue: The New British Politics* provides an important context for understanding the cultural drivers of national populism.[34]

I think that the term national populism is much more applicable to the current circumstance, where attitudes towards the question of sovereignty mark one of the most important dividing lines in contemporary politics. Despite the many differences amongst them, movements like Make America Great Again (MAGA), the Reform Party in the UK, Rassemblement Nationale in France and Frattelli d'Italia in Italy are representative members of the national-populist family.

The mythological framing of populism continues to exercise a powerful influence on how this movement is represented in the media and within institutions of culture and education. It is invariably characterized as far-right, authoritarian, xenophobic or a danger to democracy. The demonization of populism has acquired a quasi-ideological character that tries to immunize the electorate from coming under the influence of such a terrifying political movement. Nevertheless, despite their best efforts, anti-populist idealogues have not succeeded in limiting the forward march of this movement.

The contemporary anti-populist narrative should be interpreted as a sublimated critique of popular sovereignty and democratic decision making. In recent decades, sections of the Western political class have become disconcerted by the outcome of various elections and referendums across the world. Anxiety about the behaviour of citizens has intensified since the outcome of the Brexit referendum and the election of Donald Trump to the American presidency in 2016. It has become even more panic-like since Trump's re-election in 2024. In some cases, the disappointment of the ruling elites with their own capability to motivate and influence the electorate has crystallized into an anti-democratic sensibility towards public life.

It is easy to overlook an extraordinary feature of the topic of this book. Populism is a term that is mainly used by its opponents. Hardly anyone uses 'the P word' as a form of self-designation. Unlike communists, socialists, anarchists, fascists, liberals or conservatives, there are very few self-defined populists. It is tempting to follow the advice of scholars such as Ian Roxborough to abandon the term populist altogether.[35] However, what is at stake is not simply the impoverished quality of the debate on the subject and the confusion surrounding this concept. For better or worse, the criticisms levelled at populism represent an indirect attack on the foundational status of democracy. It is for this reason that the concept of populism needs to be wrested from the grip of its opponents. As an expression of popular sovereignty and democracy, populism should be defended. Challenging the pathologization of populism is necessary for rescuing the reputation of democracy from its detractors.

Populism should not be seen as a movement with a distinct political programme. Historically, the early versions of populist movements, such as the American People's Party established in the 1890s, were principally oriented towards achieving economic justice and defending the living conditions of working people. In nineteenth-century Russia, the Narodniks and later the Socialist Revolutionary Party sought to appeal to the peasantry and essentially stood for an agrarian socialist political outlook. Throughout most of the twentieth century, populist movements attached themselves to a variety of different political tendencies. Some drew on the outlook of the right and others drew on the left. In the current era, the growth of populism in the Western world is closely linked to a search for meaning and the rescue of a way of life and identity that appears to be under attack.

Virtually everyone writing on the subject of populism agrees that this movement is not ideologically disposed and lacks a coherent doctrine through which it communicates its programmatic orientation and outlook. Because there is no coherent doctrine articulating a populist worldview or ideology, I will have to reconstruct it on the basis of exploring the ideals, sentiments and motivational themes associated with it. As readers will discover, the politics of movements designated as populist and the spirit they articulate bears very little relationship to the way its opponents represent them. Indeed, some of the most important motivational concerns that have led to the emergence and consolidation of populist movements are often overlooked and barely mentioned by their adversaries.

Instead of perceiving populism as an ideology, it is more useful to represent it as a *disposition* or *orientation* towards public life. Populist movements like the one supporting Brexit, or the Rassemblement National in France, or the movement campaigning against the Irish government's referendum on the definition of the family, or the Trumpian MAGA movements, are mainly concerned with defending a way of life which is at risk of being taken away by an elite whose outlook is alien to theirs.

The populist disposition draws on the common sense prevailing in different communities. What's important about this sensibility is that it reflects the common experiences of people. What makes sense to a community is underpinned by a consciousness of its experience. Common sense expresses what people have in common and its articulation helps forge a point of contact between people. The experience of history indicates that common sense provides the ground on which true democracy flourishes. Common sense is the lifeblood of democracy and in the current era populism serves as it most direct expression.

Arguably, for these movements, the question of identity, the preservation of a way of life and its affirmation is more important than it was for the populist movements of the twentieth century. However, what the contemporary movements share with those of an earlier era is the quest for a voice, the defence of living standards and a determination to influence the direction of society. In effect, they seek to endow citizenship with meaning. I would argue that, in this respect, they represent democracy in action. It is the aspiration for a voice and a disposition towards the defence of a way of life that shapes the populist imagination. How this impulse is expressed, through which organizations and leaders, will vary from one case to another. As is the case all too often, the leaders of populist movements – like those of the mainstream – disappoint the citizens who voted for them.

Conceptually, it is useful to distinguish the populist spirit and what animates it from its political representatives. That is why many leaders that the movement supports or elects are career politicians who are anything but populist in their orientation. Someone like Juan Peron of Argentina is the exception, but most of the leaders that anti-populists label as populist – such as Viktor Orbán, Marine Le Pen or Donald Trump – would reject this designation. Often governments run by leaders designated as populists turn out to be a radical variation of the mainstream. Populist governments are no less immune to the influence of international pressures and pragmatic concerns than regimes run by mainstream governments. That is why, for example, I would not characterize the two Trump administrations or even that of Italian Prime Minister Giorgia Meloni (who is closest to possessing a populist mindset) as representing populism in action.

In this book, my defence of populism should not be construed as offering an automatic support for individual politicians and parties that are characterized as populists. Mine is a defence of the spirit that populism captures and communicates. The spirit of populism has gained definition through the advocacy of ideals such as popular and national sovereignty, majoritarian democracy, respect for tradition and solidarity. Without falling into the trap of romanticizing the spirit of populism, we must understand that, without the influence of this movement, democracy would be robbed of its representative content and become an instrument of the managerial technocratic elites.

The spirit of populism summed up

A simple definition cannot capture the meaning of the spirit of populism. Populism has no doctrinal ambition. Its spirit affirms the life world of people and the pre-political dimension of a community's existence. This spirit is fuelled by an egalitarian impulse, which unfortunately its detractors misinterpret as anti-elitist and anti-pluralist. One of the most astute understandings of the spirit of populism is provided by Arthur Borriello, Jean-Yves Pranchère and Pierre-Étienne Vandamme.[36] These authors characterize populism as 'an egalitarian impulse against oligarchic tendencies, centered on anti-elitism and the defense of a democratic common sense'.[37] They note that this egalitarian impulse is 'mainly defensive-reactive in nature and rooted in a democratic commonsense, rather than in a fully-fledged ideological worldview aiming at the establishment of a radically new social order'.

Populism draws on the pre-political resources of society – shared memory and solidarity based on a common experience – and has no ideological pretensions. As we discuss in chapter 5, populism's defence of the pre-political sphere is significant because individual rights and political freedoms emerge out of it.

The spirit of populism encourages the valuation of democratic common sense which conveys the belief that citizens possess the capacity to judge issues and policies that concern them. Populism's affirmation of common sense is not ideological. It represents a taken-for-granted assumption that affirms the common experience – past and present – on which the sensibility of common sense is constructed.

Although it lacks a systematic doctrine, there are certain attitudes and ideals that characterize the value orientation that all national populist movements possess. In the current era the populist value system often comes across as directly antithetical to those of the political and cultural establishment. As the political theorist Margaret Canovan pointed out, unlike so-called social movements, populism does not merely challenge the holder of power but also 'elite values'. Therefore, its hostility is also directed at 'opinion formers and the media'.[38] Often the challenge posed by populist movements to elite values is expressed through their defiant act of rescue, expressed through their determination to defend the customs and traditions that the technocratic-managerial class have discarded as outdated.

The sense of community belonging is the most important sentiment motivating contemporary populists. This sensibility of local or national patriotism is expressed through an attachment to national sovereignty. From the standpoint of national populism, sovereignty is significant for two reasons. First, because it provides the largest terrain that humankind has discovered so far where democratic accountability can be exercised and have real meaning. Popular sovereignty can occur within a local community, a city or a nation – but it cannot be exercised in a territory larger than the nation. National sovereignty is also regarded as essential because it provides a context for the cultivation of a real, felt identity. There are other possible ways for people to develop their identities, but for most people the nation constitutes the largest area within which their identity can be forged and gain real purchase.

Many of the reactions and attitudes associated with populism constitute a common quest for gaining meaning through the forging of pre-political solidarity. It can often express itself in affirming traditional family and community life, and in the solidarity that arises within faith communities. This attempt to re-appropriate the moral in this manner goes directly against the grain of the cultural norms that prevail in the West. In fact one of the frequent charges directed at populism is that it is moralistic.[39]

The significance of populism's moral dimension is highlighted through one of its principal ideas, which is the quest for a home, motivated by the aspiration of belonging. This love of home – captured by Roger Scruton by the term *oikophilia* – does not simply attach itself to the homeland of the nation but also to the local community.[40]

Many of the reactions and attitudes associated with populism constitute what Hannah Arendt described as a search for pre-political solidarity. This quest for solidarity is underpinned by a sense of hope about the ability of people to assume control over their lives.

In different circumstances the spirit of populism would not have so easily lent itself to becoming politicized. However, since the decline of ideologically motivated party competition, culture has served as the main sphere where political ideas are played out. And since the late 1970s the ruling classes of Western societies have pursued policies that have sought to dispossess people of their cultural heritage and their sense of home. In its current form national populism can be understood as a reaction to what Christopher Lasch characterized as *The Revolt of the Elites and the Betrayal of Democracy*. Since the most important feature of *The Revolt of the Elites* was its repudiation of society's traditional outlook and cultural roots, it is not surprising that millions of people would respond by attempting to reconnect with their past and cultural heritage. Today, the simple act of community rescue inspires hope amongst millions of people searching for a home.

The aim of *In Defence of Populism* is to explore and explain the issues and ideals that motivate millions of people to support populist parties. It will seek to achieve this by examining the outlook and motivation for the anti-populist mindset and effectively countering it. It will argue that, in this context, populism is essential for the revival of democracy and, indeed, it represents democracy in action. The focus of the book is not populism in general but its manifestation in the twenty-first-century Western world. It is also in this part of world that the anti-populist standpoint is most systematically developed and has the greatest influence on society. Although populism has exercised an important influence on public life, its impact has been mainly on matters that touch on the pre-political sphere. It is still in the phase of becoming a distinct political movement and has yet to develop a system of policies required for the governing of society. Whether it can make the transition from a movement to a governing agency is one of the big questions of our time.

One word of caution! Just as the academics and politicians involved in framing populism tend to approach it from a hostile, anti-populist point of view, in turn I am a shameless adherent of popular sovereignty and an advocate of a positive orientation towards populist politics. I will take into account the arguments of the anti-populist narrative where it raises an important point – for example, in its concern for minorities. A formidable 'empathy wall' (see below) that divides commentators from supporters of populism is evident in the debate surrounding populism. That is why it is important to challenge the dogmatic demonization of a movement whose main crime is to challenge the value hegemony of the political and cultural elites of Western society.

I take it as given that it is entirely legitimate to adopt a critical stance towards different features of national populism. Some scholars opposed to populism have made a genuine effort to understand and engage with this phenomenon. The work of the American sociologist Arlie Russell Hochschild stands out with two remarkably sensitive studies, *Strangers in their Own Land* and *Stolen Pride: Loss, Shame and the Rise of the Right*. Unlike most books written on the subject, the author makes a genuine attempt to understand the motivation and outlook of people whose views are very different to her own. In contrast to the army of academic populism experts who allow their prejudices to get in the way of engaging in an objective scholarly encounter, Hochschild possesses empathy for the people who have become, in her own words, 'strangers in their own land'.

Academic commentaries on populism tend to be distinctly hostile to their subject matter. They certainly make little attempt to overcome what Hochschild characterizes as an 'empathy wall' between them and the millions of people who vote for populist parties.[41] Hochschild defined an empathy wall as an 'obstacle to the deep understanding of another person, one that can make us feel indifferent or even hostile to those who hold different beliefs or whose childhood is rooted in different circumstances'.[42]

In her magisterial study of Tea Party supporters and Trump voters – *Strangers in their Own Land* – Hochschild, a self-professed liberal, demonstrated an exemplary capacity for overcoming the empathy wall that separated her from the people she studied. The title of her book highlights an important dimension of the outlook that characterizes people who are drawn towards movements and parties that are labelled as populist. The term 'strangers' draws attention to the sensibility of estrangement, a feeling associated with alienation, disenchantment and cultural loss. In the chapters that follow, I will do my best to explain how the motivating influence of contemporary national populism can be best understood as the quest for connection, solidarity and control.

2

A Teleology of Evil

In its contemporary usage by the mainstream media, academics and intellectuals, populism carries powerful moral and normative connotations. The term often conveys the notion of a moral hazard. Populism is often diagnosed as a dangerous phenomenon that is likely to lead to some terrifying and evil outcome. This is a teleology of evil that sometimes goes so far as to suggest that the election of a populist politician is the first step on the slippery slope to fascism.

This assertion is based entirely on the fearful prejudice of would-be doom-mongering prophets. In the academic world, this prejudice has acquired the status of an unquestioned truth, which empowers anti-populist commentators to adopt casual references to the impending threat of authoritarianism and fascism. 'I argue that it is now appropriate to describe Trumpism as a form of fascism', contends one commentator who regards populism as a precursor to a very evil conclusion.[1] In a similar manner Justin Welby, the former Archbishop of Canterbury situated the vote for Brexit within the 'fascist tradition'.[2]

An analysis of news-reporting practices regarding the representation of populism in the media concludes that, according to the prevailing narrative, this movement is 'shrill', 'angry', 'unreasonable' and 'hysterical'. The study adds that even 'more negative evaluations repeated in the media are: "hateful", "brash", "thuggish", as well as "xenophobic", "unpredictable", "vulgar", "authoritarian", "manipulative" and "aggressive"'.[3] Frequent allusions to the far-right serve to construct a subliminal and not-so subliminal connection between populism and the horrific behaviour of 1930s Fascist and Nazi movements. Consequently, as one commentator noted, 'often as not, populism sounds like something from a horror film: an alien bacteria that has somehow slipped through democracy's defences – aided, perhaps, by Steve Bannon or some other wily agent of mass manipulation – and is now poisoning political life, creating new ranks of populist voters among "us"'.[4]

It is important to note that demonization of populism has a long history. During the Cold War, populism emerged as a constant target of frustrated American liberals, who felt isolated from the everyday life and outlook of working people. Post-Second World War liberalism was afflicted with a sense of anxiety about the reliability of the working classes. The sense of insecurity that afflicted sections of the left and of liberals was expressed through an anti-majoritarian outlook.

Even someone like the radical, liberal-minded political theorist Peter Bachrach – who was critical of the elitism of mainstream political theory – concluded that the 'illiberal and anti-democratic propensity of the common man is an undeniable fact that must be faced'.[5] Bachrach himself alluded to the 'widespread support of totalitarian movements in pre-war Europe and the rise of powerful proletarian-based communist parties in post-war France and Italy, of Peronism in Argentina and McCarthyism in the United States' to explain liberalism's loss of faith in the people.[6] Evidently the 'illiberal' propensity of the 'common man' meant that it is pointless to treat them liberally. At this point in time, anti-populist ideology communicated a sense of distrust bordering on contempt towards the 'common man'.

According to one well-documented historical account, for fifties' liberal intellectuals 'populism became the paradigmatic case of American-style xenophobia'.[7] In his important study, *The Populist Persuasion*, Michael Kazin notes that in the United States during the Cold War, populism became the 'great fear of liberal intellectuals'.[8] They blamed mass democracy and an 'authoritarian' and 'irrational' working class for the rise of McCarthyism. Senator Joseph McCarthy, a scourge of liberalism and the left, created what turned out to be a moral panic about the communist infiltration of key political and cultural institutions.

Liberal hostility to McCarthyism was not simply directed at the man himself; it was also underpinned by distrust and antipathy towards 'the very kinds of white American-Catholic workers, military veterans, discontented families in the middle of the social structure – who had once been in the forefront of supporting such causes as industrial unionism, the Congress of Industrial Organizations (CIO) and the Popular Front in the 1930s and 1940s'. The former militants of progressive causes were now cast aside as enemies of liberalism.

Since the 1950s, populism has been systematically disparaged by the vast majority of academics and political analysts. With some honourable exceptions, populism has been framed as a movement that possesses a range of moral deficits. In particular, the contributions of intellectual commentators are saturated with the hermeneutics of suspicion towards their subject. As far back as 1976, the American historian C. Vann Woodward noted that:

'Populism' is a bad word in the current American political vocabulary and has been for a long time. Any aspirant for elective office who is tagged with the term or makes bold to own it himself is rendered immediately vulnerable to suspicions of a sinister sort. In circles of acknowledged sophistication, the identification is sufficient to damn a candidate's motives and associate him with a host of symbols of that which is low, demagogic, retrograde and irrational in the American tradition of democratic politics.[9]

Vann Woodward later asserted that 'the study of populism is instructive about the consequences of condescension, arrogance and ignorance on the part of elites and intellectuals'.[10] He could have added that it is also instructive about their intellectual laziness.

Since the turn of the twenty-first century, the condescending hatred expressed towards populism by supposedly objective scholars, intellectuals and media commentators has intensified. Nevertheless, there are a handful of critics of populism who recognize that their academic colleagues tend to have an *a priori* hostility towards the object of their study. As Cristóbal Rovira Kaltwasser remarked, 'those who are interested in populism assume that populism is something bad'.[11]

Even Mudde acknowledged that: 'One of the most used and abused terms inside and outside of academia is undoubtedly populism. At times it seems that almost every politician, at least those we do not like, is a populist.'[12] As Yannis Stavrakakis observed, it is partly thanks to the hostile reception of the academic commentariat that populism has become a 'pejorative concept'.[13] The sociologist Rogers Brubaker, who is no friend of populism, notes that it is a 'morally and politically charged term, a weapon of political struggle as much as a tool of scholarly analysis'.[14]

Pierre-André Taguieff concluded that: 'Significantly, the epithet "populist" appears almost exclusively in polemical expressions – the "drift toward populism", the "populist temptation", the "danger" (or "threat") of populism, even a "populist infection".'[15] He also alluded to a time when anti-populist hysteria was far less prominent in academia than today. He wrote of a 'period immediately before the term "populism" came into widespread use as a means of delegitimizing or

stigmatizing people or phenomena without having to provide any further conceptual elaboration when most political
scientists emphasized the term's conceptual indeterminacy,
focusing on its ambiguous, ambivalent, and even contradictory
nature'.[16] Ambivalence and nuance are today conspicuous by
their absence in the mainstream commentaries on this subject.

Outside of academia, the commentaries on populism are
even more unrestrained in their representation of this phenomenon. 'The repugnance with which the words "populism"
and "populist" are uttered these days is a familiar feature
of the political scene', writes the leftist Italian sociologist
Marco D'Eramo.[17] Its adversaries often refer to populism as
a 'virus' that infects the body politic. For example, the Belgian
politician Charles Michel, who was president of the European
Council until 2024, stated that 'today's populism is like a
virus'. The implication of his words was that populism preys
on democracy and therefore – to quote Michel's predecessor,
Donald Tusk – 'defending our liberal democracies is our first,
second and third obligation'.[18]

Echoing this sentiment, the title of a commentary in *Politico*
simply warned of 'The next epidemic: resurgent populism'.[19]
The demonization of populism was also communicated by
commentators for *OpenDemocracy* when they asked: 'What
causes the populist infection? How can it be cured?'[20] Writing
in *Euractiv*, Gianni Pittella exclaimed:

> We have been infected. The virus of populism, racism, xeno-
> phobia has affected Europe. This virus in Europe is named
> Le Pen in France, Farage in Great Britain, Orbán in Hungary, 5
> Stars Movements in Italy, Kaczynski in Poland.[21]

The diseasing of populist parties is systematically promoted by
the mainstream media and their political supporters. 'I think
what we have at the moment is a populist virus', complained
Alastair Campbell, spin doctor to former UK Prime Minister

Tony Blair.[22] According to one professor of politics, populism is a 'recurrent autoimmune disease of democracy'.[23] In recent times, populism was sometimes portrayed as a virus that is no less of a threat than Covid-19. Australian Labor politician Andrew Leigh's book on existential risk and extreme politics is paradigmatic in this respect.[24] Leigh claimed that the threat of existential threats like climate change, pandemics and nuclear war are not unlike the threat posed by populist adversaries. In this scenario, populism works as destructive virus with a fascist face.

The alarmist tone that accompanies the pathologization of populism constitutes a striking illustration of what I described elsewhere as the performance of fear.[25] It is paradoxical that the accusation of using the politics of fear is so often hurled at populists when arguably the use of an alarmist rhetoric is far more typical of their adversaries.

Many of those who attack populism on the grounds that it relies on scaremongering appear unaware of their own complicity in the practice of the politics of fear. Their condemnation of the use of fear by populist parties is swiftly followed by warnings about the threat that populists pose to democratic societies. As one commentator pointed out, in Europe, 'populist movements and technocracies may simply represent, albeit in an extremely polarized fashion, two sides of the same coin'. They both base their strategy 'on generating fear'.[26]

Likewise, an analysis of Swedish politics claimed that, on the one hand, the 'successes of many of the anti-immigrant and nationalistic political forces in Europe are based on manufacturing a politics of fear for the electorate'. On the other hand, the author of this article also noted that 'the strange thing in the current political situation is that even most of the left and progressive political forces construct much of their politics on fear'.[27]

The framing of populism as a toxic disease invariably invites its medicalization. 'By fighting off the current infection', the political scientist Yascha Mounk stated, 'we might just build up the necessary antibodies to remain immune against new bouts of the populist disease for decades to come'.[28] Following this line of thinking, in many parts of Europe, and especially within the institutions of the EU, populism is regarded as a legitimate target for quarantine. That is why sections of the European Parliament have sought to exclude populist parties from access to decision making and influence by establishing what they call a *cordon sanitaire*. Ostracism is the fate of democratically elected members of the Parliament who are demonized for their alleged populist affiliation.

Not a term of self-designation

The most curious feature of the discussion that surrounds our subject matter is that almost everything that is said about national populism has its origins in claims asserted by its opponents. Most of the features attributed to populism originate from the narrative elaborated by its adversaries.

As the American historian Thomas Frank observed in his book *The People, No: A Brief History of Anti-Populism*, 'anti-populism is an adversary proceeding. Our thought leaders relate to populism not so much as scholars but as a privileged class putting down a challenge to itself.'[29] Since they regard populism as an enemy that must be crushed, they are far from nuanced in their representation of their adversary. So, when they comment on movements such as the one that supported Brexit or the Brothers of Italy, they hurl terms like racist, xenophobic, authoritarian at their enemy. They frequently refer to the MAGA movement supporting Trump as far-right, nativist and racist. This narrative of condemnation is circulated ceaselessly through the media, which has provided the language through which the phenomenon of populism is interpreted by millions of people.

Given the power of language, it is not surprising that before they actually meet a living so-called populist, many people are predisposed to encounter a loud-mouth, uncouth xenophobe. You could encounter such anti-democratic prejudices in full flow following the success of anti-establishment parties in the 2018 Italian General Election. *The Sunday Times* reported from a fancy dinner on a Roman roof terrace, attended by Italian aristocrats, businessmen and cultural figures. As they sat around 'glumly digesting events', a lawyer in attendance reportedly declared that the voters were 'beasts' and 'anthropologically different'.[30] Former President Biden just calls them 'garbage'[31] and, no doubt in his imagination, a supporter of Trump evoked the image of a low form of human being.

In the current highly polarized political environment, the meaning of twenty-first-century populism is fraught with difficulty. Though there is a vast literature on the subject, virtually every contribution acknowledges the absence of a consensus on the meaning of populism. There is an interminable discussion about the need to reach such a consensus, yet these contributions are often opaque and characterized by a reluctance to acknowledge their implicit hostility to it.

The French philosopher Cathérine Colliot-Thélène has argued persuasively that the definitional problem cited by almost all the academic experts is in part due to their negative framing of populism, which contains assumptions that are implicit.[32] Colliot-Thélène noted that the 'vagueness of the notion [of populism] stems precisely from the fact that this term is above all deprecatory'. It is a morally charged term masquerading as a neutral, social-science concept.

However, despite the numerous contrasting views on how populism ought to be defined, academic experts tend to be united in their hostility to the subject of their investigation. Some of them make an exception in relation to what they describe as 'left-wing populism' – such as Podemos in Spain or the Mexican Zapatistas. These leftish academics express sympathy towards their subject, but movements that they label as right-wing are attacked as far-right authoritarian enemies of democracy.[33] Sympathetic academic accounts of national populism are conspicuously rare.

In the past, populism served as a form of self-designation and people knowingly and proudly described themselves using the term. During the nineteenth century, the Narodniks in Russia, like the People's Party in the United States, took pride in their populist outlook, which they perceived as an egalitarian orientation towards the people. In the twenty-first century, it is the advocates of anti-populism who define their opponents as populist. The political scientist Ivan Krastev raised an important question when he asked, 'who decides which policies are "populist" and which are "sound"?'[34] In the contemporary era, this decision has become the prerogative of a coterie of influential anti-populists.

Almost everything that people hear about the meaning of populism on the mainstream media originates from views developed by its opponents. As Paul James explained:

> To begin with an obvious but often overlooked point, the term 'populist' in contemporary usage tends to be applied politically and analytically to others, usually by those who are deemed the enemies of 'good' populists: journalists, academics, establishment politicians and other elites. Although occasionally a populist leader will provocatively acknowledge the term as relevant to defining their politics, there are now no self-identified national populist movements, and certainly no self-proclaimed global populist movements.[35]

The very fact that populism is a designation that its opponents assign to it indicates that, in this century, the term serves a polemical purpose. As D'Eramo explained, this term says more about those who use it to characterize their adversaries than about what the movements designated as populist represent:

[P]opulism is not a self-definition. No one defines themselves as populist; it is an epithet pinned on you by your political enemies. In its most brutal form, 'populist' is simply an insult; in a more cultivated form, a term of disparagement. But if no one defines themselves as populist, then the term populism defines those who use it rather than those who are branded with it. As such, it is above all a useful hermeneutic tool for identifying and characterizing those political parties that accuse their opponents of populism.[36]

The French linguist Marie-Anne Paveau wrote – in her fascinating discourse analysis of the use of the term populism in France – that it is 'almost always the bearer of a negative evaluation'.[37] She remarked that the words '*populism* and *populist* serve as an accusation, an attack, or even an insult'. Because of the well-established negative connotation of these words, they can be used alone, 'without the need for derogatory associations', since they intrinsically convey such sentiments. In other words, the word populist is so deeply impregnated with antipathetic connotations that it is not necessary to link it to a derogatory adjective. In such circumstances, it is not surprising that this word is so rarely used as a form of self-identification by anyone sensitive to the prevailing political language. Alexandre Dorna, the French political psychologist, echoed this point, when he wrote that populism was an 'insulting alibi for all the right-thinking'.[38]

Since the framing of populism today is motivated by a barely concealed hatred towards it, the really interesting research question is not 'What is populism?' but 'What is the driver of its demonization in the media and academia?' In other words, what is the meaning of anti-populist discourse, what are the factors that create it and why has it become so influential in public life? As Paula Biglieri, one of the few academics who identifies with populism, pointed out:

But after all these years of incessant growing interest in populism, not much has been said of anti-populism. At least we can say that compared to the amount of academic production regarding populism, the reflections about anti-populism are few.[39]

The anti-populist literature is typically uncritical of how its own political disposition influences its engagement and it rarely questions its own role in the construction of the myth of populism.

In this book, I argue that the narrative of anti-populism is the latest version of the historical phenomenon of *demophobia*. As Biglieri, notes 'hating the people' is an 'anti-populist passion'.[40] Demophobia is fuelled by anxiety and fear about the working of democracy and a sense of loathing towards the *demos*. As the leftist American political theorist Wendy Brown hinted, 'perhaps the horror of populism carries a horror of the people, especially of a politics of the people, the power of the people, real democracy'.[41] Turning populism into a term of condemnation has been an important ideological and rhetorical accomplishment of its opponents.

The Mexican political theorist Benjamin Arditi has drawn an interesting parallel between the historical career of the term democracy and that of populism. He suggested that 'populism may work better as a term of derision, as democracy was for the ancient Greeks'.[42] It is worth noting that the term democracy was perhaps, like the contemporary usage of the word populism, an invention of its opponents. Indeed, most of what we know about democracy in Ancient Greece comes from the statements of its opponents. The wealthy oligarchy that traditionally ruled Athens could never reconcile itself to the political influence of the *demos*, and regarded the city-states' democratically inspired customs, laws and institutions with hostility. The wresting of political power by the people swiftly led to the formulation of anti-democratic theories and polemics, which emerged a long time before the formulation of a coherent democratic outlook.

By the middle of the fifth century BC, opponents of the *demos* argued that what democracy really meant was the tyranny of the mob: 'the domination of the many poor over the wealthy few'.[43] Some sources have gone so far as to claim that the word 'democracy' was coined by its enemies as a term to decry the behaviour of the *demos*.[44] While the authorship of this word continues to be a matter of debate, at least within elite philosophical and intellectual discourse, the usage of the term democracy communicated negative characteristics.

Western political theory itself was born as a response to the perception of the threat posed by democracy. Greek political theory was devoted to the task of discrediting and marginalizing claims supporting democratic customs, institutions and practices. As one study on the history of the 'mob' observes, 'it could almost be said that political theorizing was *invented* to show that democracy, the rule of men by themselves, necessarily turns into rule by the mob'. John McClelland, the author of this study, argues that the Western tradition of political thought 'begins with this profoundly anti-democratic bias'.[45] The elite's criticism of Athenian democracy was promoted systematically and led to the formulation of the first coherent elaboration of political theory.

The anti-democratic sentiments expressed by the Greek oligarchy continued to influence the outlook of Western political philosophy well into the twentieth century. Alarmist accounts about the influence of mass propaganda and the media in the inter-war era anticipate the current discussion on the impact of disinformation on a naïve immature populist electorate.

These theories invariably drew attention to the moral deficiencies and irrationality of the masses. Such theories are exemplified by Gustave Le Bon's influential *Psychologie des foules* (1895), 'the people' were seen as a mass of irrationality and delusion, a wild surge of adolescence that could lay waste to established orders. In the twentieth century, psychoanalysts such as William McDougall and Sigmund Freud identified in 'the people' the suggestible and destructive instincts of a primitive epoch.

In the 1920s and 1930s, questions about the reliability of democratic citizenship were re-raised through the discussion of mass culture and mass man. Public opinion, which was always a focus of anxiety, came under new attack and was routinely depicted as a synthesis of irrational myths and prejudice. This argument was forcefully presented by the American commentator Walter Lippmann in his influential 1922 study *Public Opinion*, which declared that the proportion of the electorate that is 'absolutely illiterate' is much larger than one would suspect, and that these people who are 'mentally children or barbarians' are the natural targets of manipulators.[46]

A modern version of these criticisms continues to influence the discussion of populism to this day. During the Cold War, the American political sociologist Seymour M. Lipset, characterized populism as the political refuge of 'the uneducated, unsophisticated, and the authoritarian persons'.[47]

The anti-democratic imagination, which regarded the masses as irrational and easily seduced by the propaganda of nationalist and authoritarian leaders, dominated the outlook of mainstream political commentators across the political divide. John Dewey, one of the most important American liberal thinkers in the twentieth century, tended to regard the psychological attitudes of the masses as a threat to democracy in the United States. 'The serious threat to our democracy', he asserted, 'is not the existence of foreign totalitarian states', but the 'existence within our personal attitudes and within our own institutions of conditions which have given a victory to external authority, discipline, uniformity and dependence upon The Leader'.[48]

The hostility directed towards the people by the oligarchs of Ancient Greece was also echoed during the twentieth century by the paternalistic left. In 1950 Theodor Adorno, one of the leading thinkers of the Marxisant Frankfurt School observed that 'throughout the ages', since the oligarchy arose in Greece, 'the majority of the people frequently act blindly in accordance with the will of powerful institutions or demagogic figures, and in opposition both to the basic concepts of democratism and their own rational interest'.[49] The anti-democratic prejudices of the Ancient Greek oligarchy continue to be articulated by populism's adversaries. As one commentator wrote with approval: 'Plato is an unfashionable thinker – far too authoritarian for most 21st-century minds. But for him the key problem was epistemological: most people – "the many" – had no knowledge of truth and no clear thinking about justice in their minds.'[50]

Plato's claim that democracy inevitably leads to tyranny is constantly recycled in twenty-first-century anti-populist narratives. In an influential essay, titled, 'Democracies end when they are too democratic', Andrew Sullivan cites the warning of Plato regarding the inevitability of democracy mutating into tyranny.[51] In a voice of despair, he noted that it is 'hard not to see in Plato's vision a murky reflection of our own hyperdemocratic times'. In current times, the refrain that '2,400 years ago, Plato saw democracy would give rise to a tyrannical leader' is frequently repeated by those overwhelmed by the sensibility of *demophobia*.[52]

Today's anti-populist narrative bears all the hallmarks of its Ancient Greek predecessors. As Hamdaoui observed, 'it is often accompanied by a demophobic discourse that sees the people as overly emotional, delirious and lazy'.[53] Anti-populist narratives echo Plato's technocratic affirmation of expertise in the domain of policy making. As Voutryas observed, the 'two core normative and ideological features of antipopulism' are 'namely meritocracy and technocracy'. He added that 'both principles underpin the distinction and growing disparities between elites and "the rest"; meritocracy by producing a hierarchy of worth, and technocracy by justifying the narrowing down of political participation by ordinary citizens'.[54]

The one crucial difference between the explicit anti-democratic outlook promoted by Plato and classical anti-democrats and today's anti-populists is that now critics outwardly affirm democracy while attacking populists as a threat to it.

In reality, the ideology of anti-populism is profoundly suspicious of democracy, particularly in its majoritarian form. It prefers a form of insulated decision making, in which the governing elites are shielded from the pressure of public opinion. Indeed, it is precisely because populism represents democracy in action that it has become the ceaseless object of vilification by its opponents.

Today, it is no longer possible to be too explicit about being sceptical about democracy. Formally, we all support democratic values. Consequently, the anti-democratic impulse driving the demonization of populism is communicated through the language of bad faith. It postures as a defence of democracy against the supposed threat to freedom posed by authoritarian populists.

3

Populism versus Anti-populism

By all accounts, national populism represents the most important political movement of the twenty-first century. Its dynamism and influence in the Western world stand in sharp contrast to the mood of malaise and stagnation that afflicts the legacy parties, who appear to be living off their past. These mainstream parties – be they Socialist, Conservative, Liberal or Green – have far more in common with one another than with their *arriviste* populist opponents. Despite the many differences that separate them, they spontaneously come together to constitute an *anti-populist* bloc.

The interaction between populism and its anti-populist nemesis is a dynamic one and shapes both movements. The outcome of this interaction will have a powerful influence on the direction of travel of Western public life.

As many observers have noted, in the current era, the conflict between populism and anti-populism constitutes the main dividing line in political life. The classical distinction between left and right has lost much of its salience in the so-called post-ideological moment. Movements that still bear the old label of left or right self-consciously eschew ideology and are constantly driven towards the acceptance of pragmatic compromise. The legacy parties have embraced the fatalistic outlook that dictates that there is no alternative to a globalist-directed, technocratic-managerial style of governance.

It is important to note that in the so-called post-ideological era, with the hollowing out of the politics of the left and of the right, every serious alternative to the technocratic/managerial order is likely to be labelled as populist. The mere appeal to the people or to popular sovereignty is regarded with suspicion by the legacy media. Defiance of the technocratic declaration that There Is No Alternative invites the condemnation of the political establishment. Yet, the very existence of a populist challenge to the prevailing technocratic consensus affirms that, at least potentially, there is an alternative.

As the Austrian professor of sociology Oliver Marchart noted: 'Populism represents a quest for an alternative – [it] rejects mainstream wisdom.' The ideology of anti-populism attempts to 'draw a political line of conflict – an antagonism – between "us liberal democrats" and the "populist anti-democrats"'.[1] For the political theorist Yannis Stavrakakis, 'this "axis of populism and anti-populism" is aptly described as the dominant split over which political meaning is organized in our current political conjuncture'.[2] The point is echoed by the German sociologist Wolfgang Streeck, who wrote that this split 'between those who call others "populists" and those who are called such by them is the dominant line of political conflict in the crisis societies of finance capitalism today'.[3]

This line of political conflict runs deep inside the EU, where virtually every manifestation of the crisis that afflicts the European project is interpreted through the prism of the populist/anti-populist dialectic. That is why the EU Commission has spent vast sums on propaganda and on projects devoted to developing an effective response to the 'populist challenge'.[4] As noted in the previous chapter, in June 2024, the European Commission's ethics group issued a statement titled 'Resisting authoritarian populism'.[5] Amongst its many recommendations, it argued that identities linked to 'territory, nation, ethnicity or religion' should be challenged by anti-sovereigntist 'pluralistic' federalist ones. The mainstream political parties in the European Parliament echo this outlook and have sought to impose a *cordon sanitaire* – a political quarantine on populist parties – to isolate them from playing an influential role within this institution. Evidently the commitment of the Commission to the principle of pluralism – the acceptance of genuine diversity of beliefs and opinions – does not extend to its political adversaries.

The obsession with maintaining a line that divides the EU oligarchy from the forces of populism often assumes an obsessive character. As the Czech social scientist Petr Agha warned, the 'current crisis of the European project can hardly be explained as a simple clash between democratic values and the rule of law on the one hand, and the so-called back-sliding populist movements, on the other'.[6] However, the constant escalation of anti-populist rhetoric ensures that polarization between the two protagonists acquires greater and greater depth.

Anti-populism is not simply a spontaneous reaction to its populist opposite. It is also embedded in the outlook of the technocratic-managerial elite. In the current post-ideological era, the remnants of the dominant post-Second World War political parties have converged around a managerial ethos and the institutionalization of technocratic governance. This style of governance seeks to depoliticize public issues and turn them into technical matters. Technocratic governance draws on the legitimacy of science and the authority of expertise. It outsources decision making on the issue of the day to non-elected technocratic bodies and to international institutions.

Anti-populism presents itself as the defender of liberal democracy against the threat of populism. However, its real aim is to defend technocratic institutions, and its insulated form of decision making, from popular pressure. In this way

it seeks to restrict the scope for the exercise of representative democracy, which is actually a central feature of liberal
democracy.

A study of anti-populist rhetoric in the media noted that
'what often goes unnoticed is that the negative valence that
"populism" has acquired, and its elevation to a central political
frame may itself be contributing to polarization by solidifying
a new divide along the populism/anti-populism line'.[7] Anti-
populist ideology is fiercely committed to ensuring that its
opponents are perceived as irredeemable enemies of democracy who ought to have no place in public life. Yet as the
experience of the past two decades indicates, it is difficult to
exclude populism from the public conversation. Why? Because
it offers a credible alternative – in many instances, the only
alternative – to the political mainstream.

Populism offers an alternative to the outlook of the political
mainstream on many fronts. As I argue in the chapters that
follow, this alternative touches on many issues affecting public
life. But arguably the key line of differentiation is between the
national orientation of populism and the anti-national and
globalist outlook of the technocratic-managerial elites. As
Streeck wrote, in recent years, 'populism has been used by the
parties and media of liberal internationalism all over the world
as a general polemical term for the new opposition which is
pressing for national alternatives to that internationalization
declared to be without alternatives'.[8] Until the re-election of
Donald Trump, the quest for national solutions could be dismissed as a form of backward chauvinism. Since 2024, even
governments that were hitherto zealously committed to globalist solutions have had to have a major rethink.

'Politics is the denial of fate', argued the Austrian political
scientist, Andreas Schedler.[9] If that is so, then the populist
movements who refuse to defer to the values and ideology of
the prevailing system of technocratic-managerial governance
serve an important role in re-politicizing public life. Issues that

appeared settled or beyond discussion have become the foci of debate and controversy. The influence of populist movements is discernible on issues such as immigration, multicultural-ism, institutionalization of identity politics, green deals and the re-nationalization of public life. The political theorist Raymond Geuss has argued that 'really significant political action . . . changes a situation in a way that cannot be seen to be a mere instantiation of a pre-existing set of rules'.[10] Through calling into question the dominant set of rules, populism fundamentally disrupts the *modus vivendi* of technocratic-managerial governance. That is why it has become a target of so much condemnation and that is also why the political establishment attempts to impose a quarantine around it.

Thomas Frank, who has written extensively on the history of American populism, observed that:

From the very beginning, then, populism had two meanings. There was Populism as its proponents understood it, meaning a movement in which ordinary citizens demanded democratic economic reforms. And there was Populism as its enemies characterized it: a dangerous movement of groundless resent-ment in which demagogues led the disreputable.[11]

The movements that Frank explored in his historical study focused mainly on achieving economic reforms and the redis-tribution of resources. Twenty-first-century national populism shares some of these concerns, but its principal interest pertains to the domain of cultural and political values. In this respect, it is very different to the movements that are characterized as left-wing populist. Populist movements of the left, such as Syriza in Greece or Podemos in Spain, emerged in response to the financial crisis of 2008. These movements constituted a response to the socio-economic fallout of the global financial crisis and, unlike national populism, tend to be indifferent to issues pertaining to people's sense of cultural insecurity.

Table 3.1. Key differences in value orientation between national populism and anti-populism

Populist value orientation	Anti-populist value orientation
Upholding the principle of sovereignty	Commitment to cosmopolitan ideology of globalization
Patriotism and national consciousness	De-nationalized approach to identity
Solidarity	Social cohesion
Community	Multiculturalism
The primacy of pre-political bonds	Diversity
Cultural continuity	Presentism
Demand for a voice	Insulated decision making
Popular sovereignty	Authority of expert
Tradition	Anti/post tradition

Arguably one of the main reasons why these movements have failed to make headway was because they ignored the cultural crisis experienced by the former constituency of the old left.

Populism and its opposite, anti-populism, represent not only opposing views of democracy, but also a contrasting system of values. Table 3.1 outlines the key differences in value orientation between national populism and its antithesis.

The most important contrast between these two value systems is the principle of national sovereignty and that of a globalist cosmopolitan orientation towards the problems of the time. For populists, the nation state is valued in its own right as the site of democratic decision making and the focus for loyalty. In contrast, the twenty-first-century version of the ideology of cosmopolitanism regards the nation state as possessing no inherent moral significance. It presumes in favour of international institutions and looks upon loyalty to nation as an outdated ideal.

Patriotism and national consciousness are foundational ideals of national populism. In contrast, anti-populism is deeply hostile to the cultivation of a national identity. Most anti-populist idealogues support views that are detached from an identity associated with a nation. Arguably the most polarized debates between the two sides pivot around the status of patriotism and national consciousness.

In most commentaries the terms solidarity and social cohesion are used interchangeably. However, there is a fundamental distinction between the two. Populist solidarity – sometimes referred to as natural solidarity – is founded on pre-political bonds and is the outcome of common community experience. This is a solidarity that emerges relatively spontaneously through the day-to-day interaction between people. In contrast, social cohesion is promoted through formal policies from above. It attempts to provide a technical solution to a polarized cultural landscape brought about by multicultural policies. In practice, administrative initiatives promoting social cohesion attempt to provide a solution to the absence of natural solidarity.

The populist valuation of community is based on an attachment to a home that has evolved through the historical experience of successive generations. Its focus on what people have in common in such settings and its idea of a people are based on the community bonds that bind individuals together. Anti-populists regard communitarianism with suspicion and celebrate the value of multiculturalism. Unlike a multi-ethnic society which can come together around common values, multiculturalism presumes in favour of different outlooks inhabiting the same geographical space.

National populism is strongly attached to the relationships that emerge in the pre-political sphere. It is committed to the defence of an inter-generational community and the particularity of the cultural norms and ideals that emerge out of it. Such communities are anything but diverse; a clear distinction is made between members of families, kinship and friendship groups and those who are seen as strangers. Anti-populists possess a negative outlook towards the pre-political sphere, which they regard as exclusionary. Instead, they support diversity as a value that is good-in-itself. In their hands, diversity has become politicized and regarded as a weapon with which to challenge national consciousness and traditional values.

For populism, cultural continuity is valued because it allows successive generations to renew a community's relation with the legacy of the past. For populists, the cultivation of cultural continuity is the prerequisite for the cultivation of community identity. This continuity provides the cultural roots necessary for encouraging a sense of belonging. Anti-populists dismiss the valuation of cultural continuity as a form of nostalgia that distracts people with outdated ideals. They adopt a presentist mode and claim that breaking from the past is necessary to liberate society from the bad old days. They offer a negative account of the past and idealize the present as morally superior to it.

The demand for a voice is one of the defining features of the spirit of populism. It encourages people to speak out and actively contribute to public life. Demanding the right to be heard provides the energy for ensuring that democracy is a living force. In contrast, anti-populists prefer a form of governance based on insulated decision making, which seeks to narrow the space for political debate and attempts to turn political questions into technical ones that are the prerogative of mangers and technocrats.

Populism and anti-populism appeal to two different sources of authority. Populists claim that popular sovereignty is the source of legitimate authority. From this standpoint citizens must have a central role in the determination of the political agenda and its elected representatives should represent the views of the people. Anti-populism dismisses popular sovereignty on the ground that the *demos* lack the maturity and education to make the right choices. It regards the authority of expertise as the basis for sound decision making. Its commitment is to expert-led policy making in preference to citizen-initiated policies.

National populists take their national and historical traditions seriously. Such traditions are regarded as a precious resource that can inspire society. Populists take seriously the knowledge and insights that tradition provides and seek to develop their views on the basis of the legacy of the past. Anti-populists tend to regard tradition as an outdated relic. In some cases, they go so far as to dismiss tradition and the values associated with it as not only irrelevant but as positively harmful to contemporary society.

Table 3.1 merely touches on the most striking differences in approach between those who inhabit the different sides of the line that divides them. In the chapters to come, these differences will be elaborated and discussed.

National populism:
a response to the double betrayal of the people

Since their emergence in the 1970s, populist movements have often been dismissed and caricatured as merely parties of protest. The Western mainstream media and political establishment regarded these parties of protest as inherently fragile, temporary movements that would remain forever on the margins or disappear as soon as their supporters got fed up with wasting their votes on no-hope politicians. The UK *Guardian* typified this approach when, in the aftermath of the electoral success of UK's Reform Party in the May 2025 local elections, it offered this summary of the situation: 'Many voted for the party as protest against government, while others have detached completely from politics.'[12]

Typically, protest parties arise to express dissatisfaction with the existing political system, mainstream parties or specific policies. An illustration of a protest movement is the *gilets jaunes* ('yellow vests'), which represented a formidable movement of French citizens directing its energy against a planned rise in tax on diesel and petrol.[13] This movement began in early November 2018 and organized weekly demonstrations that ended a few days before the coronavirus lockdown in March 2020. The 'Block Everything' movement of September 2025 carried on in the spirit of the Yellow Vests. No doubt this movement demonstrated an affinity to the outlook of populism, but it self-consciously avoided adopting any political affiliations and confined its energies to protesting against the French government's policies.

In many cases, populist parties also mobilize supporters to protest against particular policies. However, these parties are not merely engaged in protesting around a specific issue, but also in advancing ideals that challenge hegemonic values. The success and resilience of populism are underwritten by a pre-existing demand for parties that can articulate and give shape or a form to sentiments that are widely held by people, but are nevertheless rejected or not taken seriously by the political establishment. Unlike left-wing protest movements, national populists are not only responding to an act of social or economic injustice, but to an underlying demand by sections of society for their values and way of life to be respected and affirmed.

It is important to situate the success and subsequent advance of populism in the context of what I characterize as the *double betrayal* of the people. This refers to two different but mutually reinforcing socio-cultural processes that led to the transformation of political life in Western societies towards the end of the 1970s. The first act of betrayal was perpetrated by the political and cultural establishment, who systematically distanced themselves from their role as guardians of the nation and defenders of its interest. During the 1970s and 1980s, a new generation of the ruling elites detached themselves from the society which their families and ancestors have traditionally governed. Instead of defending and upholding the values rooted in their national way of life, the elites embraced many of the values advocated by the 1960s counterculture. This precipitated an era of cultural disorientation where people's sense of ontological security was significantly undermined. A sense of cultural loss – discussed at length in chapter 4 – created a demand for solidarity and meaning to which national populism sought to provide an effective response.

The second act of betrayal originally emanated from the crisis of the left in the late 1970s. This development was most strikingly illustrated in November 1977, when Louis Althusser, a leading French Marxist idealogue gave his famous 'Crisis of Marxism' speech. In this speech he acknowledged that Marxism had become irrelevant. At the same time other sections of the left could no longer ignore the exhaustion of their anti-capitalist ideology. This led to the left's transformation from a movement organically linked to working people to a centrist movement of professionals associated with the public sector, charities and non-governmental organizations (NGOs). In the new playbook of the left, the concerns of working people gave way to the issues and causes embraced by the managerial and professional classes. In effect, the left reinvented itself as a coalition promoting environmentalism and identity-related issues around race, gender and sexuality.

It was during the 1970s and 1980s that sections of the ruling class began to distance themselves from the historical traditions and cultural legacy of their nation. Unlike previous generations of the political and cultural establishment, which were committed to transmitting to society the historical legacy of their nation, the new modernizing elites rejected it as outdated and irrelevant. Estranged from the past and the values of their nation, they also looked down on people who took seriously their community and national identity. Although the more conservative-inclined members of the ruling class contested this development, they were not able and prepared to challenge the cultural transformation of their society.

From the 1990s onwards, the ruling classes embraced what they saw as a post-national, globalist outlook. Their values reflected a synthesis of a technocratic-managerial mindset and identity politics. From this standpoint, ordinary people had to be managed and educated to embrace identity-related values such as inclusion, diversity and multiculturalism. The cumulative outcome of the elite's betrayal of its duty to maintain society's connection with the legacy of the past was to inflict the condition of cultural loss on millions of people.

Christopher Lasch characterized the betrayal of the people discussed above as *The Revolt of the Elites*, which he associated with what he saw as the 'betrayal of democracy'.[14] The use of the word 'revolt' highlighted the conscious refusal of this generation of elites to perform their traditional role of protecting and transmitting the values and customs of their nation to society. This revolution from above not only ignored the aspirations of the people but also sought to impose upon them values that were alien to their existence.

From the 1990s onwards, millions of people were placed under pressure to rethink their relationship to their community and the nature of their national affiliation. People were instructed constantly to redefine their understanding of the family, child rearing and sexuality. Cultural institutions took it upon themselves to call into question the language that people used and took for granted. Pre-existing forms of humour and the cultivation of society's sense of the past were discouraged by the institutions of culture and education. Members of the public were placed under pressure to embrace the latest version of identity politics, even to the point of denying the fundamentals of biology.

The Revolt of the Elites should be interpreted as a response to the so-called 'cultural turn'. The cultural turn, which will be discussed in chapter 4, referred to what can be described as the transformation of Western society's commanding system of values in the late 1970s. This led to a turn away from the organically rooted traditional value system of the West towards administratively created values, principally linked to non-material, environmental, lifestyle and identity-related politics. The outlook of the new anti-traditional elites drew on these values which assisted their attempt to cultivate an identity that distinguished them from the rest of society.

The cultural turn precipitated a series of conflicts that eventually led to a polarized value landscape associated with what we now designate as the culture wars. Throughout most of the past four decades, this war targeting the pre-existing system of values sought to discredit the way of life through which millions of people gained meaning and understood their place in the world. These conflicts of a pre-political nature helped propel populism forward. National populism emerged in response to the predicament of people who experienced this development as a form of cultural loss. Its role should be interpreted as a response to the demand for retaining community solidarity and a connection with the traditions of the past.

The betrayal by the elites ran in parallel with the left's abandonment of the working class. The unravelling of the classical left – communists and socialists – in the late 1970s led many of these movements' activists to look for an alternative political identity. Many of them became overnight converts to Green ideology. Others drew on the resources provided by identity politics to reinvent a new form of radical identity.

Their disenchantment with communist and socialist politics was coupled with a growing sense of estrangement from their former working-class base. Throughout the 1980 and 1990s, they shifted their interest from representing working people to advocating the outlook of middle-class professionals and employees of various state and parastatal institutions and NGOs. Feeling abandoned by parties that hitherto represented them, millions of working people became disillusioned with the left. Today, they constitute the political base of populism.

The double betrayal of the people by the elites and the left occurred in a context where the mainstream political institutions supporting the post-Second World War consensus in the West lost much of its force. The legacy political parties appeared exhausted and found it difficult to sustain and motivate their traditional base. Parties sought to compensate for their estrangement from the electorate by professionalizing their operations and relying on promotion by allies in the media and the institutions of state and society. In this way, they became even more distanced from the electorate and accelerated the erosion of their base. As the Swiss political scientist Hanspeter Kriesi wrote, the 'parties moved their centre of gravity from civil society to the state and have begun to shift from combining representative and governmental roles to strengthening their governmental role – at the detriment of their representation function'.[15]

The weakening of the representative role of political parties was of great concern to the political scientist Peter Mair. He was worried about the phenomenon of 'partyless democracy', a political regime where parties had lost their representative function.[16] In these circumstances, parties also lost their mass base, leading to what Mair saw as the 'hollowing out of mass politics'.[17] He rightly feared that a partyless democracy would encourage the growth of populist parties. Once people felt that their traditional parties did not represent their interest, their political loyalty could no longer be taken for granted. Consequently, the relationship of parties to society altered.

The political scientists Russel Dalton and Martin Wattenberg wrote of the shift towards *Parties Without Partisans*.[18] The phenomenon of parties without partisans can be understood through the concept of *cartel parties*, a concept developed by Richard Katz and Peter Mair to describe a trend whereby parties increasingly function like cartels that employ the resources of the state to limit political competition, thereby ensuring their own electoral survival.[19]

The weakening of the bond between voters and political parties invariably accelerated the erosion of pre-existing loyalties. This phenomenon, characterized by political scientists as party dealignment, assisted the emergence and growth of new parties. These cartel parties rely on access to the institutions of the state and become distanced from their members and supporters. Collusion between cartel parties is the norm, leading to a diminishing role of substantive inter-party competition. Cartel parties collude to limit the scope for the emergence of new parties, and recently in the EU, they have formed informal and formal pacts to prevent populist parties from gaining access to the resources of the state.

The flip side of the cartelization of party politics is dealignment.[20] Dealignment is associated with people's alienation from the party system, which in most cases reflected the loss of legitimacy of the prevailing political order. It refers to a decline in the strength of the electorate's long-term attachment to its political party. Though dealignment affects the electorate as a whole, its effect has been most pronounced among working-class voters.[21] Abandoned by their traditional parties and alienated by the new value orientation of their elites, working people formed the natural constituency for the national-populist movement.

The success of European populism is intimately linked to the implosion of the centre-left and centre-right parties that have dominated the continent since the late 1940s. Parties that used to dominate the European political landscape have become a shadow of themselves. In Austria, France, Holland, Italy and Germany, the populist parties enjoy greater electoral support than the socialists and often surpass the centre-right. So, the context for the rise of populism is the legitimacy crisis of the European political establishment leading to the unravelling of the hegemonic parties of the post-war political order.

One reason why the resilience of populism is underestimated is because most analysts fail to grasp its main driver.

They constantly associate the growth of populism with bigotry and racism. However, what they characterize as bigotry or racism is an expression of the sense of cultural insecurity brought about by people's concern about the devaluation of their national community. This problem was finally recognized by the UK's prime minister, Keir Starmer, at a press conference on immigration in May 2025, where he stated, 'we risk becoming an island of strangers, not a nation that walks forward together'.[22] It is worth noting that no sooner had these words left his mouth than he declared that he regretted using the phrase 'island of strangers'.[23]

Invariably, the cause of the populist surge is attributed to economic factors. Leftist commentators constantly argue that neo-liberal policies are to blame for the rise of populism. Economic inequality and poverty are often perceived as the terrain on which populism flourishes. That is why the German-based Kiel Institute for the World Economy argues that public investment is the antidote to populism. It concluded in its 2024 report that since regions receiving financial support see right-wing populist vote share fall by 15–20 per cent, investment is the way forward.[24]

No doubt economic factors such as the socio-economic dislocation precipitated by globalization and neo-liberal policies, the impact of the recession of 2008 and de-industrialization have played an important role in destabilizing life in many communities and creating mistrust in the political institutions of society. In the past, communities ravaged by the corrosive impact of global capitalism would have aligned themselves with leftist anti-capitalist movements. However, since these negative economic influences coincided with a pre-existing sense of cultural loss and weakening of solidarity, they were experienced through the prism of community insecurity. That is why economic factors played a secondary role in creating a demand for populism. There is substantial evidence that calls into question the attribution of the populist surge to economic factors. For example, a report by the Swedish think tank Timbro found that 'support for populist parties has grown somewhat independently of economic crises or growth'.[25]

What has occurred is not simply a loss of trust in the mainstream political establishment, but also an unprecedented level of cultural polarization – one where values imposed from above are called into question. The coincidence of a crisis of authority with the outbreak of cultural conflict has created the condition for the flourishing of populism.

In the legacy media, there is a tendency to confuse the cause of polarization with its symptoms. It ignores the responsibility of Europe's political establishment for provoking an all-pervasive cultural conflict over values. Invariably, the populist wave is blamed for the polarization of society. But the populist moment emerged in response to the attempt by an increasingly distrusted elite to impose a way of life foreign to the traditions and outlook of millions of people in Europe.

Most analysts fail to grasp the depth of this cultural tension that has created a demand for a voice. To be sure, events like the 2008 financial crisis, the Covid-19 pandemic and the refugee crisis have created important opportunities for populist mobilization. But quite independently of these events, there has been a growing demand for populist answers to the problems created by mass migration, multiculturalism, devaluation of the nation, and policies such as the celebration of LGBTQ+ ideals that threaten traditional cultural norms.

As the political theorist Margaret Canovan pointed out, unlike so-called social movements, populism does not merely 'challenge the holder of power but also "elite values." Therefore, its hostility is also directed at opinion formers and the media.'[26] In turn, the media has a real problem grasping the dynamics of populist politics. This problem is not simply the fault of its shallow analyses. As an institution, the media has become increasingly estranged from the lives of working people and is intensely suspicious of those who do not share its cultural outlook.

The long-term significance of the revolt of 2016

It was in 2016 that the populist revolt got into its stride.

That year brought a historic shift in the political balance of influence between the forces of populism and anti-populism. On 23 June 2016, the people of the UK voted to leave the EU. As Perry Anderson noted, this was the first time that 'a populist rebellion became the expression of a political majority in any capitalist country, and in so doing altered the course of its history'.[27] Brexit represented an astonishingly powerful response to the double betrayal of the people. It rejected the hitherto hegemonic outlook of technocratic-managerial elites and effectively challenged the globalist ideology that dominated the institutions of Western Europe.

At the same time, it highlighted the irrelevance of the Labour Party, whose working-class base voted for Brexit in significant numbers. Brexit showed that populism had mass appeal and that it therefore represented a formidable challenge to the political establishment. That Brexit was not a unique one-off event that went against the prevailing political current was demonstrated by the election of Donald Trump a few months later to the US presidency. The mere fact that Trump could be elected to become the leader of the most powerful nation in the Western world indicated that the influence of anti-populist ideology has reached its limit.

What the Brexit referendum and the Trump election showed was that the technocratic-managerial elites could no longer retain their grip over the electoral process. Their hegemonic authority was now seriously tested by a significant sector of the electorate. Despite their control over the mainstream media, millions of people decided to follow their instinct and reject their message. On the night of Trump's election, 8 November 2016, the legacy media was in a state of shock. As Marco Revelli reported in striking detail:

> The uncontrolled agitation of CNN's John King, standing in front of his magic touchscreen wall, when the colours of the states called for each candidate began to run out of control and he had to admit, disconsolate, that none of the news that the polls had been preparing us for had come true. Or the desperate comments of the CBS star Stephen Colbert, when at the end of a night of torture, with Donald Trump now uncatchable, he asked himself (and America): 'Were there crazier moments than what's happening right now? Or is this just the ultimate fruit of the crazy tree?' The journalist Mark Alperin beside him added, in apocalyptic terms, that 'Outside of the Civil War, World War II and including 9/11, this may be the most cataclysmic event the country's ever seen.'[28]

The triumph of Brexit in the referendum of 2016 unleashed a chain reaction that continues to haunt the political and cultural establishment of the Western world to this day. Why? Because Brexit demonstrated that the people's voice could no longer be silenced by the promoters of the ideology of 'There is No Alternative'. The year 2016 marked a turning point in the fortunes of the political and cultural elites who subscribe to the anti-national globalist worldview. It led to a condition which, in the UK, is diagnosed as 'Brexit Derangement Syndrome'.[29] This condition refers to the trauma precipitated by an entirely unexpected shift in society's political vibe. It is intuited by the recognition that after Brexit, political life could not return to the *status quo ante*.

The election of Trump just a few months after the Brexit referendum further intensified the anxiety of the Anglo-American elites. These two events in 2016 were perceived as a shock to the system. They served as an uncomfortable wake-up call to an entitled and complacent political class, which rightly felt that it and its values were rejected by a significant section of society. The election of Trump forced it to realize that it had totally misjudged the state of public opinion. Members of the elite could intuit that they were totally out of touch with the outlook of millions of American citizens.

Their shock was all the more intense because previously they seemed to be completely unaware of the scale of their isolation from sections of the American public. They were so used to influencing public opinion that they never once thought that it was possible for one of their own to lose the Presidential election. As political analyst Thomas Frank pointed out in November 2016, as the race unfurled the Washington establishment, the media continued to act as if it was business as usual. They supported Hillary Clinton uncritically and refused to acknowledge that she had many flaws. Frank described how opening a newspaper felt like 'tuning in to a Cold War propaganda station'. The American political class tried to defend its authority by pathologizing its opponents. Many thought that only 'botched humans' could support Trump.[30]

In retrospect, it is evident that Brexit constituted the beginning of the end of the smug and self-consciously paternalistic cosmopolitan order that dominated public life on both sides of the Atlantic. Transnational cosmopolitan institutions appeared confused and disoriented by the events of 2016. The global elites that inhabited institutions such as the World Economic Forum (WEF) reacted with a sense of anxiety. Davos Man, as those in attendance at the WEF annual conferences in Davos were known, ceased to be the possessor of a monopoly on wisdom about how to manage global affairs. Writing in *Forbes* a month after the 2016 referendum, the journalist Kenneth Rapoza correctly characterized this event as 'The populist revolt against "Davos Man"'.[31] Rapoza observed that 'Brexit proved once again that Davos Man isn't all-knowing', and added that Davos Man 'has the rhetoric down and he knows how to spread the gospel, but beyond that, their near-term predictions lack vision'. During the years following the events of 2016, the mood of defensiveness amongst supporters of the WEF hardened and at times acquired a panic-like form.

To this day, Brexit is rightly perceived as the launchpad for a global populist revolt. Most supporters of Brexit have no idea how much consternation their triumph caused to the global cosmopolitan network consisting of Remainers, EU ideologues and their allies in the World Economic Forum. Their sense of alarm was captured a month after the referendum by the economic commentator Anatole Kaletsky, who noted that 'Europe's fear of contagion is justified, because the Brexit referendum's outcome has transformed the politics of EU fragmentation'. He added that 'Brexit has turned "Leave" (whether the EU or the euro) into a realistic option in every European country'.[32] Though this point may contain a hint of exaggeration, it is evident that the managers of the EU's institutions are still traumatized by the events of 2016.

Back in the summer of 2016, when Kaletsky expressed his sense of alarm, the national-populist movement that led to Britain leaving the EU could still be dismissed as a one-off event. At successive annual meetings of the World Economic Forum, participants expressed the hope that the threat posed by their populist opponents had waned. The well-known Indian-American commentator Fareed Zakaria was hopeful that '2023 could be the year that exposes populism for the sham that it is'.[33]

Numerous anti-populist commentators echoed his sentiment. 'We seem to have passed peak populism', predicted Andrew Adonis, a leading British anti-Brexit voice.[34] He described Brexit as 'an absurd and damaging project based on a host of populist lies'. Adonis's association of populism with 'lies' and dishonesty expressed the main argument that his side uses to undermine the moral status of their opponent. Through drawing a contrast between the fake populist and the truthful Davos Man, adherents of globalist ideology like Adonis imagined that they could undermine the appeal of their political foes.

Many years have gone by since Kaletsky raised the alarm about the challenge posed by populism to the institutions of the EU. Subsequently, movements that are designated as populist have gained considerable momentum. According to one risk-management consultancy, Solace Global: 'An analysis conducted by more than one hundred political scientists in 31 European countries during 2022 revealed that approximately 32 per cent of Europeans voted for anti-establishment parties. This is a significant increase compared to around 20 per cent in the early 2000s and 12 per cent in the early 1990s.'[35]

Since the publication of this study, the influence of populism has continued to expand, leading to its impressive surge in 2024. The European Parliamentary elections in June 2024 showed that populism had established a formidable presence on the continent. The outcome saw 60 populist parties from 26 EU member states gaining representation in the European Parliament. These parties won 263 (roughly 36 per cent) of the 720 seats. Right-wing populist parties in France, Italy, Austria, Germany and Holland did particularly well, while left-wing ones received less support.[36]

Mainstream commentators cling to the view that populism is a passing phenomenon. 'Has Europe reached peak populism?', asked a commentator in *Politico* in 2019, before expressing the hope that 'the tide could be turning against the anti-establishment nationalist movements that have upended politics across the Continent, leaving the barbarians howling in frustration at the gates'.[37] 'Populism never lasts' (2024) is the reassuring message of another anti-populist commentator.[38] Yet – especially in the aftermath of the re-election of Donald Trump in 2024 – it is evident that populism possesses considerable forward momentum.

The election of Giorgia Meloni in Italy in 2022 clearly showed that, despite the accusation that her party relied on populist lies, her movement could become the party of government. The impressive result achieved by Geert Wilders and his Freedom Party in the Netherlands meant that he became the leader of the party that won the most votes in the 2023 elections. The populist party Chega became the main opposition after its electoral success in the 2025 parliamentary elections in Portugal. Populists constitute the largest parties in Austria and France. At the time of writing, the national populist Alternative für Deutschland (AfD) was beating all its competitors in the opinion polls. A similar pattern of growing support for populist parties is evident in Belgium, Sweden and other parts of Northern Europe. And, of course, Trump's astonishing victory in 2024 showed that populism endures.

Back in 2016, an understanding of the long-term global significance of the outcome of the Brexit referendum eluded even most supporters of the Leave campaign. At the time it appeared as a one-off, almost accidental, event. Today we can see that Brexit opened the floodgates allowing pent-up frustrations with the political system to find an outlet. Brexit had the double effect of undermining the moral authority of the political establishments within the EU and empowering those fed up with the *status quo*. Through demonstrating that there was an alternative to what at times appeared as an invincible globalist neo-liberal outlook, it encouraged people to find their voice and express sentiments that they previously imagined they were not permitted to communicate.

During the eight years between 2016 and Trump's re-election in 2024, the relationship between populists and anti-populists had dramatically shifted in favour of the former. This shift was illustrated by the demoralized response of the American cultural establishment to the election of Trump in 2024. The willingness to organize and resist the victory of Trump in 2016 stands in sharp contrast to the mood of defeatism that enveloped the Democratic Party establishment and their allies in 2024. The headline of a report in *The New York Times*, '"Get somebody else to do it": Trump resistance encounters fatigue' summed up the mood of demoralization that prevailed amongst anti-Trump forces.[39] Kim Whittaker, who was one of the organizers of the 2017 Women's March against Trump indicated that this time around she isn't taking to the street. According to a report 'she's asking, what's the point?'

Anti-populism: the contemporary form of *demophobia*

Anti-populism contains within itself a system of ideas that attempt to portray populism as a threat to a pluralist democratic society. It is essential to understand the role of this ideology since its narrative dominates the media's framing of populism. Until recently, the hegemonic status of its narrative was rarely questioned. Even now, despite its declining influence, the anti-populist narrative continues to provide the script through which the public 'understands' the phenomenon of populism. This narrative typically represents populism as an irrational, dangerous, emotion-driven movement led by authoritarian demagogues. Its objective is to delegitimize populist actors, by representing them as xenophobic, nativist and authoritarian. As Robert Howse, a professor of law explains: '"Populism" is usually and pejoratively defined by the anti-populist elites to imply nativism, anti-liberalism and anti-pluralism.'[40] That is why even individuals possessing radical right views have accepted this negative framing and insist that they are not populists.

It is now acknowledged by a group of scholars who specialize in the study of this phenomenon that anti-populism constitutes a distinct ideological orientation, and that in many respects it represents the latest version of anti-democratic thought. This new *ochlophobia*, or fear of the masses, has gained a commanding influence amongst the intellectuals and cultural leaders wedded to the technocratic-managerial elites.[41]

Critics of populist movements accuse them of practising the politics of fear. In reality, it is the fear of populism that offers the most systematic expression of this tendency. That is why critics of populism often conclude their alarmist accounts with the warning that unless it is crushed, populism will lead to the rise of fascism and another Hitler.

As Savvas Voutyras explained:

> Anti-populism is not entirely new. At its core, it comprises convictions and dispositions regarding the place and role of ordinary citizens (the many, the multitude, the people) in the political process which go a long way back. More specifically, it captures a suspicion towards the masses, and a desire to limit their political involvement, described by some as 'demophobia'.[42]

'Demophobia', or the fear of the people, has acquired a pathological form in the aftermath of the Brexit referendum and the election of Donald Trump. Since that time, sections of the Western elite have become habituated to using words like 'fascist', 'authoritarian', 'illiberal' and 'anti-democratic' as interchangeable with populism. Populism is invariably represented as a threat to democracy, yet at the same time the reaction to it is animated by a powerful mood of suspicion towards democracy.

This suspicion is particularly directed at the majoritarian dimension of democratic decision making. Critics continually warn that majoritarian democracy invariably directs its power against the interest of minorities. One monograph titled 'The rise of despotic majoritarianism' (2022) draws attention to the age-old argument which claims that majoritarianism represents the tyranny of majority.[43] To be sure, there are examples throughout history where governments harnessed their majority support against the interest of minorities. But in such cases the problem was not majoritarian democracy but the violation of its spirit of fairness. Whatever the potential risks of majoritarianism, they pale into insignificance compared to its antithesis, minority rule. Those who oppose majoritarian democracy are in fact demonstrating a preference for the tyranny of a minority.

The real reason why the technocratic-managerial elites fear populism is not because it is a threat to democracy, but because people who support it reject the moral authority of a failed political establishment. By its very existence and its growing influence, it exposes a political order that is clearly aware of its lack of legitimacy. Populist movements offer an alternative source of legitimacy, which is based on the principle of popular sovereignty. Populist movements believe that decisions affecting the public should reflect the aspirations of the people and not the outlook of experts and technocrats.

The current wave of anti-populist and anti-democratic literature is underpinned by a profound sense of anxiety about the loss of elite authority. Yet its authors find it difficult to openly acknowledge the fact that the authority of a political order that prevailed in the West during the Cold War has gradually unravelled. The 'crisis of liberalism' literature rarely interrogates itself to ask why representatives of the political establishment struggle to challenge and neutralize the appeal of its populist opponents. Instead of exploring the implications of the loss of its authority, it prefers to blame its inability to win the arguments on the moral deficiencies of voters.

Jason Stanley's book *How Fascism Works: The Politics of Us and Them* notes that 'the pull of fascist politics is powerful' because it 'simplifies human existence'.[44] Instead of raising concerns about the poverty of the intellectual outlook of those opposed to populists, Stanley prefers to point the finger of blame at an unsophisticated public who are moved by the simplistic message of the fascists. It is important to note, once again, that unceasing allusions to the threat of fascism have become a constant theme promoted by anti-populists. Typical of this literature is Federico Finchelstein's *A Brief History of Fascist Lies*, which asserts that fascist lies inform the contemporary populist narrative.[45] Trump's second term as President stimulated a genre of 'slippery slope from populism to fascism' literature.[46]

Torn from its historical context, the term fascism has been emptied of its precise historical meaning. It serves as a term of abuse to be hurled at political opponents. Jason Stanley's dishonest coupling of populism with fascism offers a paradigmatic illustration of how elite hysteria now works as a medium of academic analysis. In Stanley's fantasy world, America is in 'fascism's legal phase' and supposedly authoritarian leaders like Hungary's prime minister, Viktor Orbán, are following the script of inter-war fascists. Stanley wrote:

> Fascist ideology strictly enforces gender roles and restricts the freedom of women. For fascists, it is part of their commitment to a supposed 'natural order' where men are on top. It is also integral to the broader fascist strategy of winning over social conservatives who might otherwise be unhappy with the endemic corruption of fascist rule. Far-right authoritarian leaders across the world, such as Brazil's Jair Bolsonaro, Hungary's Viktor Orbán and Russia's Vladimir Putin, have targeted 'gender ideology', as Nazism targeted feminism. Freedom to choose one's role in society, when it goes against a supposed 'natural order', is a kind of freedom fascism has always opposed.[47]

Stanley's takeaway message is that governments who oppose the ideology of gender politics are simply following the 'fascist strategy of winning over social conservatives'.[48]

It is likely that Stanley understands that millions of people throughout the world are profoundly hostile to gender ideology.

From his standpoint the problem lies with the prejudices of the masses rather than with his willingness to ignore the biological distinction between men and women. Yet, throughout history, the biological distinction between male and female and the conviction that these were the only two biological sexes, served as a scientifically validated fact of life. Today, such beliefs are indicted as markers of authoritarian fascism! No wonder the crusade against populism appears increasingly to resemble a moral panic.

The rhetoric of 'just like Hitler' is widely circulated by politicians and media commentators who ought to know better. John McDonnell, a leading figure in the left-wing of the British Labour Party likened Nigel Farage to Adolf Hitler and described Reform UK as a 'fascist organization'.[49] He was following the example of the Attorney General, Lord Hermer who likened the attempt to 'abandon' the European Convention on Human Rights to Nazi Germany'.[50] He later stated that he regretted his 'clumsy remarks' but there was nothing clumsy about his scare-mongering reference to Nazi Germany.[51]

4

The Quest for Home

The success of national populism is predicated on its ability to provide an answer to people's quest for a home. Although the quest for home is rarely discussed as a political issue, millions of people are deeply concerned with finding a solution to their condition of uprootedness and isolation. As the American sociologist Robert Bellah famously explained in his magisterial *Habits of the Heart: Individualism and Commitment in American Life* (1996):

> Much of what has been happening in our society has been undermining our sense of community at every level. We are facing trends that threaten our basic sense of solidarity with others: solidarity with those near to us (to neighbors, colleagues at work, fellow townsfolk) but also solidarity with those who live far from us, those who are economically in situations very different from our own, those of other nations.[1]

To be sure, the predicament outlined by Bellah has plagued Western societies since the rise of modernity. However, in recent times the bonds of social solidarity have weakened to the point that in many urban settings people do not even know the names of their neighbours. Life in neighbourhoods without neighbours highlights the classical problem of alienation and estrangement in a poignant form. Another feature of the contemporary quest for home is that, since the cultural turn, it is often dismissed as a problem by an anti-traditionalist cultural establishment.

National populism promotes ideals that attempt to respond to the issues raised by Bellah. For example, the Founding Manifesto of Chega stated that this movement 'came to maintain'. It added

> To maintain our long-standing values and our ancient traditions. To maintain our identity and our attachment to our roots; to maintain our way of discreetly 'giving new worlds to the world' and to maintain our pride, in the face of everyone and everything, of having done so and of still intending to do so.[2]

The delegitimization of the home

The cultural narrative promoted by the cosmopolitan elites is that those who are concerned with home and homeland or nation are insecure and closed-minded individuals who fear facing up to the demands of a changing world. Just as the valuation of the home has become associated with conservative-minded individuals, so too has a preoccupation with alienation become linked to inflexible and backward-looking people who cannot face up to the demands of a constantly changing world.

In his discussion of the shift in attitude towards cultural loss, the University of California historian Martin Jay cannot hide his contempt for those who still take their homeland seriously. He wrote that,

> In short, alienation in the second decade of the 21st century has not actually faded away as a descriptor of human distress.

Rather, it has become most visible in the anxiety of those who bemoan the transformation of a beloved homeland into an unrecognizable nation of aliens.[3]

Jay believes that in the contemporary era, traditional attachment to homeland has no inherent virtue. He asks, 'but in an era of fluid modernity, defined by incessant change, why should sameness and identity be preferred over otherness and difference?' From this perspective the distinction drawn by members of a 'beloved homeland' between themselves and strangers is underpinned by the ideology of exclusion. He observed:

What if hospitality to the alien was privileged over the imperative to defend the homeland against alleged intruders? Accepting the stranger within, the other in the self, could then be credited as a sign of maturity. The weakening of the discourse of alienation reflected these changes in the cultural climate.[4]

From this standpoint the quest for a home must yield to a cosmopolitan narrative that suggests there is no homeland to defend.

For anti-populist critics, people's strong emotional attachment to place makes little sense. They often dismiss national borders as an arbitrary invention that has little moral significance. The American philosopher Martha Nussbaum claims that the attachment to national borders smacks of 'false moral weight and glory'. Indifferent to the individual's cultural connections, cosmopolitan commentators dismiss them as of little import. 'The accident of where one is born is just that, an accident; any human being might have been born in any nation', contends Nussbaum.[5]

The assertion that people's origin has no special significance deprives joint membership of a community of any meaning.

In effect, people become dispossessed of any special claims on their community or homeland. They become detached and uprooted from a world that they imagined as their own and lose all moral ties or rights to the territory they inhabit. This sensibility implicitly affirms an alienated existence as a normal state.[6]

In contrast, a sense of belonging and home is for most people a precondition for feeling ontologically secure. Their refusal to acquiesce to an alienated existence marks the first step towards rescuing what has been culturally lost. It also represents the first step in the very maintenance of cultural continuity with place and the past that has served as a pole of attraction for millions of voters.

The cultural turn and the reaction to it

The dictum that 'There is No Alternative' (TINA), referred to in the previous chapter, was coined by former UK Prime Minister Margaret Thatcher in the 1980s, and represented a fatalistic turn in the political life of Western societies. Since the 1980s, the political establishment has adopted the view that economic realities would always overwhelm political ambition. Like the banal slogan popularized by former US President Bill Clinton – 'it's the economy, stupid' – this view has acquired the status of an unquestioned political truth. Clinton's fatalistic statement conveyed the claim that in the end what mattered was economics and the forces of globalization. Political parties in and out of government have accommodated to this approach, adopting the view that the state is a relatively feeble institution for dealing with the problems of society.

This loss of belief in the efficacy of the state and of government policy reflected a general sense of disenchantment with politics. As such, TINA captured the spirit of the 1990s, in its assumption about the futility of the political imagination. For if indeed there is no alternative, politics can have little meaning. At best, politics can mean no more than fiddling around with minor issues on the margins of society.

Some supporters of TINA attempt to present their case as if it were based on some law of nature. This argument was advanced by former UK Prime Minister Tony Blair, when he informed his audience that 'globalization is a force of nature, not a policy: it is a fact'.[7] An enthusiastic promoter of globalist ideology, Blair has no doubt that his principal enemy is national populism. He set up his well-financed think tank, the Tony Blair Institute for Global Change, to combat what he describes as 'frightening authoritarian populism'.[8]

Others account for their adherence to TINA by arguing that material conditions have reached the stage where there is diminished scope for political life. For example, it is frequently suggested that the process of globalization has reduced the capacity of the nation state to manage its affairs. Politicians and governments have been quick to acquiesce in this outlook.

Initially, the claim that 'there is no alternative' was integral to the unconditional affirmation of the globalist economic order. In the aftermath of the collapse of the Soviet Union, even remnants of the old left accommodated to this view. However, since the institutionalization of the West's cultural turn, this claim has extended its reach, and it is now asserted that there can be no alternative to the cultural hegemony of so-called 'post-material' values. Attempts to question the relevance of post-material values to people's lives are countered by the scornful riposte that this would lead to a hopeless retreat into a world that had ceased to exist. Traditional values came to be dismissed as remnants of an outdated pathology associated with different manifestations of extremism.

Understanding the significance of the cultural turn of the late 1970s, and the reaction to it, provides the context for understanding the emergence of what would eventually crystallize into national populism. The late 1970s saw the ascendancy of the worldview associated with the countercultural movements of the 1960s. This development was led by a new class of cultural elites committed to the advocacy of so-called non- or post-material values.

According to the political scientist Ronald Inglehart, this new class was concerned with post-material needs, such as the need for aesthetic satisfaction, and what psychologists called 'self-actualization'.[9] Its members were increasingly interested in environmentalism and in therapeutic self-help groups.

More broadly, the new elite classes tended to be preoccupied with the question of identity. From the outset, the emerging post-material values were not presented neutrally, as one set of values among others. Rather, they were promoted as superior to 'outdated' traditional values, such as patriotism, nationalism, loyalty and a sense of duty to community. Inglehart himself thought that the move from traditional to post-material values was positive, because it would displace the influence of greedy materialism in society with an enlightened, emotionally correct orientation.

Outwardly, the cultural turn projected a post-materialist outlook that relegated people's concern with living standards to a secondary significance. Instead, it celebrated the authority of non-material values such as therapeutic self-realization and concern with quality of life, particularly the valuation of the environment. It contrasted its high-minded advocacy of quality of life issues with the materialist outlook of old-school parties. At the same time the cultural turn represented a turn against traditional values, which it dismissed as outdated.

From the outset, the contrast between proponents of post-material values and supporters of traditional values was underpinned by a clear class distinction, between the relatively secure and affluent beneficiaries of the so-called knowledge economy and the working classes. Five or six decades later, the cultural-political outlook of these classes has hardened and today is often expressed in a conflict between an elitist and populist political outlook.

The class basis for the clash of values was explicitly acknowledged by two of the most influential theorists and enthusiasts of the cultural turn. As Ronald Inglehart and Pippa Norris outlined in their statement of 'the silent revolution in reverse':

> From the start, younger Postmaterialist birth cohorts supported environmentalist parties, while older, less secure cohorts supported authoritarian xenophobic parties, in an enduring intergenerational value clash. But for the past three decades, strong period effects have been working to increase support for xenophobic parties: economic gains have gone almost entirely to those at the top, while a large share of the population experienced declining real income and job security, along with a large influx of immigrants and refugees.[10]

However, it is important to note that the growing tension between the economically secure and insecure is rarely expressed simply through the traditional vocabulary of class, but of culture.

The cultural turn ran in parallel with important modifications to the socio-economic and political complexion of society. Deindustrialization and the rise of the service and knowledge sectors altered the class structure of society. These trends undermined traditional affiliations and pre-existing forms of group solidarity, particularly as they pertained to social class. As noted previously, an important outcome of this development was the decline of the salience of class in political life.

These developments led to the phenomenon of party dealignment, and the erosion of traditional loyalties to political parties. The Italian political scientist Piero Ignazi highlighted the significance of the unprecedented *realignment* that occurred during the 1980s, writing that 'voting is no longer the confirmation of the belonging to a specific social group but becomes an individual choice, an affirmation of a personal value system: the "issue voter" replaces the traditional "party identification voter"'.[11]

Ignazi was one of the first scholars to notice an important paradoxical development, which was that the cultural turn that led to the rise of new anti-traditional, post-material values also provoked a counter-movement, which he characterized as a 'silent counter-revolution'.[12] Following Inglehart's thesis of a silent revolution leading to the commanding influence of post-materialist movements such as the Greens, Ignazi suggested that the hegemonic influence of the new anti-traditionalist values incited the emergence of a traditionalist counter-movement.

Written in 1992, Ignazi's important monograph on the 'silent counter-revolution' observed that 'changes in the cultural domain and in mass beliefs' favoured both movements associated with post-material values and also with what he characterized as extremist right-wing parties (ERPs). He believed that this silent counter-revolution was the outcome of a widespread disenchantment with party politics and a loss of legitimacy of the governing elites. A mood of malaise leading to a lack of confidence about the future provided the terrain on which the ERPs could grow.

This mood of malaise reflected a palpable sense of political exhaustion. Back in 1997, the political philosopher Isaiah Berlin remarked that 'for the first time since 1789, the European left does not have a project'.[13] He could have added that neither did the European right. This exhaustion of politics was closely linked with widespread pessimism towards the process of change. 'It is everywhere that ideas that were filled with hope of liberation have lost their positive charge, have lost all importance', noted Alain Touraine, one of France's leading sociologists.[14]

Ignazi stated that 'it could be said that the Greens and the ERPs are, respectively, the legitimate and the unwanted children of the new politics'.[15] Ignazi's analysis highlighted an important development that tended to be overlooked by many commentators in the 1990s: the emergence of a growing mood of cultural insecurity amongst European citizens. Integral to this mood were concerns about the very foundations on which European culture rested. Questions about the status of patriotism and the nation, the role of family and community, and values associated with tradition tended to be ignored and frequently disparaged by the political mainstream, including by conservative parties. Millions of people who still lived according to these values often felt that they had become strangers in their own society. Consequently, a space opened for a tradition-affirming, counter-cultural movement.

At the time, this 'silent counter-revolution' was frequently described as a 'backlash' to the ascendancy of post-material values. However, what began as a reaction to the cultural turn gradually mutated into a political alternative that directly challenged the prevailing system of values promoted by the technocratic-managerial elites. Over the decades, this populist challenge to elite authority gained momentum and eventually led to its transformation into a powerful political alternative.

Ignazi referred to the silent counter-revolution as the accomplishment of what he characterized as extreme right-wing parties. His use of the term 'extreme right' illustrates the way in which the mere projection of a systematic challenge to the mainstream political establishment invites a disparaging label. According to Ignazi, these 'parties share some common features which are clearly antisystem':

> These characteristics include antiparlamentarism, antipluralism and antipartism. Even if such parties do not openly advocate a non-democratic institutional setting, they nevertheless undermine system legitimacy by expressing distrust for the parliamentary system, its procedures and discussions, the

weakness of the state, the disruption of the traditional natural communities.[16]

Ignazi recognized that his ERPs do not 'advocate a non-democratic institutional setting'. Nevertheless, they were cast into the role of right-wing extremists because their critique of the political system was fundamental and drew attention to its weak legitimacy.

In effect, what Ignazi's thesis amounted to was that a serious challenge to the political system, one that exposes its crisis of legitimacy, is beyond the boundary of what is acceptable to the maintenance of the status quo and therefore deserves to be branded as extreme right-wing. His conceptualization of the term 'extreme' required that the boundary surrounding the 'acceptable' non-extreme was drawn narrowly. In this schema, there is little room for movements that question and challenge the centrist technocratic mainstream. Movements that project a serious alternative are likely to find themselves cast aside. Ignazi's charge that ERPs were anti-pluralist was clearly a case of the pot calling the kettle black. His refusal to allow populist parties a legitimate place in public life exposed his own anti-pluralist instincts.

The ideologically motivated term 'extremism' is integral to the rhetorical strategy of quarantining populist movements. The aim of deploying what is classically known as the 'politics of fear' is to discredit the projection of a genuine alternative to prevailing political norms. The lack of tolerance towards the ideas of national-populist movements encompasses an extensive range of views. Intolerance is not only regarded as a legitimate response towards the views of national popu-lists, but also as an obligatory expression of the aspiration for being seen as 'aware' and enlightened. The intolerant behav-iour of anti-populists is not only directed at views judged to be hateful or xenophobic, but also to those that simply give offence. As I noted previously, 'according to the current elite consensus, those people who do not celebrate diversity, non-judgementalism and recognition lack "awareness" and are deemed not worthy of tolerance'.[17]

Ignazi's hostility towards populism was underpinned by the concern that it appeals directly to the public and that its aim to mobilize the masses undermines the political system and its elitist institutions. As the Bulgarian political scientist Ivan Krastev observed in relation to the disputes surrounding the EU, at the 'heart of the conflict' is 'the clash between liberal rationalism embodied by EU institutions and the populist revolt against the unaccountability of the elites'.[18]

Technocratic managerialism has always shown a preference for voter apathy over populist mobilization. From the 1950s onwards, numerous liberal political commentators adopted the view that a degree of political apathy was necessary for the maintenance of a stable political regime. Christopher Lasch drew attention to this development when he wrote that, whereas formerly, 'liberals had worried about the decline of popular participation in politics', now 'they began to wonder whether "apathy" might not be a blessing in disguise'.[19] In his important study *The Populist Persuasion*, Michael Kazin notes that in the United States during the Cold War, populism became the 'great fear of liberal intellectuals'[20] who viewed apathy as its antidote.

These days, the attribution of extremism is performed so promiscuously that many ideals and values that one could take for granted are denounced as hateful, xenophobic or racist. Patriotism, which, not so long ago, was perceived as a virtue, is regarded frequently by the cosmopolitan elites as an exclusionary outlook that serves as a precursor of ethnocentrism and xenophobia. The love of nation and nationalism, which once fuelled the revolutions of 1848, are now framed as the racist ideology of the far right. The classical ideal of patriotic citizenship, which was rooted in a sense of place and community, is criticized for excluding those who do not possess this privilege.

Populist commentators who assert that there are only two biological sexes face an onslaught of criticism for their supposed transphobic outlook. Advocates of the traditional nuclear family are castigated for their narrow-minded prejudice. Populists who question mass migration are denounced as quasi-fascist. Even opposition to *illegal* mass migration is decried as a manifestation of racist nativism.

The clash of values between populists on one side, and society's cultural overlords on the other, touches on virtually every dimension of everyday life. What distinguishes populism from many other movements is that it directly challenges elite values. The very articulation of the values of contemporary national populism is perceived as a threat by a complacent elite who, until recently, did not have to face a serious alternative. Their unrestrained hostility towards populist movements is in part motivated by the intuition that their outlook is rejected, not only by populist politicians, but by a significant section of society. The recent ascendancy of populist parties in the face of so many obstacles from the media and establishment institutions speaks to the fact that there is a demand for a movement that poses an alternative to the established mainstream.

Since the 1980s, populism has been constantly attacked for investing its naïve faith in the nation state. Writers frequently highlighted trends that they associated with the 'end of the nation' or 'the demise of the nation state',[21] typically arguing that the nation state had 'become obsolete' and that the backlash to globalization by populist movements was a symptom of their visceral reaction to the 'irreversible decline' of the nation. Anti-populist commentators took delight in emphasizing the irrelevance of the nation and its supposed outdated institutions. In its place, the ideology of globalization posited superior transnational institutions that would displace narrow-minded nationalist sentiments with their superior cosmopolitan values.

During the past decade, the national-populist outlook has been vindicated by the erosion of the globalist worldview.

Now it appears that the much acclaimed, omnipotent forces of globalization are fast unravelling before our eyes. Numerous statements by economic commentators and geopolitical experts lament the 'end of globalization', as a contribution in *Foreign Affairs* puts it.[22] In a similar vein, *The Economist* comments that: 'Globalization is dead and we need to invent a new world order.'[23] Larry Fink, the head of BlackRock, one of the world's largest investment corporations, warned that the 'Russian invasion of Ukraine has put an end to the globalization we have experienced over the last three decades'.[24] Since the election of Donald Trump to his second term, the realization that the ideology of globalization has lost touch with reality is widely echoed, even among its former fans in the world of business. So although we still inhabit a globally interconnected world, the borderless fantasy of cosmopolitan idealogues has lost much of its resonance.

The alternative to globalist ideology by national populism is not confined to the issues that touch on economic matters. Arguably, the most important point of conflict relates to the significance that populists attach to both national and popular sovereignty. Implicitly and explicitly, the main source of dispute between populism and its opponents is an irresolvable conflict over the status of national sovereignty and the nation state. The transnational outlook that dominates the worldview of the technocratic-managerial class regards national sovereignty as an outdated and potentially disruptive ideal.

Cosmopolitanism versus sovereignty

Sovereigntist populism offers a coherent alternative to the hegemonic anti-sovereigntist and cosmopolitan worldview that prevails in many parts of the Western world. In the EU in particular, the standpoint that regards any manifestation of national consciousness as a form of pathology dominates its institutions. Even patriotism – the love of one's country – is frequently denounced by intellectuals possessing antinational, cosmopolitan values. The American philosopher Martha Nussbaum personifies the anti-populist and antisovereigntist worldview. She attacked 'patriotic pride' as 'morally dangerous' and exhorted her readers to direct their 'allegiance' to the 'worldwide community'.[25]

Yet the experience of history indicates that popular sovereignty, and the values associated with its exercise, is the most robust foundation on which public life can flourish. Even the political theorist Francis Fukuyama, who is well known for his adherence to globalist liberal ideals, has acknowledged that there is 'no universal principle of legitimacy other than the sovereignty of the people'.[26] Unfortunately, this principle remains constantly challenged by anti-populist opinion, which has no trust in the capacity of the people to make intelligent choices.

Illiberal opponents of populism possess two important motives for opposing sovereignty. First, they are suspicious of the moral status of 'the people'. Second, they possess a visceral dislike of national consciousness and of national attachments.

Originally, the ascendancy of anti-sovereigntist sentiments constituted an understandable response to the catastrophic events of the 1930s and the Second World War. The rise of Nazi aggression, the catastrophe of war and the Holocaust were often perceived as the inevitable consequence of nationalist rivalries and ideologies. From this standpoint, national attachments are interpreted as a cultural resource that is inherently dangerous because it can be mobilized to promote exclusionary and racial causes. In effect, all forms of national attachments, from patriotism to national pride, were reinterpreted as a potential precursor for xenophobia and racial supremacy.

Since the end of the Second World War, national consciousness was presented as a manifestation of an original sin that could effortlessly mutate into a threat to world peace.

According to this teleological conception of nationalism, what at first appears as an innocent manifestation of national identity and loyalty in the nineteenth century inevitably crystallized into menacing political ideology, of which Nazism is the most barbaric manifestation.

Hostility to national identity acquired a dominant influence amongst the Western intelligentsia in the post-war era. As Johanna Möhring and Gwythian Prins point out, 'for more than two intellectual generations, since 1945, there has been an ascendant narrative in international affairs which has represented the nation state as pathological in its very nature'.[27] The pathologization of national consciousness has been systematically pursued by idealogues attached to the legacy parties of Western Europe.

In recent decades, the conviction that national sentiments and attachments are responsible for all the woes that have afflicted modern European societies has acquired the status of a taken-for-granted truth within international cultural and political institutions. In particular, the EU promotes a political narrative that depicts nationalism itself as the cause of war and political violence. Roger Scruton referred to the 'founding myth' of European integration, the 'belief that nationhood and national self-determination were the prime causes of the wars that had ruined Europe'.[28]

Since the rise of populism, anti-nationalist hysteria has become the default response to it. Leading anti-populist politicians constantly caution against complacency and call for vigilance against the possible resurgence of the bad old days of the 1930s. Warning of the 'demons of nationalism', Jean-Claude Juncker, the former prime minister of Luxembourg and a former head of the EU Commission, said of the growth of nationalist parties in Europe: 'I am chilled by the realization of how similar circumstances in Europe in 2013 are to those of 100 years ago.'[29] In 2016, he warned of the danger posed by 'galloping populism'. When Juncker declared that 'we have to fight nationalism' and 'block the avenue of populism', he evoked memories associated with the good fight against fascism.[30]

Since the 1950s, the evocation of the threat of fascism to de-legitimate the moral status of populism has become the standard practice of its intellectual and political opponents. One of the first examples of this manipulative use of the fear of fascism is to be found in a monograph published in 1955 by Victor Ferkiss, a political scientist with a background in psychological warfare. He explicitly associated populism with American fascism, and stated that populist beliefs formed the core of Ezra Pound's philosophy, 'just as they provide the basis of American fascism generally'.[31]

Virtually every undergraduate studying political sociology during the last four decades of the twentieth century would have been introduced to Seymour Lipset's *Political Man*. In this influential classic, Lipset discussed populism in the same breath as Italian fascism and German and Austrian Nazism. For Lipset, they all constituted a generic form of extremism.[32]

In recent years the narrative of associating populism with fascism has become far more prevalent than before. Even the papacy joined the 'populism as fascism' chorus. In 2017, Pope Francis stated that 'the example of populism in the European sense of the word is Germany in 1933'. Here, the pope didn't merely compare today with the past and use the phrase '*like* 1933' – he went a step further and claimed that European populism *is* Germany in 1933.[33]

The 'just like the 1930s' rhetoric has as its target populism's unambiguous national attachment. The rhetoric that populists are fascists or fascist-adjacent is just that – rhetoric. Populism has nothing in common with fascism. There are no national-populist armed militias, nor any examples of the deployment of anti-democratic violence to substantiate the fear about the imminent rise of European fascism. Nor do populists possess an ambition to settle scores with foreign enemies.

Indeed, it is worth noting that fascism was profoundly hostile to the spirit of populism. In his account of his doctrine, Mussolini declared, 'Fascism . . . denies that this majority can govern by means of a periodical consultation; it affirms the irremediable, fruitful and beneficent inequality of men, who cannot be leveled by such a mechanical and extrinsic fact as universal suffrage.'[34] Paradoxically, Mussolini's condemnation of the rule of a democratic majority is shared by many contemporary anti-populist accounts warning about the return of fascism.

Moreover, contrary to the widely held view that associates fascism with a populist yearning for the past, Mussolini and his movement were thoroughly modernist and future-oriented. Unlike traditional right-wing movements, both reactionary and conservative, fascism was far more obsessed with novelty than with tradition. Italian fascist leaders frequently promoted the goal of a New Age and New Rome, and the creation of a New Man. The ideology possessed a distinctly anti-traditional orientation. As Paolo Orano, a prominent fascist ideologue, put it at the time, fascism was animated by a 'will to annul at all costs in us the vestiges of the past, so as to live only in the future'.[35]

Although the argument against sovereigntism is frequently peppered with references to the 1930s, what is really at stake are differences that pivot around the value conflicts unleashed in the aftermath of the late 1960s cultural turn. These differences are highlighted by diverging attitudes to territory, and the values associated with tradition. Time and again, the target of the anti-populist polemic is its celebration of the virtue of patriotism and its embrace of the national homeland.

Hostility to the ideal of a national homeland extends to the people who support this sentiment. Their rejection of the homeland co-exists with a refusal to take seriously their society's national interest; this view of the world underpinned by their emotional detachment from their own national institutions. Their cultural estrangement from identifying with their nation stands in sharp contrast to the lives and outlook of millions of citizens who are rooted in a place and possess a consciousness that associates nation with their home. From the standpoint of cosmopolitan critics, people's strong emotional bonds to territory make little sense. They often discuss national borders as an arbitrary invention that has little moral significance. Indifferent to the particularity of an individual and their cultural connections, cosmopolitan campaigners dismiss these attributes as of little import. 'The accident of where one is born is just that, an accident; any human being might have been born in any nation', declares Nussbaum.[36]

Anti-populist rhetoric is not simply directed towards negating the celebration of peoplehood, but also at the status of a citizen. They frequently assert that the people living in a particular nation state should have no special rights to the territory they inhabit. Citizens and foreigners alike should enjoy the same privileges, and the people who were born in a nation should enjoy the same rights as a recently arrived migrant.

The American historian Josiah Ober refers to cosmopolitan and global justice arguments against 'state-based restrictions on immigration and rights of citizenship', which he regards as 'inherently illegitimate'. Many argue against the 'legitimacy of national border controls or restrictions on grants of citizenship'.[37] The denial of the legitimacy of national borders in effect denationalizes the meaning of citizenship and deprives people of possessing a sturdy sense of belonging to a common home. And yet, as Canovan rightly noted, 'nationhood is actually a tacit premise in almost all contemporary thinking'.[38] The political ideals of democracy, liberalism, social justice, presuppose its existence.

The assertion that people's origin has no special significance deprives joint membership of a community of any meaning. In effect, people become dispossessed of any special claims on their community or homeland. They become alienated and uprooted from a homeland that they imagined as their own, and become deprived of all moral ties or rights to the territory they inhabit. As Scruton noted, political order 'requires cultural unity, something that politics itself can never provide'.[39]

Cultural unity is particularly important in the modern world where the flow of people between countries has become the norm. Without the cultural unity based on people with a historical connection to their nation, it becomes difficult, if not impossible, to integrate newcomers into the norms of the host society. In such circumstances the potential for multi-ethnic co-operation gives way to the polarized landscape of contemporary multiculturalism.

The mobile and globalist class of professionals and managers adopt a very different attitude to borders and sovereignty than the people whose everyday life is bounded to their community's territory. Pointing to the tension between 'globalists' and 'territorialists', one study of this conflict explains that:

> in many aspects of life, territorial allegiances have become a class-specific property; they have in effect bifurcated. Those who tend to occupy the supervisory positions in politics and the economy – in the non-profit or the electronically based economy, the research centers, financial firms, but in many units, too, of the manufacturing, agriculture and mining sectors – claim to transcend territory. They aspire to make it archaic, depriving it both of real power over their particular activities and of symbolic power, as well.[40]

In contrast, for billions of ordinary people, 'territory remains an important principle of structuring existence in the world. The protection they derive from borders is fragile, but they are dependent on them, and their sense of national or ethnic identity remains higher'.[41]

Indifference to the meaning of a particular historically defined territory tends to endow the sensibility of home with a fragile character, reinforcing the sense of homelessness and of alienation. Territory and place do not simply have a physical or geographical existence. They serve as a medium through which a common historical memory is rendered palpable. Common roots in place connect generations and provide the foundation on which a consciousness of solidarity is formed.

As noted previously, the modern feeling of homelessness – of strangeness in one's own land – is a problem that the globalist technocratic-managerial elites neither recognize nor are willing to address. One reason why sovereigntist populism has succeeded in making headway in recent years is because it explicitly addresses people's quest for a home, as something that is both very personal and seamlessly intertwined with a sense of belonging and identity. Home connects an individual with a community's historical legacy and with the accomplishment of previous generations.

Populism's quest for home constitutes a moral contrast with its opponents' estrangement from their respective homelands. In a very real sense, the conflict of values that pivot around the question of sovereignty are underpinned by contrasting lifestyles and attitudes to life between the technical-managerial elites and that of ordinary citizens.

Indeed, lurking behind the strident anti-populist rhetoric is the conviction that national sensibilities must be subordinated to the outlook of cosmopolitanism. Many Eurocrats and members of the globalist elites have become de-nationalized to the point that they feel more comfortable describing themselves as citizens of the world rather than as member of a national community. Unlike the people who support populist parties and who identify with their nation, the cosmopolitan elites have become de-territorialized. As the sociologist Manuel Castells noted, 'the elites are cosmopolitan, people are local'.[42]

David Goodhart describes the former as the 'anywheres' and the latter as 'somewheres'.[43]

Since the 1990s, the psychic distance between the cosmopolitan elite's outlook and national sensibilities has widened. Cosmopolitans self-consciously distance themselves from the valuation of national culture and posit multiculturalism as superior to what preceded it. Drawn towards multiculturalism and the sacralization of diversity, they have become invested in the promotion of identity politics.

The one identity that they consistently devalue is that of nation. The well-known American sociologist Richard Sennett went so far as to argue that 'the challenge and the promise of American society lie in finding ways of acting together without invoking the evil of a shared national identity'.[44] For someone who regards national identity as an evil, the erosion of national sovereignty is a cause for celebration.

In effect, sections of the elites have consciously detached themselves from their nations. Their alienation from the nation is often expressed through a language that exudes a patronizing sensibility of contempt towards their nationally rooted fellow citizens. Academics in particular are often prone to regard such citizens as uneducated people who do not understand their real interests. As two prominent European sociologists, Ulrich Beck and Anthony Giddens, asserted, nationalist thinking 'can be the worst enemy of the nation and its interests'.

Lasch was one of the first commentators to draw attention to the trend towards the de-nationalization of the elites, writing in 1995 that:

> Those who covet membership in the new aristocracy of brains tend to congregate on the coast, turning their back on the heartland and cultivating ties with the international market in fast-moving money, glamour, fashion and popular culture. It is a question whether they think of themselves as Americans

at all. Patriotism, certainly, does not rank very high in their hierarchy of virtues.[45]

Lasch noted that, in contrast to their lack of enthusiasm for patriotism, the elites readily embraced multiculturalism and diversity. For the de-nationalized elites, patriotism makes little sense since they do not attach much value to the bonds and relationships that bind together the people who inhabit a common territory. Having dismissed the moral status of national identity, they call into question the conviction that members of a community have a moral claim on one another. They assert that members of a community have no legitimate distinct moral claims towards one another that does not apply to all humans.

Beck argued that the duty and responsibility that members of a national community have towards one another makes little sense. 'Why do we have to recognize a special moral responsibility towards other people just because they have the same nationality?', he asked.[46] He asked 'why should they be free of any moral sensibility towards other people for the sole reason that they happened to be born on the other side of the national fence?' His conclusion is that the bonds of culture that bind people together should form the basis for privileges that are not available to those who do not belong to their community.

Beck's cosmopolitan outlook dictates that the duties that family members and kinship groups possess towards one another are no different than their obligation towards strangers living thousands of miles away. In this way, national sovereignty is turned into a form of special pleading by selfish individuals and an expression of nativism.

Outwardly, nativism is an ugly word that refers to the self-ish act of excluding immigrants from entering society. The *Oxford English Dictionary* defines nativism as 'the attitude, practice, or policy of protecting the interests of native-born or existing inhabitants against those of immigrants'.[47] Today, the term is frequently used to characterize the behaviour of people who put the interest of their fellow citizens before people from other societies. Such behaviour can certainly be represented as ungenerous and unkind. But the recognition that the connection between family and community members has a unique quality that cannot be extended to strangers without undermining those bonds is essential for maintaining its integrity.

As it happens, the call to de-territorialize citizenship and deny the moral status of borders constitutes an abstract universalism that in practice denies the substantive content of citizenship. It also goes against the grain of classical cosmopolitan ideals. Immanuel Kant, the founder of modern cosmopolitan philosophy, developed the concept of 'cosmopolitan right', which insisted that strangers who entered the territory of a foreign state should not be treated with hostility. He characterized this right as the 'natural right of hospitality'. However, the right to hospitality should not be equated with 'the right to settle'. Nor did Kant elide the distinction between community members and strangers. Kant understood the importance of community and nation and wrote that a world state would lead to global tyranny.[48]

In contradistinction to contemporary cosmopolitan idealogues, Kant claimed that laws that transcend the nation state lacked the moral depth necessary for the exercise of authority. He stated that 'laws progressively lose their impact as the government increases its range, and a soulless despotism, after crushing the germs of goodness, will finally lapse into anarchy'. Kant's vision of cosmopolitanism was very different to the outlook of contemporary anti-populists.

Technocratic, cosmopolitan-minded politicians simply fail to understand people's national attachments. Nor can they grasp why millions of Europeans have decided to support political movements that they denounce as populist. They are so far removed from the lives of ordinary people that there is no real point of political contact between these two sections of society. That is why the cosmopolitan elites do not even understand those people who are targets of their hate. Populism is about many things – but above all, it is the people's answer to those who would dispossess them of their national identity.

Democracy needs a home

'Only if people are held together by stronger bonds than the bond of free choice can free choice be raised to the prominence that the new political order promised', argued Scruton.[49] It is the spontaneously formed bonds developed through the experience of generations inhabiting a common space that provides the sense of belonging and social solidarity. What some commentators describe as 'natural solidarity' possesses an important moral significance for people. Such solidarity acquires real significance in people's lives when, as Miller noted, 'the political community conceives of itself as extended in time, indeed often as reaching back into antiquity'.[50] Cultural continuity underpins a way of life that is interpreted as both an inheritance from the past and a legacy to be passed on to future generations.

Identification with the nation helps citizens – old and new – acquire a sense of intergenerational continuity, which provides a bond that offers a sense of permanence and confidence. Historically, democrats of all shades of opinion recognized the importance of intergenerational continuity for the flourishing of civic society. Indeed, without the bonds supplied by intergenerational and other forms of community ties, it is difficult to establish a stable democratic polity. As the political theorist Bernard Yack explains, 'contingencies of shared memory and identity' are the foundations on which 'individual rights and political freedoms are exercised'.[51] The element of continuity serves as the prerequisite for achieving solidarity. As Steinar Stjerno explained, 'our interdependence in the past develops bonds that make us more interdependent in our present social organization'.[52] These bonds of solidarity find their political expression in the principle of citizenship. As the social theorist Adam Seligman wrote, 'the ties of solidarity are found within the logic of citizenship itself'.[53]

For solidarity to be effective it needs to be bounded within a pre-political cultural setting. A civil society can make an important contribution to the promotion of a feeling of solidarity and of citizenship. However, for such solidarity to flourish, it needs to become bounded so that it is not simply experienced as matter of individual choice but as a form of action founded on a community of common values. Critics of national identity fail to understand that solidarity is not simply a political but also a cultural accomplishment, and therefore its stability presupposes a connection with the experience of past generations. As Margaret Canovan explained:

> nations are not just common worlds; they are inherited common worlds, sustained by the facts of birth and the mythology of blood ... this natal element in political allegiance is crucially important, and is regularly forgotten by political theorists anxious to recommend a non-national version of political community.[54]

Boundaries are integral to the constitution of people's identity. It is through the drawing of boundaries that 'we are defined and define ourselves'.[55]

The inheritance of a common world provides the foundation for the cultivation of the bonds of solidarity. Whenever the sense of being part of a common world diminishes, solidarity becomes enfeebled. Bellah was deeply preoccupied with this problem, which is why he warned:

Yet this solidarity – this sense of connection, shared fate, mutual responsibility, community – is more critical now than ever. It is solidarity, trust, mutual responsibility that allows human communities to deal with threats and take advantage of opportunities. How can we strengthen these endangered capacities, which are first of all cultural capacities to think in certain ways?[56]

Bellah's emphasis on the need to strengthen 'cultural capacities' is fully shared by national populism. That is why this movement is so devoted to what can be best described as the politics of culture. The success and ultimately the future of populism depends on its ability to cultivate a sense of community where people take for granted their duties and obligations to one another. Getting the balance right between individual aspirations and community obligations is one of the important challenges facing national populism.

5

Populism's Defence of the Pre-political Sphere

The concept of the pre-political sphere refers to dimensions of social life and organization that exist outside formal political and state institutions. The pre-political sphere embraces informal relations, associations that shape civic life, and community interactions that are independent of formal politics. It includes neighbourhood networks, voluntary associations, community customs and more. The quality of the pre-political sphere exercises great influence on how solidarity is experienced. It is in the pre-political domain that intergenerational bonds and the valuation of tradition and its rituals and practices continue to retain their force. It also provides the spirit of populism with energy and force.

For some time now, the pre-political sphere has been subjected to great external pressure from public institutions that wish to impose their values upon it and bring it under their authority. The way of life associated with the preservation of customs, traditions and informal institutions continue to run up against the value system of the technocratic-managerial elites.

The conflicting views over the pre-political are the outcome of the fact that the new elites have very different ideas about the importance of traditional values attached to the pre-political sphere to most other people. In the past, the disputes between populists and elites rarely touched on this realm of life; until recently, the sanctity of the family and the importance of community and place were at least rhetorically upheld by both sides. There were different visions of the upside and downside of modernization, but until the 1970s, these differences did not crystallize into a sharply polarized orientation towards the lifeworld of people.

The pre-political sphere is by definition one that is inhospitable to the hegemonic value of inclusion. In this domain individuals are defined by their particularity. They are not equal nor interchangeable. Members of a family regard non-members as outsiders who are treated in accordance to a different standard than those on the inside. Similarly, members of a community possess different duties, obligations but also privileges than do non-members. Friends possess obligations to one another that they do not extend to others. Friendship groups only include friends and exclude those who are not. As Scruton explained, communities 'are by their very nature exclusive, establishing privileges and benefits that are offered only to the insider, and which cannot be freely bestowed on all-comers without sacrificing the trust on which social harmony depends'.[1]

For its critics, one of the most objectionable features of populism is its supposed exclusionary outlook. In a world where inclusion has become one of the foundational political values of the post 1960s cultural elites, those who are deemed to violate it are cast in the role of enemies of a just society. As two of the leading academic anti-populist commentators noted, 'almost all scholars of European populism stress its exclusive nature'.[2] However, as we explain below, the tendency to dismiss or condemn the exclusion and exclusionary attitudes of populism is often underpinned by an existing hostility to relations of solidarity based on pre-political bonds and informal relations. Anti-populist ideology is permeated with the conviction that it is exclusionary to draw any form of distinction between people. Consequently, the normal gesture of showing partiality for someone with whom you feel a special connection can fall foul of the exclusion police. Anti-populist ideology regards strong bonds between members of a family, kinship group, community or nation as tribalist, and finds it difficult even to tolerate appeals made to a people.

The solidarity that is based on pre-political bonds and obligations is often the target of criticism by anti-populist writers. They refer to such forms of pre-political bonds as natural solidarity, which they deem to be inferior to formal types of political solidarity. Natural solidarity is one that is forged between people who see themselves as belonging to an organically rooted common community. Such critics distinguish between 'negative and positive modes of solidarity'. They argue that 'negative solidarity connotes a given commonality without political action. Good, positive solidarity establishes a previously absent commonality through political action'.[3] In some cases, the couplet good and bad solidarity is replaced by the terms political and anti-political solidarity.[4] Jennifer Gaffney noted that 'unlike "anti-political" solidarities grounded in familiarity and sameness, political solidarities thrive on diversity, action, and spontaneity'.[5]

It is important to note that until the cultural turn pre-political solidarity was rarely a target of criticism. As one account of the history of solidarity explained:

> Whatever else solidarity entails descriptively; it entails a special commitment to one's solidarity fellows that one does not hold towards everybody else. And whatever normative consequences solidarity has for those in solidarity, it will ground *some* special claims that these fellows have on us and we on them. In this sense, solidarity, like friendship, family, and nationality, constitutes a special relationship with special obligations. Over

recent decades, a number of philosophers have raised challenges to the very idea that special obligations can be justified towards those who are not part of them.[6]

The challenge to the moral authority of pre-political solidarity is motivated by the concern that 'strong solidarity within a group can easily be accompanied by nonsolidarity and injustice toward outsiders'.[7]

The construction of a moral contrast between political and pre-political solidarity is unhelpful since there is a close connection between the two. Political life does not emerge from thin air but presupposes pre-political communities from which it evolves. The pre-political is chronologically and logically prior to the political. The basis for the emergence of a public devoted to the pursuit of politics evolves out of the experience and concerns of the lifeworld of people. That the two spheres are so sharply counterposed to one another is due to the cultural turn against a form of solidarity that is based on cultural continuity and on values that are antithetical to those of the technocratic-managerial elites. The political theorist Bernard Yack warned against the tendency to counterpose community to formal political institutions. He rightly noted, 'to the extent that one condemns our tendency to look for prepolitical sources of political identity, modern democratic political culture is part of the problem, not the solution'.[8]

Of all the value-related conflict between populism and its elitist adversaries, none is more consequential than the contrasting attitudes towards solidarity. What happens to people and their relationship to one another in the domain of the pre-political is important to millions of people. Millions of people are concerned to uphold the natural bonds of solidarity in face of the pressure to diminish their significance. More than anything else it is the quest for this form of solidarity that leads concerned citizens to support populist movements.

The weaponization of inclusion

Anti-populist hostility to solidarity runs in parallel with an obsession with the threat posed by similitude and homogeneity – in both cultural and national forms. In particular, the pre-political sphere – where everyday ties of blood and kinship and close cultural connections are forged and reproduced – is frequently criticized for being antithetical to the cultural valuation of diversity. Populism is often condemned for failing to adhere to the sacred values of diversity and heterogeneity.

The vast literature on populism has failed to notice one of the most significant defining features of contemporary populism, which is its instinctive defence of the pre-political sphere. This oversight is not surprising because the classical Aristotelian distinction between the political and the pre-political is rarely discussed by political theorists and analysts. Moreover, the importance of the pre-political is characteristically overlooked within the post-liberal and anti-populist literature.

In his seminal work *Politics*, Aristotle drew a clear analytic distinction between the pre-political and political 'in the form of the household and the state'.[9] According to Aristotle, the pre-political community is founded on natural inequality, where distinctions in terms of physicality, intelligence and other attributes are expressed in terms of what can best be described as natural principles of hierarchy. Although over the centuries the principles of hierarchy have altered, as has the relationship between household and the state, the distinction between the pre-political and the political retains its relevance. Today, this distinction often overlaps with that drawn between the private and public sphere.

Unlike the political sphere – or what Hannah Arendt characterized as public life, which is the realm of equality – private life 'consists in those exclusive attachments that form between individuals as unique persons, such as love, friendship and family'.[10] In public life discrimination cannot be accepted since it negates the principles of equality and democracy. In the private sphere matters are different since it is through discrimination that the particularity of relationships gain meaning.

Arendt argued that outside of the public/political sphere, discrimination and differentiation between people is the norm, and the rule of equality has little bearing on how people conduct themselves. She controversially wrote that in the pre-political sphere 'we become subject to the old adage of "like attracts like" which controls the whole realm of society in the innumerable variety of its groups and associations'. She added that 'what matters here' are 'the differences by which people belong to certain groups whose very identifiability demands that they discriminate against other groups in the same domain'.[11]

In contrast to the contemporary tendency to cast the act of discrimination in an entirely negative light, Arendt argued that without discrimination, society would cease to exist:

> In American society, people group together, and therefore discriminate against each other, along lines of profession, income, and ethnic origin, while in Europe the lines run along class origin, education and manners. From the viewpoint of the human person, none of these discriminatory practices makes sense; but then it is doubtful whether the human person as such ever appears in the social realm. At any rate, without discrimination of some sort, society would simply cease to exist and very important possibilities of free association and group formation would disappear.[12]

In the pre-political sphere, the attachments that are formed are, by definition, exclusive, and discrimination is its integral feature. Arendt was worried that the attempt to eradicate the distinction between the private pre-political sphere and the public political domain would deprive people of the opportunity to live their lives in accordance with their natural affinities, likes and interests.

Arendt was writing at a time when the elimination of discrimination and exclusion of all sorts was fast becoming institutionalized, and the pre-political sphere was therefore gradually falling under the spell of public regulatory procedures. She was writing decades before the regime of 'diversity, equity and inclusion' (DEI) became institutionalized, but she anticipated the threat posed by technocratic-managerial rule-makers who wished to erode or formalize the natural ties that bound people together in the informal domain of the pre-political.

The main casualties of this assault on the pre-political domain were the inherently discriminatory relations founded on bonds of affection. These bonds, which were underwritten by custom and a spontaneously developed sense of affinity, were, by definition, exclusive. Until relatively recently, people wanting to forge relations with those who are like them was seen as a normal part of human existence. However, in the aftermath of the emergence of the 1960s counterculture, the distinction between the private and the public realms became eroded and the freedom to discriminate in the pre-political sphere came under increasing scrutiny. It was at this point that discrimination was redefined as unjust and oppressive.[13] The cause of abolishing all forms of discriminatory behaviour and customs became an integral element of the cultural turn. It failed to distinguish between discriminatory behaviour in the public sphere, which necessarily represented a denial of democratic rights, with what went on in the pre-political sphere where such rights make little sense.

Today, the term discrimination has become subject to the imperative of concept creep and is often trivialized, as I discuss below.

From the 1980s onwards, the targeting of attitudes and customs that prevailed in the pre-political sphere became a central feature of anti-populist ideology. The term 'othering' gained currency in the anti-populist literature to refer to what was characterized as the exclusionary outlook of their opponents. *The Palgrave Handbook on Right-Wing Populism and Otherness in Global Perspective* is paradigmatic in this respect. It argues that 'a key characteristic of the recent rise in right-wing populist politicians worldwide is the pervasive dynamic of exclusionary conflicts and moral divisions, designated as meta-othering'.[14]

In Western cultural institutions, othering, defined as 'the act of treating someone as though they are not part of a group and are different in some way',[15] has become vilified. Yet throughout the centuries, common sense dictated that the cultivation of a sense of in-group identity was an entirely understandable way of cultivating relationships and building communities. The communitarian sensibility that underpins populism takes the act of treating people who are not part of a group differently than its members as a normal, even necessary part of life. Those who are obsessed with 'othering' cannot imagine that the cultivation of an in-group identity does not logically lead to the oppression of the 'others'. From their perspective, any form of exclusion serves as a prelude to what they perceive as an unjust act of discrimination.

The current use of the term othering elides the distinction between the deeply structured discrimination that is based entirely on race or class and acts of exclusion that spontaneously emerge through the informal interaction between people. The refusal to interview someone for a job on account of their race or gender represents a qualitatively different form of action than the reluctance to invite a colleague to your wedding.

The 1960s counterculture played an important role in undermining the legitimacy of the domain of the pre-political. It directed much of its fire on lifestyles that it regarded as disagreeable and did not hesitate to attack long-established customs and behaviours in the pre-political sphere. At the time, commentators struggled to comprehend the origins and meaning of the cultural upheaval that they were witnessing. It was evident that many features of the taken-for-granted consensus that touched on the conduct of everyday life had become a focus for conflict. Matters that had been hitherto relatively untouched by political disputes – values, lifestyles, private life – were suddenly engulfed by them.

One of the first to note this shift was the scholar Gabriel Kolko, who in 1968 remarked that 'cultural realignment', rather than class politics, led to a shift towards conflicts that were 'pre-political'. He asserted that what 'ultimately explains the realignment in America's public culture are allegiances to different formulations and sources of moral authority'.[16]

Decades later, the Italian writer and philosopher Umberto Eco recalled that 'even though all visible traces of 1968 are gone, it profoundly changed the way all of us, at least in Europe, behave and relate to one another'. He added that 'relations between bosses and workers, students and teachers, even children and parents, have opened up' and therefore 'they'll never be the same again'.[17] Eco's focus on the transformative impact of cultural change on the conduct of informal and formal human relationships captured the essence of the events of the 1960s.

The emergence of new inclusive and anti-traditional lifestyles gained cultural ascendancy in the 1970s and became institutionalized by the cultural establishments of Western societies. However, significant sections of society found theses new anti-traditional values alien to their way of life. Over the decades, these sentiments galvanized people to try to live according to the values into which they were socialized by their ancestors. Arguably, the defence of the customs and taken-for-granted forms of behaviour prevailing in communities constitutes a central pillar of national populism.

The populist solidarity dismissed as a demand for exclusion

The transformation in the 1970s of the noun 'exclusion' into a term with normative connotations was inspired by the project of endowing the word 'inclusion' with positive moral associations. Nevertheless, despite the considerable ideological investment in rendering the inclusion–exclusion couplet into an ideologically compelling binary, its meaning lacks precision. The terms are often used instrumentally to signal a preference for breaking down traditionally based social networks and informally established customs.

Exclusion is used in a variety of different contexts to ascribe negative connotations to disparaged actions and behaviour. Attempts to define the term precisely tend to flounder. One European Union document conceded that 'it is difficult to come up with a simple definition'.[18] As a review of sociological theories of exclusion explained:

> In fact, observers agree on only one point: the impossibility of having a single, simple criterion with which to define exclusion. The numerous surveys and reports on exclusion all reveal the profound helplessness of the experts and responsible officials.[19]

This point was reinforced by the French sociologist Julien Freund, who stated that, despite numerous attempts to find a definition, 'in the end, the notion of exclusion is permeated with both sense and nonsense and is liable to misinterpretation; after all, the concept can be made to express pretty well anything, including even the pique of someone who cannot get everything he wants'.[20]

The lack of conceptual clarity surrounding the meaning of exclusion does not inhibit advocates of inclusion from casually hurling the accusation of exclusionary behaviour at their adversaries. In recent decades, the meaning of exclusion has expanded to the point that, in some cases, the practice of not treating all people the same can be defined as unacceptable exclusionary behaviour. The logical outcome of this approach is that the maintenance of a distinction between a member of family and that of a stranger, or between a friend and a casual acquaintance, or a citizen of a nation and a non-citizen can be characterized as an act of exclusion. That is why the appeal by populists to 'the people' is frequently denounced for excluding those who are not considered to be part of that group. Even a nation's flag can be characterized as a symbol of exclusion and hate. 'Does America's flag symbolize exclusion and hate?', asks a commentator in *The Washington Post*.[21]

It is important to realize that the charge of exclusion is not simply directed at the politics of populism, but against the cultivation and promotion of family, community and informal bonds. The celebration of these bonds and their maintenance is often denounced on the grounds that they are discriminatory, tribal and hostile to pluralism. What lies behind these accusations is the cultural disposition to perceive the cultivation of strong attachments and loyalties in a negative light. Even friendship circles, particularly in the workplace, are regarded as potential sites for exclusion and regarded with hostility and scepticism.

According to so-called bullying experts, the failure to invite a colleague to an informal social event can be construed as an act of exclusion. So, when someone is not invited to a social occasion or to join a group chat, they may be considered victims of bullying.[22] One Employment Tribunal case in the UK found that the failure to invite an individual to a work night out organized by colleagues 'amounted to a form of victimisation'.[23] The implicit message of this judgment was that everyone had to be treated the same regardless of whether or not they are your friends. In effect, the implication of this judgment is to call into question the right of employees to decide who they wish to include in their social circle. In the UK, an NHS nurse who quit her job because she felt that she was excluded after her colleague left her out of a tea round was awarded £41,000 in compensation.[24]

There is even an attempt to characterize those who are not regarded as potential and desirable sexual partners as 'sexually excluded'.[25] One essay in the journal *Social Theory and Practice* titled 'A defence of sexual inclusion' argues that:

> access to meaningful sexual experience should be included within the set of the goods that are subject to principles of distributive justice. It argues that some people are currently unjustly excluded from meaningful sexual experience, and it is not implausible to suggest that they might thereby have certain claim rights to sexual inclusion. This does not entail that anyone has a right to sex with another person, but it does entail that duties may be imposed on society to foster greater sexual inclusion.[26]

The absurd contention that 'duties may be imposed on society to foster greater sexual inclusion' indicates that even the absence of sexual desire towards an individual can be reframed as exclusionary. This bizarre logic has been incorporated into trans identity politics. Thus, trans activists have argued that lesbians who don't want to sleep with trans women are behaving like racists.[27] The constant demand for equality in sexual attraction speaks to the impulse of corrupting the pre-political sphere.

When even informal friendship networks are assessed in accordance with the politics of inclusion, it becomes evident that the meaning of exclusion has undergone an alarming degree of concept creep. In effect, the concept of exclusion has mutated into a cultural obsession focused on the minutiae of informal relations. If people are discouraged from treating their close friends differently from people with whom there is an absence of an emotional connection, it follows that the possession of differential attitudes towards members of your community and strangers will also meet with disapproval.

Even the sharing of a joke or banter can be characterized as 'the enemy of inclusion'.[28] 'Banter can often inadvertently' result in exclusion, argues a language guide issued by the Royal Academy of Engineering.[29] When even joking at work can become a matter of interest to the inclusion engineers, it becomes evident that the weaponization of the concept of exclusion serves to legitimate the policing of spontaneous, informal life.

According to the hegemonic cultural script prevailing in Western societies, the various forms of special relations, unique attachments and solidarities – which, by definition, cannot be inclusive – are the moral opposite of the commanding values of inclusion, diversity, difference and heterogeneity. Those who identify with a nation or a particular community and who treat its members differently to those who do not belong to it are invariably accused of discrimination. Critics of populism regard a cosmopolitan, borderless and post-traditional world as morally superior to one that is nationally rooted and wedded to local custom and historically ascribed ideals and practices. They regard traditionally based pre-political communities and relationships as irrational relics. Pre-political solidarity – ties of kinship, family, friendship, religion, community membership – are dismissed as semi-archaic links that stand in the way of openness.

Habermas regards concepts like 'the people' or 'the nation' as an odious fantasy used by 'right-wing populism' to undermine diversity. He explains his antipathy to national consciousness in the following terms:

> After half a century of labour immigration, even the European peoples, given their ethnic, linguistic and religious diversity, can no longer be conceived as culturally homogeneous entities.[30]

The political philosopher Jan-Werner Müller echoes Habermas's disdain for the people, and asserts that 'the idea of the single, homogeneous, authentic people is a fantasy'.[31] However, the real fantasy is the belief that homogeneity is an essential ingredient of national consciousness or of movements that are characterized as populist. Homogeneity played a role in the racial nationalism of National Socialism. But to make a conceptual leap from the Nazi obsession with racial purity to the claim that all forms of nationalism and populism are devoted to a homogeneous ideal of the nation is an exercise in polemical acrobatics rather than a serious analysis.

National consciousness represents a form of patriotism that affirms a common cultural tradition and the territory within which it is rooted. Müller and Habermas's predilection for racializing this form of consciousness says more about their anti-populist prejudice than about the views of their foes.

The populist aspiration to preserve community and the informal attachments between its members is therefore often dismissed as an exclusivist tendency that represents the point of departure towards ethnocentrism and xenophobia. At base, the animosity directed at populism represents a pre-existing repugnance towards the values and sensibility that underpins the populist political outlook.

The ideological instrumentalization of exclusion encourages the detachment of individuals from their particular social networks, friendship groups and community affiliations. That is why the mere mention of 'the people' by populists provokes gestures of disapproval. Critics frequently argue that the claim to represent the will of the people invariably leads to an exclusionary political programme. According to one academic commentator, Marina Prentoulis, the power of national populism 'rests on putting an exclusionary principle at the centre of its project'. She condemns a populist project like Brexit because its '"we" is defined according to nationality'.[32] Like many of her co-thinkers, she assumes that the mere affirmation of an attachment to a nation implies opposition to 'others'.

The claim that a positive identification with a nation or some other cultural community automatically leads to a negative – even hostile – attitude towards the 'other' is integral to the association of populism with an 'exclusionary principle'. Critics of populism cannot comprehend the fact that the affirmation of the 'we' need not represent a gesture of hostility towards 'them'.

As one commentator explained, 'precisely because populists claim to represent "the people", they have to define the people first and that often means excluding vulnerable and marginalized populations, such as religious or ethnic minorities and immigrants'.[33] According to another account, 'when discussing migration or refugees, for instance, European populists respond with a "common sense" defence of the (native) people against a demonized out-group, namely immigrants'.[34]

The placing of the definite article before 'people' is constantly attacked by anti-populist commentators for assuming that there is a distinct group of individuals who constitute a people. Frequently, academic commentators represent the idea of a people as a myth that does not have a real existence prior to its political use. As Christos Marneros claims, 'the people' is a 'deeply problematic' construction.[35] His view – that 'the primacy which is given to "the people" as a political agent' leads 'to the formation of politics that are essentialist and exclusionary' – is widely shared by the anti-populist commentariat.[36]

According to one account, 'populist political articulation generates the people, which does not pre-exist'.[37] Another academic expert on this subject observes that the 'process of constructing a people is key to the performance of populism'.[38] In recent times, numerous academic contributions have adopted an idealist and extremely subjective interpretation of the term 'people'. At times, it seems that they are more interested in playing with words than in understanding whether a people can be both historically rooted and possess a social existence. Instead, they associate 'the people' with a 'discourse', a 'discursive construct' or an 'invention'. Apparently 'a people does not exist *as such* before it is discursively *named*'![39]

Constant references to 'the people' as an invention or as a construction indicates that writers on this subject find it difficult to imagine that there are individuals who genuinely perceive themselves as part of a people connected to a common culture and way of life and organically linked to a common historical past. It is as if they cannot reconcile themselves to the fact that there are numerous cultural and ethnic groups who see themselves as a people possessing a distinct identity.

This is why even academics who take a relatively neutral stance towards populism struggle to acknowledge the fact that the people have a very real physical and cultural existence. The radical academics Ernesto Laclau and Chantal Mouffe, who are sympathetic towards leftist populism, argue that the people do not have a fixed identity, but rather should be considered as the outcome of 'constructing a new subject of collective action'.[40]

As it happens, the constitution of a people need not have a fixed identity. In any case in the modern world identities evolve and do not remain static and fixed. Indeed, in some circumstances a people can include a variety of different ethnicities who share a commitment to a common sense of values. In recent times when I attended meetings and festivals organized by such populist movements as the Rassemblement Nationale or Reform, I was struck by the enthusiastic participation of people with an African or Asian heritage.

To be sure, the constitution of a people faces many challenges, the most important of which is the relatively fragile sense of a common culture. In the contemporary polarized landscape the task of rescuing what has been culturally lost faces formidable obstacles. Populist movements need to serve as a focus for cultural unity and encourage members of society to participate in the renewal of a common culture.

Estranged from the kind of solidarity that spontaneously emerges through the sharing of a common world, many commentators tend to regard the people as an abstraction – the accomplishment of a political invention rather than as an expression of a *demos* inhabiting a common world. The tendency to detach the people from their historical roots and represent it as a product of an invention is often motivated by the goal of discrediting the populist claim that there exists a people possessing a common legacy and characteristics that distinguish them from anybody else. That this legacy needs to be reappropriated to make it relevant for our times should not distract us from taking it seriously as a resource from which a people can continually draw inspiration.

The principal reason why anti-populist ideologues are keen to discredit the idea of the people is to undermine the legitimacy of popular sovereignty. This point is emphasized by the political theorist Ochoa Espejo, who contends that the normative authority of the people as a collective body is lost, if it turns out that it is 'solely' an 'accident of history'.[41] If 'the people' is indeed an artificially constructed entity or a product of a historical accident, then its moral authority is significantly undermined. Since populism is so closely entwined with representing or giving voice to the people, its very foundation becomes discredited if what it claims to stand for is merely an invention.

Critics who regard the concept of 'the people' as an invention also condemn it on the ground that it is a 'closed' community. In the same way, the idea of citizenship is frequently attacked for its exclusivist character. Citizenship is not an abstract transnational concept which can be distributed across national boundaries. Since not everyone is entitled to the citizenship of a specific nation, it is inconsistent with the cosmopolitan criteria of inclusivity.

Since a person is a citizen of a specific nation and bound to its territory, national citizenship fails to meet the criteria of inclusivity. Citizenship based on birth, cultural affiliations and loyalties is particularly decried. But even the status of achieving citizenship through voluntarily committing to a common civic identity – such as when immigrants are accorded such status – runs counter to the cosmopolitan vision of open borders advocates.

The anti-populist critique of the people is closely linked to a line of argument that directly calls into question the moral standing of citizenship, proclaiming that the distinction between citizens and others is morally wrong. This claim asserts that citizenship is based on an accident of birth, and that citizens therefore should not possess privileges and resources that are denied to others. Cosmopolitan critics of national citizenship, such as the philosopher Seyla Benhabib, regard people as if they were interchangeable abstract individuals. In her vision they are abstracted from their unique and distinct particularity and argues that 'legally, cosmopolitanism considers each individual as a legal person entitled to the protection of basic human rights in virtue of their moral personality and not on account of their citizenship or other membership status'.[42] A 'legal person' has no particular cultural roots and of course their pre-political affiliation is irrelevant.

Benhabib possesses a sensibility that is estranged from community. She also despises the idealization of the people on the ground that they are 'increasingly viewed as a homogeneous mass'.[43] Her hostility to populism is articulated through a language that is deeply suspicious of the people's role in democratic decision making. In particular, she is hostile to the proposition that the people should be 'identified with the electoral majority of a particular election cycle'.[44] Her argument is not only anti-majoritarian – it also seeks to replace democracy based on a nation-based constituency with one that is transnational. In this way, the role of the *demos* is all but annulled.

What the critics of populism characterize as the politics of exclusion can be best understood as a positive *quest for solidarity*. In contrast to the dominant cultural ideals, populism presumes in favour of close, organically created bonds among people who share a common heritage and way of life. It rejects the notion that membership of a nation or a community is arbitrary and accidental. It is true that human beings are not responsible for the circumstances of their birth. But once they are born, they become biologically and culturally part of their family and the citizens of their community and nation. It is through the bonds that attach them to these institutions, and the generations that preceded them, that people develop their moral sensibility and their individuality.

As the historian Gertrude Himmelfarb explained, 'the givens of life: parents, ancestors, family, race, religion, heritage, culture, tradition, community – and nationality are not the '"accidental" attributes of the individual'.[45] Individuals can leave their homes and move to another part of the globe and adopt a new identity, but what they cannot do is to be born again 'in any nation'.

For national populism, the pre-political attachments of community life provide the foundation for political solidarity. In contrast, the adversaries of populism attempt to render the particularity of community ties irrelevant. Instead of embracing the natural affinity that members of a community possess towards one another, it is rejected and an important opportunity for cultivating relations of solidarity is overlooked. Throughout the ages the central role of pre-political bonds was affirmed by thinkers and commentators across the political spectrum. Bonds of solidarity founded on an organic connection with the past were rarely dismissed as a foundation on which the politics of exclusion would flourish. With the politicization of inclusion, the meaning of pre-political attachment was radically reinterpreted and pathologized.

The views of the nineteenth-century liberal political philosopher J.S. Mill on this issue are paradigmatic in this respect. In his *Considerations on Representative Government* (1861), Mill pointed out that 'the common sympathies of fellow nationals eased political co-operation among them, whereas lack of "fellow-feeling" and common culture was bound to inhibit the formation of public opinion'. For Mill 'popular sovereignty and national self-determination are intertwined'.[46]

The sympathy and fellowship that exists between people based on shared experiences or feelings provide meaning to a group. Solidarity is easier to realize when people have a common background and interest. A kind of instinctual neighbourliness facilitates the kind of collaboration that is not possible to achieve without pre-existing emotional bonds or fellow-feeling. We know from numerous studies that 'successful societies are actually existing things based on habits of cooperation, familiarity and trust and on bonds of language, history and culture'.[47]

Studies such as the one conducted by the Harvard political scientist Robert Putnam show that diversity creates major trust issues among different groups in society. His work suggested that diversity damages civic life and can create a climate of mistrust.[48] Putnam explains his findings as the flip-side of cultural diversity. In his study *Bowling Alone*, he found that the greater the diversity in a community, the fewer people vote, and the less they volunteer, the less they give to charity and work on community projects.[49]

There is little point in attempting to speak on behalf of 'the people' if this concept is conveyed as an abstraction that could be applied to all human beings. The drawing of a line around a culturally defined people does not demand hostility towards those who are not part of this community. Similarly, the distinction between citizen and non-citizen is essential if this concept is to possess meaning. Contrary to those who advocate an inclusive interpretation of this concept, there is no citizenship without non-citizenship.

The spirit of populism seeks to recover the moral significance of solidarity based on a community of belonging, and to provide it with voice and visibility. Far from being an abstraction or an invention, the people are the foundation on which democratic life is conducted. In contrast, the anti-populist imagination regards the concept of the people with open hostility. Anti-populists are deadly serious in their attempt to render the people invisible.

The British philosopher Anthony Grayling asserts that 'the phrase "the people" should be proscribed in the discourse of democracy', since it is a 'demagogue's term'. That's another way of saying that only a *demos*-free democracy is acceptable to the technocratic-managerial worldview. Taking the *demos* out of democracy by making the people disappear is a principal aspiration of the present-day anti-populist imagination.

The spirit of populism inevitably provokes a nervous anxiety amongst those possessing an anti-democratic disposition. As Paolo Gerbaudo explains:

> Democracy, as it has developed in modern national-popular states, is a process that is encased within a specific territory to which a certain people is seen as belonging, and over which it is seen as capable of asserting this will. Therefore, sovereignty is necessarily predicated on a level of exclusivity. It needs to prescribe a sphere of action, or territory, that is discrete and delimited by borders.[50]

That democracy itself is 'predicated on a level of exclusivity' is an insight that, over the centuries, generations of democrats – including populists – have internalized. It runs counter to the way that exclusivity has been pathologized by the contemporary mainstream cultural and political establishment. The future of populism depends on the prospects of this form of democracy. In turn, a resilient populist voice is essential for protecting democracy from capture by the technocratic-managerial elites.

In defence of what we have in common

For J.S. Mill, the nation provided the common bond that underpinned democracy. The fellow-feeling previously alluded to by Mill emerges through the interaction between people of similar history and background. The crystallization of such a sentiment presupposes a public that possesses common cultural norms. A society that lacks internal cultural divisions is more likely to have a more powerful sense of community and place than one that is made up of different cultural groups. The possession of a common culture facilitates communication, the development of mutual understanding and a taken-for-granted way of doing things.

The spirit of populism encourages the preservation and cultivation of the shared grammar of meaning that a common culture provides. It is disposed towards a communitarian sensibility that assumes that social cohesion requires shared assumptions that are deeply ingrained in daily life. What sociologists characterize as folkways – the norms that are rooted in social conventions and traditions, which do not require the sanctions of formal laws – are morally significant for the populist worldview.

The folkways, the emotional connection and the fellow-feeling produced within a community are not easily transferable to those who are not party to the experiences that produced them. Such sentiments emerge within the emotional lifeworld of a particular community and resist being transformed into a generic emotion of sympathy that can be mechanically applied to different situations. That is why even when people adhere to a universalistic outlook – such as Christianity or Liberalism

– they understand that people's experience and identity are rooted in a distinct and particularist cultural terrain.

Opponents of populism are uncomfortable with the fellow-feeling that emanates from a common culture, perceiving such sentiments as tribal. Anti-populist ideology possesses a strong distaste towards what it characterizes as a culturally homogeneous society and a strong preference for a heterogeneous one. The language with which they transmit this preference is one that constantly evokes an association between homogeneity, racism and xenophobia.

Even a superficial review of the commentaries authored by anti-populist writers indicates a fixation with using the concept of homogeneity as a weapon to discredit their opponents. According to their definition of populism, an adherence to homogeneity is one of the principal features of this movement. For example, Christos Marneros claims that the 'term "people" of the right-wing populist discourse' is 'constructed around a sense of an identity, which is characterised by homogeneity'.[51] At times, it seems that virtually every twenty-first-century anti-populist publication feels an obligation to chide their political opponents for their commitment to a homogeneous people. Even Chantal Mouffe, who claims to support a left-wing version of populism, feels obliged to remind her readers that 'the people is not a homogeneous subject in which all the differences are somehow reduced to unity'.[52] Others accuse populism of a naïve belief in 'the existence of a pure and homogeneous people'.[53]

Critics of the idea of a homogeneous people frequently draw on the writings of Mudde, whose definition of populism we discussed earlier. They constantly cite Mudde's assertion that populists divide society into 'two homogeneous and antagonistic camps – a "pure people" and a "corrupt elite"'.[54] Mudde's construction does not simply draw attention to the anti-elitist orientation of populism, but also frames this tension through a language of homogeneity, purity and corruption. As noted in chapter 1, the language of homogeneity and purity evokes memories of the kind of racial theories favoured by the Nazis and other racist movements. One struggles to find references to a 'pure people' in the literature produced by populist movements.

The term 'pure people' has emerged from the imagination of anti-populist zealots who intentionally or unintentionally confuse the language of sovereigntist populists with inter-war racist movements. Purity works as a rhetorical device used by opponents of populism to discredit and caricature. The critique of the idea of a 'homogeneous people' always concludes with the claim that the people are heterogeneous and that any attempt to speak on their behalf is likely to exclude a minority. In this way, populism's claim to represent the people can be framed as both invalid and discriminatory.

There is no abstract formula for determining the composition of a people. What's important is not homogeneity but a commitment to common cultural norms, to the common bond that Mill discussed. Anyone who has viewed the proceedings at a MAGA rally will be struck by the heterogeneity of members of the audience and yet these individuals regard each other as part of the same movement.

The critique of homogeneity also serves to question populism's failure to uphold the value of diversity. This was the intent of the political theorist Andrea Baumeister, who wrote, 'ultimately the idea of a pre-political, homogeneous community rests upon a myth that can only be sustained through the suppression of heterogeneous elements of the population'.[55] From her standpoint, it follows that the suppression of heterogenous elements leads to the 'suppression of difference and diversity'. This charge is echoed by other anti-populist writers, who maintain that populism's 'fictional belief in the homogeneous unity of the political community generates a logic which disregards the idea of otherness at the heart of democracy and aims at the suppression of diversity within society'.[56]

Its critics assert that populism 'cherishes the fiction of the substantial homogeneity of the identity and the will of the people and, thereby, aims at the suppression of diversity'.[57] Populism's acclamation of a 'pure' and 'homogeneous' people is portrayed as a threat to diversity and democracy. As one observer states, '"We stand for the people" quickly turns into "We alone stand for the people", which is an excluding populism against diversity and pluralism, both core values of democratic systems. Hence populism is potentially undemocratic.'[58]

As was the case with the mendacious attribution of purity to the populist voice – so too with the tendentious association of an ideological version of homogeneity. Terms like homogeneity and heterogeneity are most likely to come out of the mouths of anti-populists, who are typically characterized by a form of inverted racial thinking. Populism affirms the people not for their homogeneity but because they share a common world rooted on a cultural connection with previous generations. Its goal is to sustain that continuity and develop it to make it relevant for the contemporary world.

No doubt there are individuals who have attached themselves to the populist camps who share the racial obsessions of their anti-populist adversaries. But these individuals do not represent the movement to which they attached themselves. As a movement, populism can appeal to a variety of ethnic constituencies, not based on celebrating heterogeneity but on the foundation of uniting around a common political culture. Unity around shared views and normative judgements and beliefs provides a common grammar of meaning that can motivate people from different ethnic backgrounds.

The hostility directed towards the concept of a homogeneous pre-political community represents an almost visceral reaction against the notion of a political community that possesses a pre-political foundation. The pre-political underpinning of a political community touches on the foundational conditions that are logically and chronologically prior to the constitution of formal political structures and institutions. The domain of the pre-political is based on the particularity of kinship and community ties, which provide their members with a sense of identity and belonging. As we noted previously, these are cultural resources that assist the emergence of solidarity, and which provide formal political institutions with legitimacy.

The key argument used to discredit the particularity of pre-political relations is to counterpose the supposed moral superiority of heterogeneity to homogeneity, and of diversity to sameness. It is worth noting that these terms, which were used historically as neutral terms of description, have become politicized and, since the 1970s, have acquired an ideological character.

One frequently used argument against the so-called populist myth of a pre-political homogeneous people is the assertion that such communities never existed but were always heterogeneous. To justify this argument, its advocates the claim that, far from being homogeneous, European societies were always 'nations of immigrants'. Anti-nationalists proudly refer to Britain as a 'mongrel nation'. As a former Labour Home Office minister, Barbara Roche, argued, the UK is 'a country of migrants and we should celebrate the multi-cultural, multi-racial nature of our society, and the very positive benefits that migration throughout the centuries has brought'.[59]

Others go further and argue that the Britain was populated by black people for 7,000 years before whites arrived.[60] One exhibition on 'diverse' history declared that as far back as Roman times, 11 per cent of York was black. A children's book, *Brilliant Black British History* by the Nigerian-born British author Atinuke, asserts that 'every single British person comes from a migrant' and 'the very first Britons were black'. Turning history on its head, this reframing of the nation's past contends that Stonehenge was built by black people, while Britain was a black country. The fiction of black origins has also been promoted in nations like Denmark and Sweden. Through reimagining a nation's history as one where diversity, multiculturalism and heterogeneity always trumped homogeneity, the populist version of pre-political solidarity loses its legitimacy.

The project of imposing the ideology of diversity on the pre-political sphere calls into question the particularist cultural connections and values that bind people together. That is why the defence of the culture of the pre-political represents the antithesis of the project of turning diversity into a political ideology.

The politicization of diversity and its aim of turning it into a first-order value invariably leads to the balkanization of society. The challenge confronting all contemporary multi-ethnic societies is how to establish a common civic culture around which everyone can unite. In contemporary debates civic culture is often mistakenly contrasted with a national one. The relation between the two can be profitably conceived as one of creative tension. How? The pre-political sphere is both logically and chronologically prior to the political one. A flourishing and authoritative pre-political sphere provides the foundation for the emergence of a political culture around which all sections of society – old and new can unite. That is why the affirmation of the pre-political by populism is so important. It represents the first step towards the forging of a common civic political culture.

6

A Response to the Condition of
Cultural Insecurity

The term *insécurité culturelle* (cultural insecurity) emerged in French public discourse in 2010.[1] The concept refers to the unease that members of a society experience in response to perceived threats to their cultural identity, values and way of life. This sense of cultural disruption and discontinuity is best captured by the term 'ontological insecurity' frequently associated with the work of British sociologist Anthony Giddens, who used this concept to highlight the sense of anxiety and uncertainty that people experience when their identity, place in the world and sense of continuity is threatened.[2] Giddens highlighted the relationship between ontological insecurity and the loss of the taken-for-granted dimensions of life that people need in order to engage with existential questions.

Typically, cultural insecurity and ontological insecurity tend to be interpreted as a response to modernization, and the rapid pace of change that comes in its wake. Alternatively, the powerful forces of change unleashed by the process of globalization are depicted as the cause of widespread disruption to people's lives, leading to existential anxiety. From this perspective, change itself is depicted as an all-powerful force that destabilizes or decentres people's identities. It is often represented through a language that hints at a fundamental rupture with the ways of the past. In the social sciences, terms such as globalization, risk society, new modernity, late modernity, post-modernity and liquid modernity draw attention to a runaway world of ceaseless change and fluidity, which unravels hitherto taken-for-granted individual and social arrangements.

The tendency to attribute the pervasive condition of ontological insecurity to the forces of modernization and globalism overlooks the fact that cultural insecurity is, in historical terms, a relatively recent development in Europe. No doubt, the rise of modernity in the eighteenth century had a major impact on social life and disrupted prevailing routines and practices. In the nineteenth century, terms such as alienation and anomie emerged to capture the sense of estrangement experienced by sections of society. However, neither alienation nor anomie defined the epoch or enveloped society in the thoroughgoing way that cultural insecurity does in the contemporary era.

The all-pervasive sense of ontological insecurity experienced today only kicked off in the wake of the institutionalization of the 1960s counterculture. The challenge to pre-existing values by the counterculture was far more extensive than any other disruption to people's taken-for-granted assumptions prevailing in the modern era. Suddenly, the commanding status of the nuclear family, marriage, heterosexuality and romantic love was called into question by the emergence of groups of activists who took great delight in delegitimating what they denounced as outdated conventions. Their ideas steadily gained a commanding influence and contributed to the creation of the conditions for the emergence of the cultural turn explored in previous chapters. This development ran in parallel with the erosion of national identity and the rise of mass migration, leading to the emergence of multicultural societies.

Back in 2010, I was involved in an EU-sponsored research programme, which explored European people's opinion of their sense of security.[3] Along with colleagues from different parts of Europe, we were interested in finding out the effects of high-profile security threats such as global terrorism, global warming, crime and other frequently cited fears on people's consciousness. We were surprised to discover that the available surveys indicated that fears about their culture being under threat were widespread amongst the citizens of the EU. Perceptions of feeling culturally threatened could assume many different forms, such as fear of crime, loss of community feeling, anxiety about the impact of mass migration, or the corrosive influence of multiculturalism on national attachments.

Since the completion of this research, it has become even more evident that cultural insecurity has played a central role in the emergence of a sizeable constituency sympathetic to populism. This point is recognized by arguably the most influential exponents of the cultural turn, Inglehart and Norris, who state: 'Declining existential security explains why support for [populist] movements is greater now than it was thirty years ago.'[4]

Inglehart and Norris draw a direct connection between cultural insecurity and the growth of populism. They claim that 'insecurity encourages an authoritarian xenophobic reaction in which people close ranks behind strong leaders, with strong in-group solidarity, rejection of outsiders, and rigid conformity to group norms'. They further assert that 'the proximate cause of the populist vote is anxiety that pervasive cultural changes and an influx of foreigners are eroding the cultural norms one knew since childhood'.

Inglehart and Norris's argument, which draws a direct and unmediated causal connection between cultural anxiety and the growth of populism, is echoed by numerous influential commentators on this subject. According to one account, 'studies indicate that threats to social identities which result from large-scale social changes contribute significantly to the emergence of populist attitudes'.[5]

At first sight, the drawing of a direct causal connection between social change and the development of populist attitudes makes sense. But social change does not itself produce populist attitudes. Change has both subjective and objective dimensions. Its impact, and how it is interpreted, depends on prevailing social and cultural norms, and its effect is mediated through institutional responses. It is when these norms and institutions are not able to endow change with meaning that the condition of anxiety gains force.

It is important to understand that populist sentiments do not emerge as a *direct* response to an abstract general condition of anxiety. People's subjective experience of ontological security is mediated through political and cultural conflict. Thus, supporters of populism are not responding to abstract omnipotent psychological forces so much as reacting to, or pushing back against, the actions and attitudes of the political representatives of the cultural turn who regard their way of life with contempt.

As Arlie Russell Hochschild explains in her insightful study *Strangers in their Own Land*, the people drawn towards populism feel disrespected by their elites. They believe that their way of life is threatened by powerful individuals and groups with whom they feel that they have nothing in common, and feel under constant pressure to adopt values and lifestyles alien to their way of being. In the United States, people who have not come to terms with their supposed unconscious bias and racism are arrogantly instructed to 'educate yourself'. Those at the receiving end of such patronizing instructions often feel that their language and opinion do not have any value in the eyes of their cultural and political overlords.

Unlike the people who feel like strangers in their own land, the technocratic-managerial elites are not particularly negatively affected by the condition of cultural insecurity. Though they feel detached from a historically rooted stable community, they do not experience it as a problem. Instead, they regard community obligations as a burden, and contend that it is undesirable to be stuck in the ways of the past. These elites – particularly those who inhabit cultural institutions – uphold values such as flexibility, adaptability and a willingness to question prevailing customs, and assume that a healthy and autonomous personality demands liberation from outdated moral norms. Their aspiration to 'free' their personality from the past appears as an end in itself. As the psychologist Roy Baumeister notes, their 'desire for identity appears to be an increased desire for differentiation not continuity'.[6]

The technocratic-managerial elites are far less concerned with overcoming atomization and forging relations of solidarity than most citizens. What they seek is differentiation from others, and to be seen as ahead of the curve. Playing at being different has also become a constant theme in consumer culture. Advertisers promote their products by appealing to potential customers to 'dare to be different'. A Europe-wide sales campaign for Honda Civic cars 'outlines a path that pushes the boundaries' of a Honda Civic driver. A voiceover instructs would-be drivers to go 'where different takes you'. The message of 'dare to be different' has become a theme that is ceaselessly promoted by the advertising industry.[7] So has the call to reject 'old' social norms and adopt new ones. That is why a report directed at the advertising industry exhorts its members to 'push the boundaries of gender stereotyping' and 'help' consumers 'break free from the shackles of identity norms'.[8]

From the perspective of the intellectual wing of the technocratic-managerial elites, it is not merely impossible to achieve a stable identity, but it is also undesirable in the so-called post-modern world. Where the loss of stable identity used to be presented as a problem, the difficulty of adopting a stable identity is now frequently portrayed as a positive development by commentators whose preference is for identities that are constructed or invented.

Post-modernist writers dismiss what they depict as traditional ideals of the self and of identity. They assert that 'the fixed subject of liberal humanistic thinking is an anachronism that should be replaced by a more flexible individual whose identity is fluid, contingent and socially constructed'.[9] Within the academic world – where these sentiments exercise considerable influence – such writers make a virtue out of the destabilization of identity.[10]

Unaware of the damaging consequences of cultural loss, they regard those who are concerned about its consequences as simply lacking the capacity to deal with cultural change. They make an exception when it comes to the predicament of indigenous people in places like Australia and Brazil. But when it comes to people facing cultural loss in Western communities, instead of responding to the problem posed by cultural insecurity, they acquiesce in it, even making a virtue of their adaptation to the contemporary condition of estrangement. This leaves the field wide open for populist movements that aim to provide people with an answer to the condition of cultural estrangement that has been imposed on them. Unlike the mainstream parties of European societies, populist parties highlight the threat to their constituency's culture and attempt to project a way forward to contain its disruptive effects.

The culture war that turned its fire on traditional values was not the outcome of the autonomous power of rapid change, but of the purposeful political behaviour of political institutions and cultural entrepreneurs seeking to undermine them. Referring to this development, the Marxist historian Eric Hobsbawm wrote of a 'cultural revolution', which he described as 'the breaking of the threads which in the past had woven human beings into social textures'.[11] Hobsbawm stated that, as a result, 'what children could learn from parents became less obvious than what parents did not know and children did'.

While the cultural turn was welcomed by a new class of countercultural elites and eventually by the technocratic-managerial

classes, it caught millions of people unaware. Older generations, in particular, found it difficult to understand what had
happened, and millions of others lacked a language through
which they could express their concern with what they experienced as a condition of cultural insecurity. Even when the scale
and the depth of the cultural revolution became apparent, millions of disaffected people lacked the clarity and confidence to
voice their disaffection.

Conservative movements and parties were appalled and
unnerved by the sight of their world being turned upside-down.
Upholders of traditional values were defensive. The chair of
the German Christian Democrat Adenauer Foundation went
so far as to state that 'the revolt of 1968 destroyed more values
than did the Third Reich'.[12] It was clear to many conservative
thinkers that by this time, their values could only survive on
life support.

Instead of making a serious effort to address this problem,
conservative parties acted in the hope that it was a temporary
deviation from the norm and deflected their attention to deal
with economic matters. They underestimated the impact of
the cultural revolution on the web of meaning through which
people made sense of their place in the world. They did little to
provide support for the millions of people whose lives were disrupted by the atomizing effects imposed by their condition of
ontological insecurity. Indeed, in some cases – such as during
the Thatcher–Reagan era – they implemented economic policies that intensified the disruption of community life.

In the 1970s and 1980s, the conservative parties' lack of
comprehension of the dynamics of the cultural turn was highlighted by their absorption in old ideological battles between
the Cold War left and right. To this day, many conservative
thinkers misguidedly interpret the cultural turn as the nefarious accomplishment of a left-wing political project. Inglehart
and Norris are far clearer on this point than conservative
commentators stuck on the battlefields of the Cold War.

They note that 'the new non-economic issues introduced by postmaterialists overshadowed the classic left-right economic issues, drawing attention away from redistribution to cultural issues'.[13] The old left, no less than conservatism, was caught out by this development.

The reaction to the cultural turn

Organized political reaction to the cultural turn first emerged on the fringes of political life. As previously noted, the emergence and subsequent success of European national populism can best be understood as a response to this shift; and commentators frequently sought to dismiss the emerging voices of populism as merely a negative backlash against the ascendancy of post-material values. During the decades that followed, commentators assured themselves and their readers continually that, like all protest movements, the high tide of populism had been reached and that it was only a matter of time before these protest movements disappeared. 'Dead, disgraced or deluded. Is this the end of populism?', asked a commentator in 2023.[14] 'Populism never lasts', predicted an anti-populist a year later.[15]

The numerous premature obituaries about the imminent disappearance of populist protest movements failed to comprehend that they represented a widespread demand for their societies to hold a line against the perceived onslaught on their way of life. The aspiration to maintain intergenerational continuity with the past and the security afforded by the taken-for-granted ways of being have deep roots in European societies. The strength of these feelings was often overlooked by supporters of the cultural turn, which is why they tended to see populist parties as mendacious external actors devoted to stirring up problems.

In an important contribution to this topic, Margaret Canovan wrote that 'populism is not just a reaction against power structures but an appeal to a recognized authority'.[16] The consequence of its appeal to a recognized authority is that populism is not a manifestation of 'simple political discontent and frustrations', but a medium for conveying a 'politics of hope'.[17]

To be sure, the different populist parties of the 1980s and 1990s bore some resemblance to protest movements. At the time, they were finding their feet and tended to be reactive rather than proactive. Their political programme tended to be inchoate and unconsciously expressed a lack of self-confidence in the possibility of gaining cultural hegemony. Nevertheless, these parties could count on a stable – if modest – constituency of electoral support, which ensured that these movements had more than the fleeting existence that characterized many protest groups. So long as populist parties were able to project a commitment to offer a way out of cultural insecurity, they could be assured of the loyal support of a section of society.

From the very moment that populist movements began to gain influence on the political stage, they faced a systematic attempt to marginalize them and delegitimize their existence. The populist parties were accused of exploiting the very conditions that they were attempting to overcome. Time and again, commentators asserted that support for populist parties had grown in line with the deepening of cultural and ontological insecurity. They reported that these conditions drove people towards populism. Academic commentators acknowledged that 'ontological insecurity' has 'the potential that people turn to populism', adding that:

> As populist movements offer to restore traditional values, they should attract those people who feel socially disintegrated due to their cognitive overload and their ontological insecurity. The appeal for these people is to retain a stable positive social identity with clear role expectations in a proven recognition order with strict definitions of social categories.[18]

The attitude communicated to describe people's reaction to the threat they faced was typically one that a doctor or psychologist uses to diagnose the mental state of a patient. It is always 'these people' whose psychological deficits lead them to embrace the simplistic solutions offered by demagogic populists. Adversaries of the *demos* often use loaded terms such as racism and xenophobia to describe the attitudes of people drawn towards populist parties.

Critics of populism contend that 'right-wing populists exploit people's existential anxieties by peddling crisis narratives'.[19] They also assert that populists stoke up anger in order to manipulate the culturally insecure,[20] and that 'populists have been able to skilfully exploit the anger of the anxious'.[21] Time and again, they insist that populists exploit a backlash against a variety of different cultural threats such as mass migration or the imposition of gender ideology on society.[22] The premise of these charges is that the real problem is populists' exploitation of grievances, rather than the conditions that gave rise to those grievances in the first place.

Often, critics do not accuse populists merely of exploiting a crisis, but also of artificially creating such a condition in order to manipulate people's fears. The political scientist Benjamin Moffitt argues that a 'crisis does not just trigger populism, but that populism also attempts to act as a trigger for crisis'.[23] This claim is elaborated by Moffitt and his colleagues in the following way:

> Populists tend to benefit from crises. A state of crisis provides populist actors with the opportunity to nurture public disaffection with the political status-quo. This is why populists do not stand idly by until a crisis occurs, but actively seek to create a sense of crisis through carefully crafted statements and performances.[24]

This narrative focuses on the manipulative behaviour of populist politicians. It displaces attention away from the widespread concerns about the cultural threats facing a community, focusing instead on the malevolent, performative role of actors stirring up trouble. If only populism did not exist, it seems, people would not feel anxious about the threats facing their culture.

It is worth reflecting on the thesis that posits populism as a parasitical force feeding off the anxiety of millions of culturally estranged citizens. This argument has the advantage of relieving its proponents of any responsibility to engage with the content of the arguments put forward by populists. If what populists say is designed to exploit, manipulate or deceive, there is little point in engaging with their deception.

'Why Europe's new populists tell so many lies – and do it so shamelessly' declares the title of an article by the political analyst Catherine Fieschi, author of the book *Populocracy*.[25] She adds that 'my research on populism' in Europe 'confirms that lying is a constant feature of populist politics'.[26] The tendency to represent populism as a medium of dishonesty and bad faith serves to justify the marginalization of populist movements. Its other, arguably more important, rationale is to deny, or at least minimize, the nature of the cultural threats, which populists supposedly 'exploit'. Thus, time and again, anti-populist politicians deny the reality of uncontrolled mass migration and fail to acknowledge its destructive consequences for the lives of millions. Concerns raised about its disorienting impact on community life are dismissed as dishonest exaggerations underpinned by xenophobia.

The rhetorical strategy of denying the scale of the cultural threat experienced by millions of people on both sides of the Atlantic often leads to the representation of people's anxieties as the consequence of the populist-promoted politics of fear. A paradigmatic example of this self-deceiving approach is advanced by Ruth Wodak in her study *The Politics of Fear: The Shameless Normalization of Far-Right Discourse*.[27] The book conveys the naïve conviction that the normalization of what

Wodak characterizes as 'far-right discourse' is the outcome of the conscious pursuit of fear. It never occurs to her to investigate the social and cultural conditions that give rise to support for populist parties. If she had, she would have discovered that this discourse represents a normal response of culturally insecure people to the conditions they face.

Despite their reluctance to undertake a genuine exploration of the relationship between cultural insecurity and its so-called backlash, many anti-populist commentators recognize that there is a genuine problem of declining existential security facing people who are patronizingly referred to as 'left behind'.[28] Since the triumph of Brexit and the election of Donald Trump in 2016, it has proved difficult to avoid recognizing that these unexpected events constitute a response to a demand that many professional commentators failed to anticipate and understand.

Some critics are forced to acknowledge the fact that populists represent a response to a demand expressed by millions of people. Babst and colleagues note:

> Populist movements meet the demand of the emerging recognition vacuum. They promise to fulfill the nostalgic wish for a restoration of the traditional status order through their rhetoric and political programs.[29]

But the question that such researchers seldom pose is: 'Why it is that only national populists are prepared to respond to people's understandable demand for cultural security?'

One reason why mainstream parties and their ideologues tend to avoid engaging with the question of cultural security is that they both lack empathy with the people who are struggling with this problem, and assume that there is something illegitimate about people's aspiration for order and security. This sentiment is clearly expressed in Babst and colleagues' reference to 'the nostalgic wish for a restoration of the traditional status order', which implicitly dismisses the relevance of this aspiration to contemporary realities. Through delegitimizing the outlook that creates a demand for the kind of politics offered by populist movements, the mainstream political establishment is spared the responsibility of engaging with this issue.

The psychic distance between the dominant cultural elites and people concerned with their place in the world was highlighted by their reaction to a speech that Giorgia Meloni made in 2019. In this speech she passionately shouted; 'I am Giorgia, I am a woman, I am a mother, I am Italian, I am a Christian . . . you won't take it from me'.[30] The reaction of Italy's cultural snobs was one of hilarity. Meloni's statement was ridiculed and set to a disco beat by two Milanese DJs. Though their aim was to make fun of Meloni, the video became a club hit and 'made Meloni "cool"'.[31] Meloni's detractors attempt at irony was lost on millions of Italians, who were spontaneously receptive to her message. Meloni's plea for upholding Italian tradition may have been alien to the outlook of the dominant cultural elites, but its message struck a chord with people feeling culturally insecure.

It may well be the case that populist parties and leaders, like other political movements, seek advantage by 'exploiting' particular issues. However, they did not create the problems that they are accused of exploiting. They could, like Europe's mainstream parties, remain quiet or ignorant about the corrosive impact of uncontrolled mass migration on society. The accusation of exploitation hurled at populist parties implies that the world would be a better place if nothing was said about contentious issues like gender ideology, Net Zero policies or multiculturalism. If so, the cultural hegemony of the managerial-technocratic elites would remain unchallenged and intact.

The obverse of challenging the problems that emanate from the condition of cultural insecurity is to acquiesce to them. Indeed, the ideologues supporting the values of the political and cultural establishment make a virtue of their disconnection from their home and the traditions into which their ancestors were socialized. They possess a borderless sensibility, and pride themselves on their fluid personalities, which allows them to be open to change. They regard supporters of populism as limited individuals who are unable to yield to new experiences and keep up with a changing world, and they regard strong attachments to community as a form of outdated tribalism. As Hochschild observed in her study of a blue-collar way of life in Louisiana: 'The liberal upper-middle class saw community as insularity and closed-mindedness rather than as a source of belonging and honor.'[32]

From this perspective, the damaging conditions that give rise to ontological insecurity – community and family break-down, loss of solidarity and social cohesion – are not a big deal, and the response should be to normalize some of the consequences of this development. For example, the decline of intact families is normalized by the statement that there is no longer one 'dominant family form'. The decline of what is now referred as the 'traditional family form' is happily followed by what the Pew Research Center describes as an 'increasingly diverse and, for many, constantly evolving family forms'.[33]

The internalization of the condition of cultural insecurity as a normal feature of life means that those invested in the elite outlook have become psychically distant from the 'left behind' people who are reacting to the loss of their world. They also regard attempts to overcome the condition of cultural insecurity through affirming traditional attitudes and modes of behaviour as regressive and misguided. Inglehart and Norris appear delighted that norms that were once widely accepted, such as 'sexual abstinence before marriage, readiness to fight for one's country and regular church attendance now seem quaint to a growing share of society'.[34] From their perspective, the benefits of cultural change far outweigh the problem of cultural loss experienced by millions of people.

What a close inspection of the academic literature on populism reveals is not only a tangible sense of ideological zealotry that leads its authors to represent their subject in the worst possible light, but also a strong determination to build a psychic wall between themselves and the objects of their animosity. As discussed in chapter 1, this adversarial mode of intellectual engagement leads to the construction of what Hochschild characterized as an 'empathy wall', a barrier or obstacle to connecting with others on an emotional level.[35] Hochschild used this term to refer to the intense polarization of American society, where millions inhabit a segregated echo chamber and lack the capacity to empathize with people outside their political community.

However, the term 'empathy wall' can also be used to explain the psychological disposition of the cultural elites and their anti-populist intellectuals, who spontaneously adopt a contemptuous conspiratorial analysis towards their subject matter. In this way, their lack of empathy towards the predicament facing the millions of people supporting populist parties leads to a lack of comprehension about what makes populist movements popular.

Powerlessness and the quest for a home

As noted previously, in the nineteenth and early twentieth centuries, the sensibility of powerlessness was often interpreted through Karl Marx's concept of alienation or Émile Durkheim's term, anomie. Alienation referred to the feeling of estrangement and disconnection from society and the product of one's labour. Anomie emphasized the state of normlessness, where community norms had become diffuse, and highlighted the erosion of solidarity and a lack of moral guidance. The relevance of the concept of alienation for understanding the sensibility of cultural insecurity is its stress on powerlessness and the feeling of a lack of control over one's circumstances and life. In turn, anomie draws attention to the importance of the erosion of moral norms leading to what can be best characterized as a crisis of normativity. Lack of clarity about prevailing norms undermines people's capacity to understand their place in the world, which in turn disrupts their sense of identity.

The feeling of alienation and anomie are often experienced through a sense of disconnection from others and of a lack of control over one's life. The consciousness of disconnection, irrelevance and especially powerlessness is widespread in our era, and serves as an important driver for the growth of populism.

As the LSE academic Michael Cox explained in his essay, 'Understanding the global rise of populism', 'populism is very much an expression in the West of a sense of powerlessness: the powerlessness of ordinary citizens when faced with massive changes going on all around them; but the powerlessness, too, of Western leaders and politicians who really do not seem to have an answer to the many challenges facing the West right now'.[36] Numerous researchers have rightly drawn the conclusion that 'anomie is one of the strongest predictors of populist voting and of populist attitudes'.[37] Research suggests that 'a perceived alienation from the symbolic architecture of a society may decrease levels of psychological need satisfaction, which may catalyse into anxiety and anger', leading to support for populist movements.[38]

The sense of powerlessness that, in recent years, has been voiced through the populist demand to 'Take Back Control', is arguably far deeper and more pervasive than in the days when the concepts of alienation and anomie were invented. Until the cultural turn of the late 1970s, the alienation and disconnection that people experienced was mediated through circumstances where moral norms and social ideals still possessed a degree of formal and institutional existence. These ideals might have lost some of their force, but they nonetheless provided people with guidance about their place in the world. Though sometimes violated in practice, society's values and ideas about expected forms of behaviour were rarely questioned, and they were formally shared by all classes and sections of society. Since the cultural turn, values have become subject to the imperative of polarization.

Indeed, advocates of the cultural turn have been at the forefront of this process, by demeaning the moral outlook of their adversaries. They frequently dismiss traditional values as stifling and outdated, and regard those who adhere to them as morally inferior. As Paul Stoneman and James Wright noted, 'commentators and political elites often exaggerate' the differences in values 'creating a fertile ground for polarisation'. They add that the '"populist turn" has breathed fresh political life into cultural differences'.[39]

Since the cultural turn, the moral bonds and values that provide people with guidance have been called into question by precisely those members of the elites who used to serve as their guardians. Bereft of this guidance, people's sense of belonging became an issue, which, as we will discuss, led populists to embrace the politics of home.

The contemporary sensibility of powerlessness has assumed an acute form because of the emergence of what I have previously characterized as *the moral disarmament of the West*.[40] Moral disarmament is the outcome of a process when a nation's elites reject or fail to take seriously the norms and values upon which their society was founded. It leads inexorably to the demise of moral authority and erodes the capacity of society's rulers to act decisively.

One of the most disturbing expressions of this process was the willingness of the West's elites to detach themselves from their own nations and regard themselves as globalist citizens of the world. Commenting in *The New York Times*, Oren Cass wrote of America's political class that it was in 'the final stages of self-righteous detachment from the economic and social conditions of the nation it ruled'.[41] The elites' casual betrayal of their duty and responsibility to their nation severely weakened the self-understanding that society has of itself.

Emotionally distanced from the problems facing their society, the cultural and political establishment of the Western world made matters worse by belittling the idealization of a homeland. They barely hide their disdain for the idealization of patriotism. The legacy of their casual indifference towards nation and home for millions of people is the intensification of the problem of belonging and the quest for a home.

The unwillingness of the managerial-technocratic elites to help people find an answer to the question 'Where do I belong?' offered populist movements an opportunity to champion this issue. These movements have turned the issue of belonging and the necessity for celebrating and protecting a home into a central feature of their political programme. This emphasis on the homeland is not merely a defensive reaction to mass migration, as some observers have suggested; it also represents an attempt to cultivate intergenerational relationships rooted within a familiar space. Anti-populists dismiss what they caricature as the 'visceral power of place' that animates the politicization of the home by populists.[42]

The quest for a home is typically dismissed as constituting a refusal to face up to the consequences of a rapidly changing society. As the American theologian Rusty Reno noted, some say that 'homelessness is an intrinsic feature of modernity' while others contend that 'homelessness and disquietude are the inevitable price of technological progress and free markets'.[43] The fatalistic tendency to normalize homelessness and alienation from space serves to reconcile people to the condition of deracination. It also constitutes the flipside of divesting the home of its moral content.

Critics of populism dismiss its 'ideology of home' as representing an illusory 'vision of a lost homeland', which 'represents nostalgia for a reconstructed past and, in turn, provides a sense of security against the perceived loss of identity'.[44] Yet the quest for a home is not so much an exercise in nostalgia as an attempt to create and consolidate the foundation for the exercise of solidarity. In the first instance, national populism aims to ensure that the national home serves as a focus for people's loyalty and exercise of solidarity. What critics label as populism's 'ideology of home' simply represents an attempt to overcome the condition of cultural insecurity through the forging of strong bonds within the familiar setting of a homeland. The relationship between a nation and home is well explained by the political analyst N.S. Lyons:

> A nation is a particular people, with a distinct culture, permanently bound together by shared relationship with place, past, and each other. A house becomes a home through relationship with the family that lives in it, a connection forged out of time and memory between concrete particularity of place and the lives of a specific group of people present, past, and yet unborn. We can say *this* house is home because it is *our* home. In much the same way, a country becomes our homeland because it is ours – and the *we* of that 'ours' is the nation, which transcends geography, government, and GDP.[45]

The particularity of place serves as the precondition for the possession of a sense of belonging. This is a point that national populism fully grasps, since people's sense of existential security emerges within the boundary of a particular place.

In her fascinating study *Close To Home: Local Ties and Voting Radical Right in Europe*, Jennifer Fitzgerald explains the significance of local attachments for people's lives. She notes that:

> local ties, community attachment, and rootedness are terms that connote feelings of connection to certain geosocial areas

and their residents. They also typically go hand in hand with a sense of solidarity with other members of a particular community. Research from several disciplines signals that these collective attachments can be important for people's self-conceptions and self-esteem.[46]

Recent elections in Western Europe showed that there is a close connection between an attachment to place and an identification with a locality and populism. The sociologist Elisa Bellè noted that there is much empirical evidence which 'confirms the importance of the local dimension'. As examples, she cited the case of Brexit, where many coastal cities and former industrial centres possessing a sense of pride voted to leave the EU. In Italy, the *Lega* has since its origins 'established its most rooted electoral presence in small to very small municipalities, becoming the voice of the "deep province"'.[47] Bellè added that 'several studies have recently highlighted the radical right's emphasis on feelings of local attachment and identity'.

Numerous studies confirm that populism's appeal to place, locality and community has played an important role in the growth of its electoral popularity. Research indicates that 'individuals who embrace idealized local sentiments tend to be more likely to support' what they call 'the radical right'.[48] According to Fitzgerald, 'in many places where the locality is a source of pride and identity', people have altered their voting behaviour and opted to vote for populist movements.[49] When a locality faces marginalization and a threat to its way of life, its inhabitants often opt to support populist parties.

Some studies acknowledge a connection between populism's affirmation of home and the enhancement of people's sense of self. According to one monograph: 'Through cross-national and country-level data analysis of Switzerland and France, the research demonstrates that people can derive a sense of self-esteem, security, and emotional attachment from the locality in which they live.'[50]

Typically, the study above raises the caveat that 'while this localist form of identity can blossom into genuine social connection, it can also coalesce with darker, more exclusionary urges that become heightened when one's home or community is perceived as being under threat by external forces'.[51] Studies focused on the relationship between localism and populism often find it difficult to desist from delegitimizing this relationship. They either call into question the motive of populist movements cultivating local pride and identity, or raise scepticism about the moral status of localism and strong community bonds.

Bellè writes of a 'forced folklorisation of the local', which has 'proved ideologically effective, binding the populist, the reactionary, and the authoritarian elements'. She comments that 'it has exploited one of the most seductive suggestions of radical-right populism: namely, nostalgia for a mythical past, an invented golden age of harmony, order, law, and tradition'.[52] In this way, the appeal to place is casually dismissed as the manipulation of people's aspiration for a home by using dishonest fantasies about an invented golden age. Others question populist parties for 'their proclivity to romanticize a nostalgic vision of community whereby true locals are distinguished from outsiders'.[53]

The delegitimization of the home

It is paradoxical that at a time when consumer culture continually celebrates the local – locally produced food, local farmer markets, local community – there is so much suspicion directed towards strong local bonds and identities. Rural communities and small towns are continually represented as inhabited by close-minded, religious and prejudiced individuals who are suspicious of outsiders and any form of change. Numerous films are devoted to exposing the dark side of small towns and suburbs.

The patronizing sentiment directed at the local was unambiguously articulated by the former president of the United States, Barack Obama, in his famous Bittergate speech at a fundraising event in San Francisco on 6 April 2008. When referring to working-class voters in old industrial towns decimated by job losses, he said: 'They get bitter, they cling to guns or religion or antipathy to people who aren't like them or anti-immigrant sentiment or anti-trade sentiment as a way to explain their frustrations.'[54] Obama's casual and knowing putdown of smalltown folk sent a very clear message about the cultural fault line that divides America today. He is blue (Democrat and liberal), they are red (Republican and traditionalist); he is enlightened, they are bitter.

The language used by Obama to describe the people of the Rust Belt implied that they inhabit a different moral universe to that inhabited by the individuals he was addressing in San Francisco. In his words, when 'they' get 'bitter', they 'cling to guns or religion or antipathy to people who aren't like them'. From this standpoint, insecurity, religion, guns and xenophobia all come to be associated with 'the other', defining the way of life of what Europeans refer to as the 'little people'. Significant sections of America's cultural elite have bought into this caricatured representation of their smalltown citizens. They have adopted a sneering sense of moral superiority towards the outdated and dysfunctional attitudes of the 'little people'.

During the 2008 election campaign, elite attitudes towards 'them' were on full display. Far from being apologetic about Bittergate, many of Obama's supporters upped the ante when the controversy kicked off. 'These people don't turn to God and guns and mistrust of foreigners because of a downturn in the economy', argued TV host Jon Stewart; rather 'those are the very foundations those towns are built on'. In short, prejudice and backwardness are built into the very foundations of small communities.

What is significant about the unapologetic prejudice directed at small towns and communities is that their target is the people who inhabit them. Critics of 'these people' draw a connection between their backward attitudes and their support for populism. In this way, it becomes evident that the hostility directed at populist movements also extends to the kind of people that support them.

In a world of unstable identities, where identity assumes unprecedented importance, people's local community identity is, in effect, devalued. At the same time, their local identity is represented as a form of prejudice and often castigated as a source of excluding the Other. Local attachment and strong social bonds are rendered as dark.

Populism's quest to re-enchant people's lives

The cynical derision communicated by the dominant cosmopolitan cultural script towards community identity can be interpreted as an expression of what the sociologist Max Weber referred to as the 'disenchantment of the world'. Weber used the term disenchantment to capture the process of rationalization that led to the elimination of the spiritual/magical dimension of human experience. From this standpoint, 'intellect becomes the sole arbiter of meaning and judgment'.[55] In relation to our subject, the process of disenchantment works to deprive community – and for that matter any group, such as members of a nation, bound together by strong natural and emotional ties – of intrinsic meaning. From this perspective, relations between people and their wider affiliation and loyalty become transactional.

The spirit of populism is spontaneously drawn towards the re-enchantment of dimensions of human life. For populists, the community or nation is not simply a conglomeration of individuals, but a group of people drawn together by a common historical legacy, connection with generations who have long been deceased, and emotional bonds reinforced by rituals and symbols of commonality. Populist politics seeks to endow community with meaning – a sensibility that transcends the immediate physical/material aspects of collective existence. Re-enchantment represents an alternative to the 'this is it' of contemporary pragmatic fatalism. It is for this reason that Margaret Canovan referred to populism as a kind of 'redemptive politics'.[56] It is also why the spirit of populism strives towards the politics of hope.

The reaction against the communitarian promise of populism by the political mainstream is founded on its technocratic-managerial prejudice against institutions based on historically founded, spontaneous and natural bonds, underpinned by sentiment rather than calculation. This prejudice is widely promoted in the contemporary social sciences, where community, like the nation or 'the people', is often deprecated as an artificial invention or as an illusion. This standpoint is clearly expressed by Zygmunt Bauman, one of the most eloquent sociologists of recent times, in his essay, *Community*. Bauman declared that:

> 'Community' is nowadays another name for paradise lost – but one to which we dearly hope to return, and so we feverishly seek the roads that may bring us there. Paradise lost or a paradise still hoped to be found; one way or another, this is definitely not a paradise that we inhabit and not the paradise that we know from our own experience.[57]

For Bauman, a community is the product of imagination, and those who possess such a dream are in fact pretending to be part of something that only exists in the mind. He aims not only to demystify the idealization of community, but also to warn about its downside. It is worth citing his warning at length:

a collectivity which pretends to be community incarnate, the dream fulfilled, and (in the name of all the goodness such community is assumed to offer) demands unconditional loyalty and treats everything short of such loyalty as an act of unforgivable treason. The 'really existing community', were we to find ourselves in its grasp, would demand stern obedience in exchange for the services it renders or promises to render. Do you want security? Give up your freedom, or at least a good chunk of it. Do you want confidence? Do not trust anybody outside your community. Do you want mutual understanding? Don't speak to foreigners nor use foreign languages . . . There is a price to be paid for the privilege of 'being in a community' – and it is inoffensive or even invisible only as long as the community stays in the dream. The price is paid in the currency of freedom, variously called 'autonomy', 'right to self-assertion', 'right to be yourself'.[58]

The dark picture of community life drawn by Bauman is one that constantly reappears in the anti-populist literature. He believes that there is a human need for the security offered by community, but that the possession of that security comes at the expense of the capacity to act freely. No doubt Bauman has a point which is why people – particularly young people – feel the need to leave their home and explore the world. However this aspiration to break free can and usually does co-exist with the desire for the security experienced in a community setting. The populist reply to Bauman's freedom–security trade-off is that the exercise of real freedom is based on the security offered by the solidarity derived from community.

To paraphrase Johann Wolfgang von Goethe, one of Germany's greatest writers, the two most precious bequests we can give to our children are 'roots and wings'. Populism recognizes the significance of roots for the cultivation of stable identities. Its affirmation of community is not designed to deprive people of their freedom but to provide the foundation on which freedom can be exercised. Roots provide the young with the strength needed to fly. From this standpoint, the re-enchantment of community and becoming a free people are intimately linked. Without a home, the exercise of freedom becomes dispossessed of meaning.

The attempt by populist parties to respond to the condition of cultural insecurity is often dismissed as an appeal to nostalgia. In the next chapter, we will explore the cynicism directed against nostalgia and suggest that what is really at issue is the attempt of populism to retain a community's connection with its past.

7

Championing Cultural Continuity

Aside from the charge of being authoritarian, xenophobic and racist, one epithet that is constantly attached to populists is that they promote the politics of nostalgia. In recent times, the charge of nostalgia serves as form of moral condemnation. In the Western world, particularly among the intelligentsia and the cultural elites, nostalgia has gained a bad press. As one study of how this label is used and its likely effect states: 'To have one's ideas, programme, policies or style labelled "nostalgic" is to be on the end of one of the most enduring and non-negotiable insults in modern political discourse.'[1]

Writing in *The Hedgehog Review*, Charlie Tyson sums up America's cultural attitude towards nostalgia by stating that it 'is a debased emotion', which is 'widely dismissed as regressive and reactionary'.[2] Agnes Arnold-Forster, the author of *Nostalgia: A History of a Dangerous Emotion*, notes that 'even outside academia, nostalgia has a poor reputation'.[3] She added that:

For many, it is a fundamentally (small-c) conservative emotion, one held by people unwilling to engage with modern life

– the proverbial ostriches with their heads in the sand. It is, according to sociologist Yiannis Gabriel, 'the latest opiate of the people'. At best, a mostly harmless condition experienced by antiquarians and sentimentalists. At worst, a kind of reactionary delusion, one blamed for a range of perceived social and political sins.[4]

As a non-negotiable insult, nostalgia worked first as a rhetorical idiom to discredit conservatism. As Lasch explained in 1984:

> The notion of the 'nostalgic American' served liberals as an ideal whipping boy at a time when the intellectual foundations of liberalism were beginning to erode. As the dogma of progress became untenable, the 'party of hope' salvaged something of its self-confidence – the appearance if not the substance of hope – by deploring the nostalgic mood that allegedly made so many Americans afraid to face the future. By the Sixties, the denunciation of nostalgia had become a liberal ritual, but such skirmishes provided only a foretaste of the campaign that followed.[5]

For the anti-traditionalist cultural critic, the term nostalgia served as an idiom connoting out-of-touch, outdated, irrelevant people who sought escape from reality by hiding in the past. For the anti-conservative and anti-populist ideologue, branding opponents as nostalgic serves to delegitimate them and to close down discussion.

As Professor Michael Kenny of Cambridge University argues:

> Nostalgia is regularly depicted as an indication of a flawed political argument or allegiance and framed as a virus more likely to take hold in places that are 'left behind'. Its prevalence has been linked to the rise of populism in Western politics, the vote for Brexit and the election of Donald Trump.[6]

The weaponization of the term nostalgia against populist electoral opponents has now become a regular feature of our polarized political landscape. Its use was on full display during the debate surrounding Brexit, where supporters of leaving the EU were constantly diagnosed as suffering from the disease of imperial nostalgia. Similarly, a columnist for the *Guardian* tried to explain away the success of the Rassemblement Nationale in the 2014 European election by asserting that 'the country fell for the far right's siren song of fake nostalgia'.[7]

Commentators worried about the growing attraction of national populism to the electorate regard nostalgia as a standalone, dangerous emotion. The argument that nostalgia has become a 'dangerous political force' was well put by the political researcher Sophia Gaston. She regards nostalgia as 'this most profoundly emotional force seemingly corrupting politics and intoxicating society', and worries that 'with 63 per cent of Britons believing that the country is in a state of decline', nostalgia can become a remedy in which 'people find comfort'. What they hope for is not 'transformative change' but 'the restoration of a lost society. In effect, the propensity to believe in the "doctrine of progress" has evaporated.'[8]

The assessment of nostalgia as an all-purpose political threat is frequently repeated by anti-populist voices:

> It's a growing and worrying movement. Recent studies reveal that around two-thirds of the European public feel nostalgic about their nation's past. Take that alongside the move to the right among Euro voters, and you can see the power of a widespread sense of loss. It provides fertile ground for political demagogues and fire breathers who promise a return to an imagined golden age, presenting themselves as the architects of a return to 'the good old days'.[9]

Many anti-populist commentators attach the label of nostalgia to any movement that is concerned by the erosion of national identity, community solidarity and the legacy of the past. Gaston observed that:

> The national story politicians have tried to weave during a time of immense change has been exposed as febrile – insufficiently robust, mobilising and securitising. These fundamental questions, about pride, patriotism and identity in an age where community is no longer defined by the physical proximity but by the proximity of the mind's shared values, have not been answered.[10]

As it happens, the fundamental questions alluded to by Gaston are precisely the ones to which national populism attempts to provide answers. That is the main reason why nostalgia has become defined as a dangerous political force.

At first sight, it may seem curious to address the role that the term nostalgia plays in the anti-populist narrative. The emotion of nostalgia has been part of the human condition for a very long time. But I contend that it is not possible to understand the discussion surrounding populism without exploring the assumptions that lie behind the politicization of nostalgia. Adversaries of populism claim that that this movement's flawed strategy seeks to mobilize people around a world that no longer exists and, in all likelihood, never existed. In this way, populists are dismissed as not only fantasists, but also as dishonest manipulators of the past.

It is also important to note that the caricatured representation of populism that dominates mainstream commentaries and the academic literature has acquired an extreme unrestrained form in its attribution of nostalgia to populists. Consequently, any statement that is remotely positive about any aspect of a community or nation's past can be characterized as an expression of nostalgia. Anyone who makes a positive reference about the way that people lived their lives in previous times can invite the charge of falling into this trap.

The main impulse behind the anti-nostalgia bombast is the hostility that its authors possess towards those who seek to uphold a sense of continuity with a community's past. As we noted previously, critics of populism often attack this movement for possessing what they describe as an ideology of home, one that upholds the value of community. They denounce populism's supposed nostalgia as a vain attempt to return to a world that has been lost. In effect, their attitude represents a preference for the atomized and highly individuated world of social estrangement. What they advocate is an acceptance of estrangement – a willingness to live in the condition of alienation. The spirit of populism refuses to accept this cultural condition, and seeks to forge bonds that will contain its most corrosive effects.

Populists seek to develop a political culture that situates the concept of authority and legitimacy on the foundation of the past. They expressly attempt to consolidate a powerful sense of tradition and continuity because they believe that, by drawing and maintaining an organic continuity between successive generations, a robust sense of the past will contribute to the development of solidarity and stability. Their quest for continuity represents an important element of the populist spirit. In reference to this 'conservative reaction', Davis wrote 'how admirably the phenomenon furthers the continuity of identity'.[11]

The construction of the narrative of populist nostalgia

One of the first post-1960 polemics directed against populism, titled *Populism: Nostalgic or Progressive?* (1964), described it as 'an irrational emotional reaction to a loss of status', at the heart of which was 'a deep nostalgia for an imagined simple past'.[12] Since that time, the anti-populist cultural script regularly repeats this assertion. It constantly decries the traditionalist inclinations of its foes. The alarmist message conveyed by this script is that nostalgia is a dangerous form of escapism – one that springs a lethal political trap for gullible people. Adversaries of populism have even invented the term 'authoritarian nostalgia', which they claim is a powerful emotional and ideological tool for 'populist radical right (PRR) parties'.[13]

After the electoral triumph of Giorgia Meloni's Fratelli d'Italia in 2022, academic commentators frequently alluded to her 'highly nostalgic' election manifesto.[14] As proof of her sin, one commentator cited the following statements from the party's manifesto: 'natural resources and artistic heritage of the nation are an inheritance to be guarded and enhanced' and 'the elderly represent our history: a heritage of experiences, skills, talents that have helped to the birth and growth of our nation'.[15] One would have imagined that a statement by Italy's prime minister expressing pride in her nation's artistic heritage would be seen as unexceptional. However, in the current climate, the mere reference and affirmation of Italy's cultural legacy invites condemnation on the ground that it expresses nostalgia. The implication of this statement is that it is illegitimate to take pride in a nation's past.

In response to the death of Jean-Marie Le Pen, the former leader of the French National Front, his detractors identified him as 'a fascist, a racist, and nostalgic for many things'.[16] Their casual coupling of nostalgia with fascism and racism speaks to the weaponization of nostalgia, implying that it is the default emotional style of the fascist.

In Portugal, the electoral success of the populist party Chega was attributed to past authoritarian 'legacies and nostalgia'.[17] A similar diagnosis was made in relation to the success of populist parties in the Netherlands. As two Dutch academic commentators noted, 'political campaign slogans, such as "Make America Great Again" or "The Netherlands Ours Again", indicate that right-wing populists in Western countries use nostalgia to depict the national past as glorious'.[18] It seems that one is guilty of nostalgia unless a nation's past is painted in the darkest of colours.

The obsession with the problem posed by the appeals of populist to nostalgia often turns into a caricature of itself. In Germany, the right-wing *Alternative für Deutschland* (AfD) party was accused of harnessing AI technology to win votes, by artificially generating clips that served as 'nostalgia machines and emotional cliché amplifiers'.[19] The fantasy of using a 'nostalgia machine' to win elections exposes the insecure sensibility of this narrative's authors.

One of the most unattractive features of the anti-nostalgia cultural narrative is the ungenerous and cynical manner in which it frames people's celebration of their history. Expressions of genuine affection and loyalty are negated through attributing it to the unattractive prejudice of nostalgia. This attitude was on full display in the aftermath of the death of Britain's Queen Elizabeth II. Her popularity with the British public was frequently attributed to its nostalgia for the old Empire by commentators who could not imagine that the public's affection for her was based on the appreciation of the conscientious way in which she executed her role.

American critics, in particular, confused their own fantasy regarding nostalgia with the alleged fantasy of the British public for imperial greatness. 'Some of [Queen] Elizabeth's domestic popularity can likely be attributed to a sense of colonial nostalgia that has surged in the UK in recent years', claimed an article in *Smithsonian* magazine, quoting historian Brooke Newman.[20] One *New York Times* columnist noted that 'My hope is that as the screen of Elizabeth falls away, Britons may find it easier to recognize the unhealthiness of a dependency on imperial nostalgia for self-esteem.'[21] Another wrote of 'a vision of Global Britain steeped in half-truths and imperial nostalgia'.[22]

As it happens, imperial nostalgia is conspicuous by its absence in most parts of British society – it is principally a fantasy that preoccupies the imagination of the cultural elites. What provokes the cynical orientation of the anti-nostalgia brigade is the prevalence of British people searching to retrieve and develop the historical sources of identity, agency and community. Yet what drives people to gain clarity about their roots is not the sentiment of nostalgia but the search for meaning.

The verdict that populism dislikes 'the present and the immediate future' by seeking 'to mould the further future in accordance with its vision of the past' has acquired the status of an incontrovertible truth amongst academic experts on this subject.[23] According to this narrative, national populism is 'a backward-looking reactionary ideology, reflecting a deep sense of nostalgia for the good old days'.[24] The media commentator Andrew Sullivan asserts that the rise of populism is closely related to 'acute despair at the present moment and a memory of a previous golden age'. Populists aim to destroy the current status quo and 'return to the past in one emotionally cathartic revolt'.[25]

Time and again, populists are criticized for inventing and promoting the delusion of a 'golden age' in order to manipulate an insecure and disoriented public. The Turkish academic Ezgi Elçi wrote that 'populist figures utilize nostalgia by referring to their country's "good old" glorious days and exploiting resentment of the elites and establishment'. The theme of conscious manipulation is advanced by Elçi, when he claims that 'populists instrumentalize nostalgia in order to create their populist heartland, which is a retrospectively constructed utopia based on an abandoned but undead past'.[26]

The thrust of the argument put forward by this spiteful narrative of populist nostalgia is that what is at issue is a backward-looking movement, which is unable to engage with the issues confronting present-day society and which therefore seeks to find refuge in a mythical golden age.

A subsidiary theme proposed by the narrative of populist nostalgia is that people drawn towards the comfort zone of the past tend to be the moral and intellectual inferiors of their forward-looking, progressive opponents. Writing of the almost clichéd denunciation of nostalgia by left-leaning liberals and radicals, Fred Davis remarked that they assert that it is, at best, a 'fatuous indulgence of the elderly and fearful of even mild social change' and at worst, 'a kind of moral soporific of the masses that blinds them to their true class enemy'.[27]

The personality deficits of the nostalgic populist are conveyed through the psychologization of the nostalgic mind. This simplification of the populist imagination is achieved by framing it as glib and shallow. For example, an explanation of the 'narrative genre of the populist myth' contends that 'the temporal organization of all populist myths follows the same structure: there is a people who in the past was wronged by a nefarious "them"; it suffers in the present, but, aided by a redeemer, it will be vindicated in the future'.[28] In this account, a simplistic, almost childish, representation of populist attitudes relies on a language designed to provoke the cynicism of the morally superior reader. The story of the 'redeemer' versus the 'nefarious them' serves as a polemical device that highlights the gullibility and crassness of a movement drawn towards black-and-white explanations.

Through narratives conveyed about unsophisticated nostalgic people, the moral superiority of the storyteller is implicitly affirmed. Populist politicians are said to rely on using crude demagogic arguments to seduce their gullible and unworldly audience. It is claimed that 'populist politicians have the potential to attract audiences since they use simplified rhetoric, present themselves as ordinary people ("one of us"), adopt entertaining performances, and create spectacle'.[29] Spectacles drawing on what some researchers characterize as 'nostalgia deprivation' invariably highlight a 'golden past'.

According to such narratives, the reappropriation of this golden age, or what has been called *retrotopia*, is based on the impulse of rectifying the failings of the contemporary era. It is said to rely on 'visions located in the lost/stolen/abandoned but undead past, instead of being tied to the not-yet-unborn and so inexistent future'.[30] The concept of *retrotopia* was developed by Bauman to highlight the tendency to retrieve the failed potentials of the past.[31] It represents a kind of utopia-in-reverse, where the way that life was lived in the past serves as the populist model of the good life for all eternity.

Time and again, attacks on nostalgia are accompanied by the claim that the past did not possess any redeeming features. Moreover, those who wish to retain the way of life practised in the past are sometimes attacked for wishing to negate the many social advances that were achieved in recent decades. In this way, nostalgia is framed as a reactionary cultural weapon directed at undermining the fruits of social progress. According to one version of this argument, 'conservatism is just weaponized nostalgia', and there never was a 'good old days':

> So much of what goes on in right-wing circles is based on a past that has been idealized to the point where it has no basis in reality or fact. They have this image of some sort of sitcom-based 1950s, where men were men, women were women, and kids were endearing and mostly out of the way.[32]

The implication of this line of thinking is that the populist *retrotopia* evokes an aspiration for a world where traditional hierarchical family values and white Western hegemony possessed commanding influence and were the unchallenged norm.

The conflict over cultural continuity

In the twenty-first century, the antagonism directed against nostalgia can best be understood as motivated principally by a powerful mood of estrangement from cultural continuity, driven by the assumption that the way we live now is in every respect morally superior to that of previous generations. In contrast, national populists are devoted to the cultivation of cultural continuity. They regard the maintenance of a connection with their community's past as a vital component for forging a consciousness of solidarity with members of society. From their standpoint, the renewal of a community's social memory assists the development of a sense of common origins, which heightens people's sense of belonging.

The general assault on nostalgia should be interpreted as representing an assault on the past, with the aim of rupturing cultural continuity. This trend gained force during the cultural turn, when the sense of moral continuity gradually gave way to a consciousness of disconnection from community traditions. Since that point in time, the sense of cultural and historical continuity has been attacked by sections of the technocratic-managerial elites, whose hostility towards the past was motivated by the aspiration to detach society from its influence. This motive forms an important part of the culture war against the past, which I have discussed in a previous book.[33] In numerous accounts, the past of various Western nations is presented as a story of shame: not a golden age, but a dark age.

According to the anti-populist imagination, 'misguided faith in ideas that defined people's attachment to history and tradition' leads populists to possess a distorted sense of contemporary reality.[34] The premise of the anti-populist critique of nostalgia is that, rather than providing a positive guide to life, the customs and traditions of the past represent negative and toxic conventions and practices.

Anti-populist commentators often ridicule the targets of their polemic as simple and gullible people who, unlike them, actually believe that the past possesses some redeeming features. 'Populists will pine for an imaginary, whitewashed past until politicians offer a credible future', asserts Cas

Mudde.[35] The critique of nostalgia does not merely caution people about the problem of living in the past: it also seeks to delegitimate the values and customs that prevailed in yesteryear. The aim of the anti-populist critique of nostalgia is to distance society morally from its history.

This point was exemplified in an article by Javier Solana, the former secretary general of NATO. Solana wrote:

> The European Union has a dangerous case of nostalgia. Not only is a yearning for the 'good old days' – before the EU supposedly impinged on national sovereignty – fueling the rise of nationalist political parties; European leaders continue to try to apply yesterday's solutions to today's problems.[36]

For Solana, nostalgia is 'dangerous' because it draws people towards gaining meaning from the values of the past – such as national sovereignty. From this standpoint, the very search for meaning in tradition is likely to encourage opposition to the value system of the technocratic-managerial defenders of the cultural status quo.

Since the growing influence of the national populist movement, it has become increasingly difficult to argue that people have transcended their need for cultural continuity. People's concern with the darkening of America's history by culture warriors intent on reinterpreting the past through the prism of identity politics no doubt played a role in motivating people to vote for a second Trump presidency.

Trump understood the need to settle the score with the advocates of the bad-old-days version of American history. On 27 March 2025, he signed an executive order titled 'Restoring truth and sanity to American history',[37] which stated its intention to challenge a movement that 'seeks to undermine the remarkable achievements of the United States by casting its founding principles and historical milestones in a negative light'. In particular, the order took exception to the project of reconstructing the 'Nation's unparalleled legacy of advancing liberty, individual rights and human happiness' as 'inherently racist, sexist, oppressive, or otherwise irredeemably flawed'.

However, American society does not need an official top-down version of history. It is unlikely that an executive order by itself can do much to restore respect and pride in a nation's historical achievements. What is required is community commitment for helping people to strengthen their connection with their nation's past.

The upside of nostalgia

The phenomenon of uprootedness implied by the metaphor of 'homelessness', discussed in the previous chapter, refers to the unravelling of the threads that connect people to the generations that preceded them. Nostalgia often serves to sustain the connections that are under threat. Davis writes of the 'nostalgia-borne dialectic of the search for continuity amid threats of discontinuity'.[38] He believes that nostalgia plays a useful role in relation to identity affirmation, and wrote that nostalgia 'is one of the means – or, better, one of the more accessible psychological lenses – we employ in the never-ending work of constructing, maintaining and reconstructing our identities'.[39]

The sense of historical continuity plays an important role in the constitution of the self. Understanding where we come from influences and strengthens individuals' sense of who they are. A feeling of continuity with the experience of previous generations lends stability to a people's identity. Continuity across time is mediated through the intergenerational transmission of a community's way of life and its ideals. It is difficult to develop a sturdy sense of collective identity without a shared memory and a common attachment to conventions or customs that are rooted in the past.

The sense of continuity across time is, as the psychologist Roy Baumeister stated, one of the defining criteria of identity.[40] This point was echoed by the American social psychologist Kenneth Keniston, when he stated that 'one of the chief tasks of identity formation is the creation of a sense of self that will link the past, the present and the future'.[41]

The common ground on which people live requires a shared understanding of where members of a community come from. Learning about the past helps children to know their place in the world and develop their identity. The German psychoanalyst Erik Erikson, who formulated the concept of an identity crisis, attached great importance to providing young people with a sense of cultural continuity. He noted that 'true identity . . . depends on the support which the young individual receives from the collective sense of identity characterizing the social groups significant to him: his class, his nation, his culture'.[42]

For socialization to occur successfully, adults draw on the experience of previous generations to provide young people with a meaningful account of adulthood. Erikson remarked that the values with which children are trained 'persist because the cultural ethos continues to consider them "natural" and does not admit of alternatives'. He observed that:

> They persist because they have become an essential part of the individual's sense of identity, which he must preserve as a core of sanity and efficiency. But values do not persist unless they work, economically, psychologically and spiritually; and I argue that to this end they must continue to be anchored, generation after generation, in early child training; while child training, to remain consistent, must be embedded in a system of continued economic and cultural synthesis.[43]

The socialization of children is key to the transmission of this legacy of the past. It is integral to an intergenerational transaction in which moral norms are communicated by authoritative adults to the young. Though this form of socialization is likely to be perceived as impregnated with nostalgia by the technocratic-managerial elites, it is essential for providing the young with roots.

Nostalgia can be understood as the cultural antithesis to the loss of a sense of the past. As Davis noted, nostalgia 'leads us to search among remembrances of persons and places of our past in an effort to bestow meaning upon persons and places of our present'.[44] From the anti-populist standpoint, the very search for meaning in tradition and the experience of the past is likely to encourage opposition to the value system of the defenders of the cultural status quo.

Instead of responding to the critics of nostalgia by dismissing the charge of being drawn towards it, it is preferable to embrace it. Nostalgia refers to a yearning for home. It expresses an understandable and genuine sense of cultural loss underwritten by the belief that values which had once provided the unity of social relations and personal experience have become marginalized. Populists are on solid ground when they seek to reconnect with the legacy of their nation's past. Those who possess a positive orientation towards the past should not be seen as emotionally illiterate, naïve simpletons. A positive orientation towards the past does not mean its uncritical romanticization. It simply means taking it seriously – warts and all.

The attempt to forge a sense of historical continuity is a prerequisite for providing the present with the sturdy foundation needed to face the future. Those who have become detached from the past inevitably become obsessed with inventing an identity to the point that they become detached from the project of facing the future. The attempt to forge a consciousness of historical continuity makes an indispensable contribution to the creation of a bridge between the past and the present, and the present and the future.

It is an effective way of cultivating a genuine sensibility of belonging.

Nostalgia is not only good for society but also for the well-being of individuals. Studies suggest that those who 'reminisce are more likely to keep friends and expand social networks',[45] and are able to forge closer and more durable relations than those who are indifferent to their past. Common sense suggests that the individual's attempt to forge and maintain a sense of continuity with the past assists the development of an individual's identity and feeds the soul of society.

Without a close connection with the past, we become prisoners of fate. Why? Because we can only truly understand what humanity has achieved so far and acquire insight into what it can achieve in the future by evaluating the experience of our forebears. The legacy of the past provides the moral and intellectual resources for developing a twenty-first-century narrative of what solidarity and community looks like. Very importantly, it also provides the foundation for freedom.

The social psychologist Clay Routledge makes an important point when he stated that 'nostalgia helps people thrive in the present and build a better future'. He wrote that 'I and many other scholars have come to this conclusion after conducting a wide range of studies, including laboratory experiments and quantitative and qualitative surveys involving a large variety of people from all around the world'.[46] In other words, taking seriously the continuity of culture serves as an important moral resource for facing up to the challenges that lie ahead. As Routledge argues, 'nostalgia is, counterintuitively, a future-oriented endeavor. We draw on it to resolve our dissatisfactions in the present and to move forward with hope and determination'.

Populists do not want to go back to a golden age, but nor do they want their communities to be dispossessed of the customs and ways of being that made them who they are. Keeping alive the traditions, customs and rituals that have inspired their communities over the generations provides populism with the cultural power to motivate millions of people. It provides the foundation for the kind of cultural security that allows people to face the future.

8

Giving People a Voice:
Giving Meaning to Democracy

A few days before voting occurred during the 2015 General Election campaign, I heard a remarkable exchange on BBC Radio 4's flagship news programme *Today*, discussing the issue of immigration in Northern Ireland.[1] The BBC presenter said that the traditional hostilities and tensions between Catholics and Protestants had been suspended, giving way to a new division between the Irish and immigrants. Interviews with people from Catholic and Protestant communities seemed to back up the claim that they no longer felt threatened by the 'other side'.

What was truly fascinating about the interviewees' comments was the language they used to describe their new concern. Time and again, they used a variation of the expression 'We are not allowed to say what worries us'. In the end, after failing to extract what it was that people were 'not allowed to say', the reporter suggested, 'You mean immigration?' 'Yes, immigration!', replied a female interviewee vehemently.

Something about this exchange struck me as very disturbing, and stuck in my mind for several days. Is it not worrying that, in a free society, citizens felt uncomfortable with publicly expressing their true opinions? Especially opinions that are widely held by members of the public? What I found even more unsettling was that the BBC reporter did not express any surprise about the hesitant manner in which her questions were being answered. One would have thought that the frequently expressed comment 'We are not allowed to say' was itself newsworthy, and worthy of explanation. But it was just nodded through, capturing the view that, yes, it is understandable that people should feel they are prohibited from saying certain things. Evidently the phenomenon of large-scale self-censorship is not newsworthy.

People's reluctance to acknowledge their concern about the impact of immigration on their communities is understandable. They feel under pressure to keep their true opinions to themselves because the very mention of the word immigration can be interpreted as an expression of bigotry – or, at best, a marker of being old-fashioned and out of touch with modern society. The Irish interviewees on this episode of *Today* may well have remembered how, during the 2010 UK General Election campaign, the then prime minister, Gordon Brown, dismissed an elderly lady – who had asked about his views on immigration – as a 'bigoted woman'.[2] Brown later apologized to the woman he slandered, but everyone got the message that you should not mention the 'I word'. More recently, Keir Starmer, while still the leader of the Labour Party in opposition, reprimanded one of his MPs, Rosie Duffield, for daring to say that 'only women have cervixes'. He told a BBC interviewer: 'It is something that shouldn't be said. It's not right.'[3] Sadly, these days there are far too many facts and views the language police believes 'shouldn't be said'.

Significant sections of the political and cultural establishment would rather that people always felt constrained in what they feel they can say. This is the twenty-first-century version of the old oligarchical ideal, 'know your place'. Putting the people on mute allows the powers-that-be to possess a monopoly over the conduct of public conversation. Populist movements challenge this demand to 'watch your words' and play an important role in encouraging people to find their voice.

The quest for voice

Throughout the Western world, many people feel alienated and estranged from their governments and institutions. They feel patronized by technocrats, and they have become sceptical towards supposed truths communicated by professional politicians and experts. Many representatives of the cultural elite claim that the people no longer care about the truth, but the real truth is simpler: they don't care about *the elites'* version of the truth.

So, when the French celebrity philosopher Bernard-Henri Lévy declared that people have 'lost interest in whether politicians tell the truth',[4] he was really describing an electorate that no longer shares *his* values. The people who Levy patronized feel that their habits, customs and traditions are constantly being ridiculed by an oligarchy that acts as if it has a right to dictate how people should lead their lives and behave towards each other. Lévy's contempt for people was expressed in a relatively nuanced form. Other anti-populists hurl abuse at people who question their values by calling them 'deplorables' or 'garbage'.

As Thomas Frank argued in his fascinating account of the history of populism: 'Western elites increasingly reject the authority of the people, many of whom they consider to be intellectually benighted, culturally backward and morally grotesque.'[5] That is one reason why many people are drawn to movements that promise to take them seriously. In this way, populist movements play an important role in giving more and more people the confidence to publicly express their true opinion.

Citizens whose values are antithetical to those of their political and cultural overlords are often forced to keep their thoughts to themselves. In recent times, there have been numerous examples where individuals who raised criticism about the content of their children's education, uncontrolled mass migration or political Islam have been silenced, censored and even criminalized. Take the example of Karina Conway, a British mother who was banned from her daughter's primary school after raising complaints that staff were teaching 11-year-old pupils about transgender identity.[6] Eight months after her ban, she was told that she could come back if she agreed to 'refrain from posting negative posts about the school' and its 'staff'. In other words, if this mother was prepared to keep her views to herself and promised to remain silent about her criticism of her child's school, she would be allowed back on the grounds of this institution. Imposing silence on controversial matters – such as whether or not only women can have cervixes – is how the cultural placemen of the technocratic-managerial elites attempt to prevent their view of the world from being seriously challenged.

Conway was prepared publicly to criticise a school that she believed was indoctrinating young children to take on board the assumptions of gender ideology. But for every Karina Conway, there are tens of thousands of people who feel unable to express their views on the public issues of the day. These are people who have not found their voice. Yet many of them want to be part of the conversation and wish to have their views taken seriously.

According to the anti-populist narrative, the populist voice thrives on demagogic scaremongering and is responsible for exploiting people's fear and creating conflict. No doubt some populist politicians and their supporters use dramatic rhetoric to highlight their cause, but if their views fail to resonate with the public, they are unlikely to make much headway. It is precisely because populists are often able to give voice to citizens' genuine, pre-existing concerns that they have made such impressive gains in recent years.

One way that populist movements have sought to give people a voice is through supporting referendums as a means of expressing their political preferences. The 2016 referendum on Britain's membership of the European Union, which led to the vote for Brexit, serves as an exemplar. The referendum was not merely important in its own right. It also gave permission to many people to voice opinions that they hitherto kept to themselves – opinions that, of course, the British establishment would rather not hear. That is why so many opponents of Brexit demonstrated such venomous hatred towards the Leave camp. Unable to acknowledge that the people who voted to leave the EU knew what they were voting for, many Remainers suggested that the people were deceived, because they lacked the intellectual resources required to make an intelligent, considered decision.

In other instances, referendums have revealed the contrast between the outlook of a significant section of the public and that of the political and cultural establishment. The rejection of the Irish government's proposal in 2024 to change the nation's constitution, by widening the definition of the meaning of a family, was a case in point.[7] As far as the ruling parties of the Irish political establishment were concerned, the outcome of the referendum was a foregone conclusion. But unexpectedly, people found their voice and insisted that they regarded upholding the traditional family as their cause. It is evident that the Irish political establishment did not believe that the nation's citizens could think for themselves and opt to support values that were the opposite to theirs. They also did not count on the fact that the mobilization of populist activists could play an important role in encouraging hitherto-silent members of the public to find their voice.

An earlier important illustration of the way that a referendum can become a medium where people find their voice occurred in France in 2005. The French people rejected the European Constitutional Treaty, which aimed to increase the power of the European Commission at the expense of the governments of the EU's member states. The proposed constitution was presented as far too complex for ordinary people to understand the issues at stake. As the leftist French social theorist Jacques Rancière pointed out, 'the Constitutional Treaty was truly a kind of monster, where you are governed by people without even knowing who chose them'.

Yet French voters rose to the situation and found their voice. 'People turned into jurists, and they began to speak without worrying about having the right qualifications or diplomas', noted Rancière. He added that 'what was interesting there was that we saw what I would call a kind of popular intellect, a democratic intellect, as opposed to the official one'.[8] Ordinary people discovered that they could have a sensible opinion and chose to reject the advice of almost the entire French political class.

Populists tend to be more in favour of institutions of direct democracy such as referenda than their political opponents. They argue that direct democracy provides greater opportunities for people to express their views than is possible within institutions of indirect representative democracy, because it is more difficult for the political classes to implement policies – such as the promotion of Net Zero, mass migration, transgender ideology – that are not supported by the majority. In contrast, anti-populist elites are opposed to different forms of direct democracy because they believe that it represents a threat to their position in society; they prefer different forms of *insulated democracy*. Insulated democracy aims to protect the political class from the impact of popular pressure.

Many mainstream commentators mistakenly accuse populist movements of supporting direct democracy because they are opposed to representative democracy. In fact, populist movements are broadly supportive of representative and parliamentary democracy, although they may sometimes be critical about how the institutions work. Indeed, populists tend to look upon parliamentary elections as an opportunity for gaining support through engaging in a dialogue with the electorate. What populist activists object to is the way that the political elites subordinate decision making to the institutions of insulated democracy. The principal aim of this form of governance is to insulate the political class from accountability to the electorate and to restrain the voice of the public. It achieves this objective by depoliticizing political issues through rendering them as technical ones.

Insulated democracy relies on outsourcing political decision making to administrators in state institutions, the judiciary, expert bodies, NGOs and international organizations. In this way, many controversial issues become depoliticized and are taken outside of the influence of public opinion. The success of insulated democracy relies on administrators of state bodies being able to convert political questions into technical or managerial ones. In this way representative democracy becomes subverted since it is not people's representatives but unelected managers who get to make policy decisions on many issues.

The conversion of political issues into technical ones is usually achieved through what Habermas has characterized as the 'scientization of politics'; the transference of responsibility for decision making on many key issues to scientists, experts and administrators.[9] Political questions are no longer resolved through argument and debate by parliamentarians, but by the pronouncements of scientists and administrators; and the role of citizens is reduced to that of spectators of the drama of decision making by unelected individuals.

The authorities' response to the Covid-19 pandemic offered a striking illustration of how insulated decision making operates. Responsibility for the management of this crisis was transferred from politicians to scientists and experts.

Throughout the population-wide 'lockdowns' imposed in many nations, government officials insisted that they must 'follow the science'. After a while, even some scientists became frustrated with the 'follow the science' mantra as it became clear that politicians used it to avoid taking responsibility for making vital decisions.

This episode revealed the problem with the contemporary subordination of democratic decision making to technical expertise. The main argument for supporting the authority of political expertise is the claim that we live in an increasingly complex and rapidly changing world, which raises problems that ordinary citizens can neither understand nor deal with. The fetishization of complexity implicitly devalues the role of democratic deliberation.

For example, opponents of referenda in the European Union argue that the issues facing the public are too complex to be grasped by ordinary people. This argument was widely expressed during the debates that followed the referendums on the EU constitution in France and the Netherlands. Margot Wallström, then the vice president of the European Commission, commented on her blog that the constitution is a 'complex issue to vote on', which can confuse many citizens. In this confused state they may be led to 'use a referendum to answer a question that was not put to them'.

Similar views were communicated after the referendum in which British people supported Brexit. 'If there are issues on which the populace at large should be trusted to vote, something as complicated and economically sophisticated as EU membership is definitely not one of them', stated the biologist and professional atheist Richard Dawkins.[10] As far as he was concerned, complicated issues are way beyond the intellectual capacities of ordinary people, and therefore allowing a vote on such matters is a violation of the natural order of things. Dawkins's message communicates a patronizing disdain for the apparently easily manipulated masses.

Anecdotes about the stupidity and irrationality of voters speak to a view of democracy as an inconvenience that very intelligent people like Dawkins have to put up with. His argument echoes the rhetoric that says, 'I am a democrat, but. . .!' As he commented: 'I'm a democrat, but we live in a representative democracy, not a plebiscite democracy.'[11]

The claim that the issues are too complex for the people to grasp constitutes the principal justification for endowing expertise with political authority. For example, some leading environmentalists argue that many ecological problems are far too complex to be left to the unpredictable outcome of democratic decision making. They assert that, unlike scientists and experts who take a long view of environmental threats, a short-termist public will resist taking the steps necessary to save the planet.[12] It is not surprising, therefore, that during the Brexit referendum campaign, anti-populist commentators reacted with outrage to the statement made by the Conservative cabinet minister Michael Gove that, 'I think the people of this country have had enough of experts.'[13] The palpable sense of horror with which the anti-populist media responded indicated that, from its standpoint, the authority of the expert stood between civilization and the dreaded populist masses.

According to the narrative of anti-populism, the greatest sin of this movement is its willingness to question the judgement of the expert. In a tone of disbelief, Pippa Norris and Ronald Inglehart observed that populists embrace the voice of 'ordinary citizens' even 'when at odds with expert judgements – including those of elected representatives and judges, scientists, scholars, journalists and commentators'.[14] If that is the case, the anti-democratic hierarchical pyramid that situates the expert at the top and 'ordinary citizens' at the bottom is turned upside down when their epistemic authority is rejected. This is a matter of utmost concern to the technocratic-managerial class, since the maintenance of the supreme authority of the expert is essential for the legitimation of its rule.

If not the expert, who else will exercise authority over the *demos*? This was a question that was formulated a long time before the emergence of the current anti-populist cultural script. The conviction that the people are morally and intellectually inferior to their enlightened superiors constitutes the historical foundation of the anti-populist imagination. This approach towards public life reduces the role of the people to that of election fodder. Ideally, what they would like to see emerge is a democracy without a *demos*.

Since the growth of support for the populist movements during the past decade, arguments about upholding the sanctity of expertise have become increasingly shrill. For example, some opponents of populism were pleased that Covid-19 provided an opportunity for otherwise ignorant people to appreciate the importance of expertise.

There has even been a return of the old class-supremacist arguments that indict the mental deficits of citizens for making the wrong choices. Citizens who display mistrust towards political expertise or who vote the wrong way are not so much criticized for their mistakes but condemned as intellectually and mentally deficient people.

According to a blog published by the LSE, the distrust displayed by voters towards expertise in the United Kingdom and the United States is evidence of their anti-intellectualism. Its author stated that his research of survey data indicates that 'anti-intellectualism is linked to voters' support for candidates and political movements that are skeptical of expertise'.[15] Not only do sceptics of expertise suffer from anti-intellectualism; they also allegedly have lower levels of verbal intelligence than citizens who place their trust in experts. That's another way of saying that people who mistrust experts are likely to be thick. This is the latest version of nineteenth-century crowd psychology's narrative regarding the mental inferiority of the masses.

Far from resisting the tendency for professional administrators and experts to colonize areas of decision making that were hitherto their prerogative, centrist politicians are often keen to outsource this responsibility to experts. Official announcements regarding a particular policy are followed by the assertion that 'we are following the science', or 'research shows . . .' or 'our policy is evidence-based'. In effect, the outsourcing of policy making to experts signals the idea that the issues they deal with are not political.

The most important consequence of the scientization of politics is that it effectively depoliticizes public life and truncates the space within which decisions can be questioned. Unlike a policy based on political choice, the 'evidence' cannot be a subject of debate, and the role assigned to citizens is to listen and not question the wisdom of the experts. Important areas of decision making are thus transformed into no-go areas for democratic accountability.

The aim of insulating governance and decision making from the pressure of public opinion is to limit the space for the exercise of people's voice. In his discussion of 'populist democracy vs party democracy' at the turn of the twenty-first century, the political theorist Peter Mair drew attention to the fact that 'so many theorists' now 'focus so much attention on the apparent need to balance the voice of the demos'.[16] Mair highlighted the growing trend among political commentators to consider how the voice of the people 'might be restrained'. Since he wrote this essay, arguments directed against democratic decision making have proliferated and become increasingly shrill – especially since Brexit and the Trump election of 2016.

The call to restrain democracy is closely linked to the growing influence of populist parties over sections of the electorate. An analyst associated with the Hoover Institution, Morris Fiorina, noted that 'today's crisis of democracy reflects too much democracy'.[17] His argument about 'too much democracy' is linked to his concern that people do not seem to trust the cultural elites and experts. Fiorina wrote that 'some commentators contend that not only do citizens now discount expertise but consider the supposed holders of expertise as a negative reference group'. He added that 'Trump owes his success in some part to popular resentment of so-called cultural elites'. The calling out of the American cultural establishment by the MAGA movement showed how populists could both call into question the politicization of expertise and gain validation for the authority of public opinion.

The manufacture of consent

The legacy political establishment relies on a voiceless public. Therefore, it is not surprising that discouraging the public from speaking out – especially on controversial matters – is widely practised by anti-populist ideologues. Through a variety of stratagems – political and cultural pressure, assuming control over the use of language, direct and indirect forms of censorship, legal measures taken to curb free speech – controversial views are silenced and, in some instances, the voice of the people becomes inaudible. Views that are widely associated with populist concerns are routinely the targets of cultural silencing.

It does not much matter exactly what populists say – even a relatively innocent remark will be represented by their opponents as an expression of racism, fascism or as one of the many phobias. Critics of populism often examine their opponents' words for a hidden meaning. Populist speakers are often accused of dog-whistling – that is, communicating a hidden message – through using euphemism and outwardly unexceptional words. For example, someone expressing concern about the introduction of Sharia law can be accused of conveying an Islamophobic message. In fact, any statement that hints at a problem with Islamic culture risks being mercilessly denounced as Islamophobic

Take the case of Italy's prime minister, Giorgia Meloni. She is frequently accused by her detractors of being a closet fascist. According to *Guardian* commentator Roberto Saviano:

> Meloni dog-whistles to her neo-fascist ancestors with the Mussolini era slogan, 'God, homeland, family'. She did it 2019, screaming from the stage at a rally in San Giovanni: 'I am Giorgia, I am a woman, I am a mother, I am Italian, I am a Christian.'[18]

As far as Meloni is concerned, her slogan 'God, homeland, family' is a 'beautiful declaration of love'. However, Meloni is denied the right to have her comments interpreted at face value. Her anti-populist critics regard her as a dog-whistler and likely to be a closet fascist. In effect, the charge of dog-whistling is used to delegitimate people's public statements. The meaning of dog-whistle politics is defined in the following way:

> 'Dog-whistle politics' refers to the use of ostensibly innocuous discursive cues that prime more insidious outgroup hostilities, particularly among those who share the ideological predilections of the speaker. In practice, such coded language often evokes racially charged attitudes, but it has also been used in religious and anti-immigrant discourse. The metaphor is a reference to high-pitched dog-training whistles that use frequencies inaudible to humans.[19]

The charge of dog-whistling hurled at populists empowers their opponents to decide what their statements mean. The term conveys the claim that populist rhetoric cannot be taken seriously since it always communicates a hidden appeal to racist or xenophobic sentiment. In effect, the charge of dog-whistling serves as a weapon designed to gain control over how a statement made by a political opponent should be interpreted.

The premise on which the concept of dog-whistling is based is that there are ideas, assumptions and words that should not and ideally cannot be said in public. Its intention is to prevent certain voices from being taken seriously. In particular, the charge of dog-whistling is used to shut down discussion on matters about which the political and cultural establishment feels insecure.

The British Labour government minister Lucy Powell adopted this stratagem when she reacted to a member of the populist party Reform raising the problem of the grooming-gang scandal during the course of a radio debate in May 2024. The scandal refers to the mainly Pakistani rape gangs that preyed on white working-class girls in England from the early 2000s, which was covered up for years due to the reluctance of the authorities to face accusations of 'racism' and acknowledge the scale of tensions caused by multicultural policies. Powell responded by dismissing the scandal as a 'dog-whistle issue' and hoped that her comment would close the discussion down.[20] In this instance, it had the opposite effect, leading to public outcry led by the families of the victims.

In some instances, repressive laws have been enacted with the explicit objective of silencing populist voices that are critical of the political establishment. The situation in Germany represents a very disturbing illustration of this trend. Laws supposedly aimed at preventing hate speech have been used to stop citizens from voicing criticism against the government.

In her study, *Silencing Alternatives: Germany's War on Free Speech*, Sabine Beppler-Spahl noted:

> Under the guise of defending democracy from the threat of the far-right, the German government attempts to systematically silence and punish critical voices. Not only politicians and journalists, but an increasing number of ordinary citizens face police investigations, heavy fines and even prison sentences

for posting a single critical comment online. Such forceful silencing of opposing views, however, is deeply anti-democratic and violates the basic rights of German citizens.[21]

Beppler-Spahl offers the following examples:

1. Section 188 (Criminal Code) criminalizes 'insults' to politicians, leading to prosecutions of ordinary citizens for social-media posts or protest letters;
2. Section 130 ('incitement of masses' law), repeatedly amended and broadened in the past few years, resulting in prosecutions for criticism, such as of Germany's immigration policies;
3. The Office for the Protection of the Constitution (BfV), which monitors citizens' speech and can designate groups as 'extremist', effectively stigmatizing political opposition. The climate of stigmatization and exclusion has impacted public debate.

She describes a 74-year-old woman who was among those convicted under Section 130 after commenting:

> We need skilled workers, not asylum seekers who just want to make a nice life here without respecting our values and culture. Send those who are here to work. We don't need idlers and scroungers, and we certainly don't need knife artists and rapists.[22]

The pensioner's comment was posted on Facebook in response to a statement by Robert Habeck, the former vice-chancellor of Germany, on the nation's need for migration. The Düsseldorf district court sentenced the woman to 150 daily fines of €53 each, totalling €7,950. Evidently, critical voices on the issue of migration invite criminal proceedings and a severe financial penalty. This elderly lady's case is by no means exceptional. Hundreds of other German citizens have been punished for daring to question the wisdom of their political overlords.

The policing of speech in Germany is reinforced by a compliant mass media, which possesses a strong pro-establishment bias. Moreover, as Beppler-Spahl wrote, the German media 'has also been profoundly shaped by the establishment's declared war against populism and the far-right'. Tragically, a 'stifling anti-free-speech climate has infiltrated newsrooms, muzzling critical reporting'.[23] It is not therefore surprising that millions of German citizens self-censor. A study by the reputable Allensbach Institute has shown that less than half of Germans now feel they can freely express their political opinion.[24]

Self-censorship in the Western world – the reluctance to air opinion on matters of public importance – is by no means confined to Germany. The pressure to conform, and the fear of social isolation, can lead to what the German social scientist Elisabeth Noelle-Neumann identified in 1980 as a 'spiral of silence'.[25] According to this theory, people's assessment of the opinions held by the majority influences and modifies the way they express their own views. Some individuals feel anxious about expressing sentiments that differ from the consensus outlook, as expressed in the political and media realm, and it is thought that, 'prompted by a "fear of social isolation"', some are 'less likely to express their own viewpoint when they believe their opinions and ideas are in the minority'.[26]

Surveys indicate that the spiral of silence exercises a powerful influence in the contemporary world. In 2013, 61 per cent of Americans reported that they have avoided saying things that they believe because others might find them offensive.[27] According to the 2024 *Social Pressure Index: Private Opinion in America*, one 'underappreciated consequence of perceived social pressure is that it can lead individuals not only to self-silence but to publicly misrepresent their private views (what scholars call "preference falsification")'.[28] Research indicates that preference falsification is far more prevalent among conservative and populist citizens than those at the other end of the political spectrum. Why? Because of the social and cultural pressure to conform to the hegemonic mainstream views.

In virtually every social setting there is always an element of self-censorship. But in contemporary Western societies, the all-too-understandable impulse to conform is continually reinforced by the message 'You can't say that!' Increasingly, it seems that the only time many people feel confident enough to express their true opinions is in the secrecy of the polling booth. This is why, from time to time, populist and other dissident voices do far better in an election than was predicted in the opinion polls.

In recent decades, the spiral of silence that nurtures self-censorship has acquired a formidable presence. According to a study titled 'Keeping your mouth shut: spiraling self-censorship in the United States' by James Gibson and Joseph Sutherland: 'Over the period from the heyday of McCarthyism to the present, the percentage of the American people not feeling free to express their views has tripled.'[29] They reported that, in 2020, more than four in 10 people engaged in self-censorship. Increasing political polarization meant that 40 per cent of Americans chose to keep their 'mouths shut rather than express their opinion'.

Another national survey found that 'nearly two-thirds – 62 per cent – of Americans say the political climate these days prevents them from saying things they believe because others might find them offensive'.[30] The survey indicated that the share of Americans who self-censor has risen several percentage points since 2017, when 58 per cent of Americans agreed with this statement.

In November 2024, another survey, by the non-partisan think tank Populace, found that 'a majority of Americans (58 per cent) think that most people cannot share their honest opinions about sensitive topics'. Additionally, 61 per cent of Americans admit to self-censoring for fear of offending others.[31] To make matters worse, what this survey found was that 'not only are Americans declining to say what they think, they're also *misrepresenting* their actual beliefs'.[32]

A similar development is evident in the UK, where the so-called 'shy Tory' effect confounds opinion-polling organizations.[33] In recent times, opinion polls have tended to underestimate the proportion of the electorate voting for the Conservative Party and right-wing causes on the ground that 'shy Tories' are reluctant to tell pollsters their true intention. Self-censorship in the UK also touches on other matters. Young people between the ages of 16 to 34 tend to hold back from sharing their views with one another.[34] According to a survey conducted by the London-based Free Speech Union, 62 per cent of the respondents were self-censoring in the workplace. They either stated views that they did not believe or were refusing to acknowledge things that they did believe.[35] The culture of 'you can't say that' exercises a chilling effect on public life.

The American academic and commentator Glenn Loury has described self-censorship as 'the hidden face of political correctness'.[36] As Loury noted, what is at work in this scenario is not the imposition of force by a 'thought police', but the internalization of the fear of the consequences of saying the wrong words. He wrote that:

> For every act of aberrant speech seen to be punished by 'thought police', there are countless other critical arguments, dissents from received truth, unpleasant factual reports, or non-conformist deviations of thought which go unexpressed, or whose expression is distorted, because potential speakers rightly fear the consequences of a candid exposition of their views. As a result, the public discussion of vital issues can become dangerously impoverished.

This point is affirmed by Auron MacIntyre in his fascinating book *The Total State*. He contends that 'despite the lack of gulags or internment camps, people in liberal democracies are increasingly terrified to speak their minds', and contends that what is at work is both a powerful cultural pressure to self-censor and its acceptance by a significant section of society.[37] As he explains:

> An errant word on social media or an awkward interaction at work can end a person's career and make them the target of a hate campaign that will strip away their friends and family. The progressive outrage machine combs through every human interaction seeking out wrongthink. The impressive part is that the machine trains the population to do most of the monitoring and policing for it.[38]

In present-day society, the policing of speech is pursued through the work of devoted activists employed by educational and cultural institutions, charities and NGOs. These institutions are fiercely committed to the cause of linguistic engineering and believe that intolerance towards those who voice dissident ideas is entirely justified.

The attempt to dispossess people of their language

In the current culture wars, language has become an important site of conflict. The technocratic-managerial elites have succeeded over the years in ensuring that language consonant with its cosmopolitan outlook retains its commanding influence. As noted previously, the main way of achieving this is by the application of social and cultural pressure, which forces millions of people to 'mind their language' and in many cases self-censor. Social pressure is reinforced through the work of institutions of culture and the media, which are leading the business of linguistic engineering.

Linguistic engineering has directed much of its energy to delegitimating words that reflect traditional and conservative ideals. For example, it dictated that the word 'prostitute' should be displaced with that of 'sex worker'. In this case, a word that possessed negative moral connotations was replaced with one that was morally neutral. Similarly, linguistic engineers sought to discourage the use of words like 'husband' and 'wife' that communicated traditional norms regarding the value of marriage, preferring the term 'partner'.

People have been warned off from using the word 'female' to refer to women. 'Stop calling women "females"', warns the headline of the *Daily Nexus*, the student newspaper of the University of Californian at Santa Barbara.[39] In case you have doubts about the necessity for ceasing to use this term, *BuzzFeed* offers '6 reasons you should stop referring to women as "females" right now'.[40] Most normal human beings who have used 'female' and 'woman' interchangeably throughout their lives would be surprised to discover that they had behaved rudely and weirdly. However, for the supporters of the crusade against traditional language, abolishing the usage of the word 'female' from everyday conversation is mandatory because 'not all women are biologically female', whereas when 'you use "woman", you include all people who identify as women'.[41]

At the same time, linguistic engineers have been busy inventing new words and phrases that put into question traditional norms regarding the conduct of human relations. 'White privilege', 'toxic masculinity', 'heteronormativity' and 'cisgender' have entered the lexicon. Individuals who fail to use the correct transgender pronoun are called out for misgendering. Although most people feel estranged from this artificially manufactured vocabulary, many are worried about expressing their true opinions – particularly in their place of work.

The significance of dispossessing people of their language is particularly striking in relation to terms that touch directly or indirectly on the issue of national identity. The anti-populist cultural script frames national sentiment as an outdated, dangerous and irrational prejudice. This representation of nationalist consciousness has gained widespread traction in elite culture, where it tends to be derided as the bigotry of ordinary people. Anti-populist ideology continually signals the idea that, if awakened, this narrow-minded sensibility will inevitably have harmful consequences. In contemporary Western political discourse, nationalism and its cognate terms – national attachments, national identity, national sentiments – have acquired the kind of negative qualities that usually invite moral condemnation.

As previously discussed, even the word 'patriotism' has become tainted because of its association with the nation. So when Viktor Orbán, the prime minister of Hungary, stated that EU member states 'should not be afraid of being good patriots' and added the 'idea that nationalism is a danger for Europe is an idea I cannot accept', he implicitly drew attention to the sentiments that divide the camp of populism from that of the anti-populist.[42] The term 'good patriot' no longer translates into a positive vision in the political vocabulary of the EU elites. For the political elites who are invested in European unification, nationalism represents the 'bad old days'.

Amongst the people who inhabit the cultural establishment and run the mainstream media, the de-nationalization of identity is perceived as a sacred cause. The ideological hegemony of this outlook has led to a situation where many feel uncomfortable about voicing their identification with their nation.

In the European context, the anti-populist narrative constitutes a clear response to popular pressure. Since such pressure implicitly calls into question the accountability of the European Union's institutions, it threatens to expose their shallow base of democratic legitimacy. In the context of European political life, hostility toward the unaccountability of the elites frequently assumes the form of Euroscepticism, and has earned over the years the sobriquet of 'the democracy deficit'. The response of EU propagandists to Euroscepticism has been to condemn it as *ipso facto* xenophobic, racist and a threat to peace and stability.

The EU's uncompromising anti-populism is, at least in part, stirred by an apprehension towards the reliability of national electorates. That is why Habermas, one of the most fervent intellectual advocates of the European Union, could so casually write off national electorates as 'the preserve of right-wing nationalism' and condemn them as 'the caricature of national macrosubjects shutting themselves off from each other'.[43] This typically contemptuous reaction runs parallel to a deep reluctance to engage in a battle to win the hearts and minds of the public. The elites find it easier to blame the ignorance and prejudices of the people than to acknowledge their own difficulty in elaborating a compelling normative foundation for their political project.

Populism helps people find their voice

The success of populism in the sphere of electoral politics and the increase in the number of people who have been able to find their voice is a mutually reinforcing process. Many people now ignore the warning that 'you can't say that'. Through motivating people to find their voice, populism contributes to the revitalization of democracy.

Despite the growing influence of populism, people who have over the decades lost their voice find it difficult to regain it. Take the sudden emergence of the grass-roots movement promoting the flying of the national flag during the summer of 2025 in England. Operation Raise the Colours seemed to have come from nowhere. This movement was a patriotic social media protest that objected to the reluctance of local institutions to value the English flag of St George.[44] Participants in the movement indicated that they were fed up with the situation where local councils were happy to fly the Palestinian and LGBTQ flags but not that of their nation. This was a grassroots movement that spread from Birmingham to towns and cities throughout England. 'Let's bring back patriotism once and for all', stated the Facebook page of Operation Raise the Colours. It urged members to post images of the assorted national flags of the four British nations 'being raised around our great towns and cities'.[45] In response, individuals decided to form groups who took it upon themselves to go out and do what they called 'flagging' around their town.

The mainstream media and legacy political parties attempted to take control of the narrative surrounding this 'fly the flag' populist movement. There were frequent suggestions that this was a movement organized by the far right and that the nation's flag conveyed racist and xenophobic connotations. The Leader of Dorset Council, the Liberal Democrat Nick Ireland, personified this response to the movement. He told the BBC that some residents found this explosion of patriotism 'intimidating' and added that it was 'naïve' to suggest that the flying of the flags had not been 'hijacked' by far right groups.[46]

There is little doubt that the mainstream media's accusation that this movement was racist and organized by the far right had an impact on the participants of Operation Raise the Colours. When I interviewed the people going around and raising the flag of St George on the lamp post of my home town of Faversham, Kent, I was struck by their initial defensive explanation of their action. They spent the first two minutes of our discussion trying to reassure me that they were not racist, but patriots fed up with the way their flag was devalued. It was only after I explained that I was on their side and supported their objectives that they felt confident to drop the 'we are not racist' rhetoric and discuss their objective. They explained that they were hoping to bring back patriotism so that people could feel pride in their community and in the achievements of their ancestors. This point was echoed by Joseph Moulton, one of the organizers of Flag Force UK, who told a television interviewer that he encouraged people to not just do the flagging but to use it as a 'gateway to actually building the communities . . . doing the litter picking, helping the food banks, looking after vulnerable people'.[47]

What struck me about my conversation with the Faversham flaggers was that they were a group of committed men and women who were struggling to find their voice. None of them were previously politically active. They knew that what they were doing mattered and was important to their community, but they also understood that they were confronted with powerful forces that were ready to belittle their behaviour and distort their message. In such circumstances standing up to such a pressure and finding your voice required courage. I felt that they were halfway there. They had taken a gigantic step forward, but they had not yet been able to work out a compelling argument justifying their cause.

I have no doubt that this grassroots action would not have burst on the scene if it had not been for the growing prominence of the Reform Party during the previous five to eight months. Reform had nothing to do with this social media driven initiative, but the very fact that it existed and at least temporarily challenged the multicultural and anti-patriotic outlook that dominates the cultural and political institutions of Britain emboldened people to raise their concerns and in this situation to act. The very presence of a strong populist movement emboldens people to take a stand on matters that concern them.

Trump's 2024 electoral victory can also be seen as a triumph for common sense language. Most of the American people did not merely reject the Democratic Party and its candidates but also the language they used. In August 2025, the American think tank Third Way issued a memo to Democratic Party activists about the need for them to change their language.[48] The authors of this report were clearly concerned about the inability of the Kamala Harris campaign to use a language that could connect with the electorate. It accused Democrats of using 'an awful lot of words and phrases no ordinary person would ever dream of saying'.[49] It added that 'the effect of this language is to sound like the extreme, divisive, elitist, and obfuscatory, enforcers of wokeness'.

The implication of Third Way's warning about the use of 'seminar room language' by the Democrats was that the language of common sense rooted in the experience of American communities could not be censored out of existence. The very existence of MAGA encouraged people to express themselves in a language that made sense to them. And the more that people feel that their voice counts, the more likely it is that public life will come alive and enhance the quality of our political imagination. The ability of populism to communicate with people in a language that gives meaning to their lives will – in the long run – determine the future of this movement.

Populism's ability to communicate with people was also significantly enhanced through its use of the social media. Social media has played an important role in allowing national populism to gain a hearing. Studies indicate that national populist movements were able to 'effectively leverage' platforms like X, Facebook and LinkedIn to disseminate their views.[50] Francis Fukuyama has gone so far as to conclude that 'technology broadly and the internet in particular stand out as the most salient explanations for why global populism has arisen in this particular historical period'.[51] For populist movements having access to media platforms that assist them to communicate with their electorate without restrictions allowed them to make significant gains. When their message is not mediated through the legacy media, populist communications cannot be distorted by their adversaries. Social media has served to amplify the populist message. It has also played an important role in politicizing members of the public and giving them the confidence to speak out. The new media land-scape has served as a fertile terrain for the flourishing of the populist voice.

9

Conclusion: Taking Control

Whereas until recently commentaries tended to speculate that populism would soon reach its peak and become exhausted, today they express the fear that this movement is likely to increase its influence in the future. It is now recognized – even by adversaries of populism – that this movement has a point and that many of the issues raised by its leaders need answers.[1] The failure of democratic institutions to provide opportunities for participation is frequently recognized as a problem that has created an audience for populism. Certainly, after Trump's re-election as President in 2024 there can be little doubt that populism is here to stay. That is why some argue that 'populism needs to grow up' and that what 'we need is a rational populism'.[2]

In recent times, despite numerous attempts to place populism in a political quarantine, this movement has been able to grow and exert influence over the direction of public life. Of course, there are still numerous initiatives in place that attempt to isolate and ostracize populist voices. At times anti-populists go to great lengths to achieve this objective. For example, in September 2025, in Cologne, the governing mainstream parties signed an electoral pact committing them to speak only positively about migration.[3] In this way they hope to isolate the voice of the populist party, the AfD, from the public conversation. The German newspaper *Bild* referred to this as a 'bizarre gag order'.[4] There is something desperate about a pact that aims to prevent discussion on migration to undermine the populist AfD.

Despite the attempt to isolate populism from the mainstream of public life, this movement has succeeded in influencing the contemporary political agenda. Its success has been most evident in relation to the challenge posed by mass migration and the dysfunctional consequences of multiculturalism. Within the EU, populist parties have also successfully pushed back against the Green Deal, particularly in relation to its expensive energy policy. Populism has also forced various governments to at least pay lip service to patriotic values. There is a definite shift in political vibe if not a dramatic change in government policies in Europe. In the United States there is a veritable flood of policy declarations by the second Trump regime that are framed in a populist language. Just how effective these policies prove to be remains to be seen. However, what is indisputable is the great upheaval that post-Second World War political institutions and culture have experienced because of the pressure they face from their populist opponents.

For the first two decades of this century, the technocratic elites and their allies within institutions of culture were able to dominate the public conversation to the point that the opponents of their views and values could be effectively silenced. But the spirit of populism can no longer be bottled up. This spirit is best captured by the name of the Portuguese populist movement, Chega – meaning 'Enough!'. Chega barely existed a few years ago. In the May 2025 legislative election, it gained 60 seats in the 230 seat National Assembly of Portugal and became the main opposition party.[5]

Enough captures the spirit of defiance that motivates the people's revolt against the value system that emerged from the elite-influenced cultural turn of the late 1970s. In a remarkably short period of time, Chega managed to alter the Portuguese political landscape from a relatively stable two-party system to an unpredictable triparty one. More significantly, Chega succeeded in exerting a significant impact on the political agenda. Its emphasis on issues like corruption, crime and rural neglect rather than on the environment has forced the two legacy parties on the defensive.[6] In this way it has succeeded in raising the salience of issues like immigration, law and order and national identity in parliamentary debates.[7]

During the last quarter of the twentieth century, when the outlook of the technocratic-managerial elites gained ascendancy and became institutionalized, it faced little opposition. However, once the implications of this ideology became evident, it began to provoke a serious reaction from people who realized that they could no longer take for granted the continuation of the way of life that they were born into. This reaction first took the form of a mood – a populist mood, if you will – which gradually became politicized and turned into a movement.

For its part, the technocratic-managerial elite appears oblivious to the impact that its policies have had on society. It has been entirely indifferent to the way its policies have undermined the pre-political bonds of solidarity in working people's communities. Their callous disregard for the way these policies damaged people's cultural security was paralleled by their patronizing and insulting behaviour towards people who resisted the imposition of their worldview. This spirit of defiance in the face of the elite's patronizing behaviour continues to fuel the populist resistance.

The open display of contempt for people often represents the contemporary version of the elite's hatred for the masses that periodically emerged throughout modern history. As the political philosopher Michael Sandel wrote in *The New York Times*, 'disdain for the less educated is the last acceptable prejudice', and 'it's having a corrosive effect on democratic life'.[8] As the author Batya Ungar-Sargon explained, America's elites hate working people, 'and the working class is noticing'.[9]

Disdain for ordinary people is most explicit in the United States, where sections of the cultural elites make little attempt to hide their feelings. Take HBO host Bill Maher mocking working people living in what he called 'flyover states'. He declared that 'the flyover states have become the passed-over states'. His America is one 'where the cool jobs are, where people drive Teslas and eat artisanal ice cream'. While Maher may have thought he was speaking up for the American equivalent of the 'left behind', he went on to observe:

> We have orchestras and theater districts and world-class shopping. We have Chef Wolfgang Puck. And they have Chef Boyardee. Our roofs have solar panels. Theirs have last year's Christmas lights. We've got legal bud. They've got Bud(weiser).[10]

In other words, if only poorer Americans had more money and better opportunities, they would be less 'crazy' and more like 'us'. It doesn't occur to Maher that people in these communities might actually have some attachment to the way they live.

Remarks like those by Maher speak to a taken-for-granted arrogance towards the most basic aspects of people's lives. From a sociological perspective, these remarks can be interpreted as an example of what Max Weber called the 'stylization of life'. Through the embrace of particular lifestyles, people set themselves apart, reinforce their status and draw a moral contrast between their styles of life and those of others. As Pierre Bourdieu noted in his magisterial sociological essay *Distinction*, 'aesthetic intolerance can be terribly violent'. He explained that 'aversion to different lifestyles is perhaps one of the strongest barriers between classes'. Struggles over the 'art of living' serve to draw lines between behaviour and attitudes considered legitimate and those deserving moral condemnation.[11]

The elite's contempt for people who are not like them has played a significant role in the activation of populist consciousness. Paradoxically, it has also weakened the legitimacy of the technocratic-managerial elites. *Populism 2024*, a global survey of 28 nations, found that the majority of people felt that the 'elites in their country make decisions based on their own interests over the needs of the rest of the people in their country'.[12] As Nathanael Blake observed, 'because liberal Western democracies are ostensibly rooted in the theory of popular sovereignty, elite disdain for the people creates another legitimation crisis', and it 'also unmoors elite authority'.[13]

The attitude of derision towards the people also expresses contempt towards the legitimacy of popular sovereignty, the basis of democracy. What's at issue here is not the normal snobbery that sections of the ruling elites have always possessed, but an expression of scorn and ridicule towards people who are not like them. These sentiments communicate the feeble valuation that democracy enjoys in elite circles. In these circumstances, populism serves as the most effective line of defence of democracy.

The people's revolt against the imposition of a way of life that is alien to them can best be understood as a new form of counterculture. However, it is much more than that. The rejection of the cultural norms favoured by the technocratic-managerial elites is underwritten by a powerful democratic impulse of people taking control of the direction of their community. The democratic impulse driving populist aspiration forward expresses the mood of 'Enough!' regarding the dilution of democratic political life. People are fed up with being told what words they can and cannot use. They are tired of having to live in accordance with political decisions about which they were not consulted.

It was not the citizens of Western societies who demanded open borders, multiculturalism, the institutionalization of LGBTQ+ culture, Net Zero and a variety of other policies that go against their values, interests and ways of life. These are all top-down decisions that were not voted for by the electorate. Yet these are decisions that people must abide by. For many people, the institutionalization of policies about which they were never consulted is experienced as a loss of control over the conduct of their lives.

Since the *demos* plays a conspicuously marginal role in decision making, the status of citizenship has in practice been undermined. Citizens can still vote, but their capacity to influence policy outcomes has been seriously constrained. Moreover, since many of their views are ignored and, in some cases, ridiculed by the media and institutions of culture, many citizens feel that they are not part of the national conversation. Not for nothing was Trump's re-election attributed to a 'revolt of the working class'.[14] Once people feel looked down upon and patronized, they will support politicians who are prepared to voice their concerns. The pressure they exert provides the energy that democracy needs to be a genuine living force.

The constant questioning of the capacity of 'low-information' citizens represents an attack on the authority of democratic decision making. By calling into question the capacity of people to play the role of intelligent and responsible citizens, the moral authority of democracy is called into question. The frequency with which the reliability of citizens is questioned is one of the most important features of what I previously characterized as the 'anti-democratic moment'.[15] This anti-democratic moment is, to a considerable extent, a reaction to the populist one.

In recent years, the electoral success of populist movements and causes has led elite policymakers and commentators to voice anxiety about what they perceive as the fragility of democratic decision making. That is why 'many authors maintain that populism is first and foremost a democratic disease or pathology'.[16] In many cases – at least among the anti-populist commentators and elites – the previously begrudging acceptance of democracy has given way to a democracy panic.

In its current form, national populism is a political medium for expressing the viewpoint of a section of society whose interest is not represented within political institutions and the mainstream media. The double betrayal of the people has created a demand for a new direction and leadership to which populism responds. The electoral success of populist parties is proportional to their ability to give expression to the widespread aspiration for control over the direction of public life. As the British journalist David Goodhart wrote:

> One of the implicit promises of modern democratic citizenship is some degree of control over one's life. This translates most easily into a right to stop things happening, the right, at its most basic, to some stability and continuity in the place and the way one lives.[17]

The ability to maintain 'some stability and continuity in the place and the way one lives' has been called into question by the advocates of globalism who have self-consciously sought to undermine and negate the moral status of national sovereignty. Their policies have attempted to de-territorialize people's identity. And in all but name, they seek to denationalize the status of citizenship. In this way, they deprive citizenship of moral content and undermine the capacity of human beings to think of themselves as part of a community and act as a people.

The authority of citizenship, which has played a foundational role in the emergence of representative democracy, is now widely contested, and the distinction between citizen and non-citizen is frequently condemned as unjust and exclusionary. Implicitly, and in some cases explicitly, these arguments are directed at the normative foundation of a territorially based system of democracy.

Taking control

Cultural insecurity and the sense of powerlessness that it entails have created a demand for a voice and for taking control. That is why the participants in the wave of demonstrations that broke out in England in August 2025 chanted 'Whose Street: Our Streets'. That they felt the need to remind the world that the streets were theirs highlighted their aspiration of control.[18] The populist aspiration to take back control does not merely signify a desire to regain what has been lost, but also to assert the role of people as active citizens. Control pertains to two interrelated goals. In the first instance, control relates to the aspiration to exercise sovereignty to the full; in the second, it expresses the objective of resisting domination.

More than any other motif, the goal of taking control represents the most important feature of the spirit of populism. This point is echoed by the leftist academic supporter of populism, Paolo Gerbaudo, who wrote that 'the notion of taking control and its connected political imaginary involving ideas of democracy, power, sovereignty, etc., have become a dominant motive in contemporary politics in the "populist era"'.[19]

As noted, the slogan 'Take Back Control' gained prominence during the Brexit referendum and was swiftly popularized by the Vote Leave campaign. Above all, it meant leaving the EU in order to regain sovereign control over the conduct of Britain's political and economic life. The slogan communicates a call to action and reminds people of the value of sovereignty and freedom from foreign interference in the business of the nation state. In the context where the ideology of globalism had achieved hegemonic status, this was a slogan that called for the subversion of the prevailing political order. Above all, Take Back Control assumed that people possessed the agency to enact an important change to the circumstances within which they lived. This exercise of human agency indicated that people were prepared to take responsibility for the future of their community.

The slogan resonated with people in Britain, but also more widely. This was demonstrated on 18 August 2016, when the soon-to-be-elected American president, Donald Trump tweeted: 'They will soon be calling me MR BREXIT!'[20] Arguably Trump's MAGA slogan, 'Make America Great Again' – used in his 2024 election campaign – echoes the same spirit expressed by Take Back Control. As one political commentator, Steve Richards, reported, 'Donald Trump noted the potency of the slogan and made it a central theme' of his campaign. Richards argues that the left should adopt such a resonant idea.[21]

The political scientist Tim Haughton wrote: 'Take back control effectively combined not just a sense of a positive future, albeit never defined or elaborated, but also suggested a sense of rightful ownership. Moreover, it helped to mobilize the anti-establishment support of voters who felt let down by their politicians.'[22] What many observers of populism failed to grasp is that this slogan was not invented by a public relations agency or even dreamt up by political activists, but was the direct reflection of a sentiment that people voiced.

According to an analysis produced by Dominic Cummings, who became Vote Leave's campaign director, the question of control was frequently raised by the focus groups of floating voters he organized.[23] The following quotes from voters who participated in these focus groups highlight this aspiration:

Man in North Warwickshire – 'If Cameron's so weak that he can't get control of immigration – then I'm OUT.'

Woman in Hendon – 'If we leave the EU, we will save a fortune and we can spend that on the NHS or tax cuts.'

Man in Thurrock – 'We've lost control – because of Europe.'

In a discussion of this 19-page report, Paul Goldsmith notes that 'control' is mentioned 37 times and 'take back control' appeared five times.[24] It is precisely because the demand for control came out of the mouths of people that it became such an effective slogan. That people spontaneously took the issue of control so seriously spoke to a mood, to which populism could provide a measure of coherence.

Throughout history, the aspiration for control has been a central feature of populist movements. In a fascinating essay, 'Machiavellian democracy: controlling elites with ferocious populism', political science professor John P. McCormick draws attention to the contribution of the late Renaissance political philosopher Niccolo Machiavelli to our understanding of the centrality of taking control in populist thinking.[25] Machiavelli perceived the populace as the genuine 'guardian of liberty' because of people's desire not to be dominated, and to achieve this objective he advocated 'more direct and robust modes of direct political action'.[26] In effect, Machiavelli argued for the perpetual contestation of power and influence by the people to ensure that self-government had real meaning.

Machiavelli had an ambiguous attitude towards the masses. At times, his view of the people was one of disdain: he wrote that 'men are so simple, and governed so absolutely by their present needs, that he who wishes to deceive will never fail in finding willing dupes'. But in his *Discourses*, Machiavelli adopted a more positive account of the people and claimed that 'the populace is more prudent, more stable, and of sounder judgement than the prince'.[27] Machiavelli concluded that when the multitude is governed by laws, it is no less wise than the ruler.

Machiavelli believed that the state would benefit from the contribution of the masses and was prepared to incorporate them into the institutions of public life. He felt that the people could contain the arbitrary and impulsive behaviour of the ruler, and his proposals provided a space for the conduct of debate and public activity, and a widening sphere of political participation. In his Renaissance version of the importance of people taking control, Machiavelli highlighted what would become the dominant feature of modern populism. His identification with what Hazel Heiman has described as the 'populist impulse' shows his empathy with the spirit that motivated ordinary men and women to resist being dominated by the power of the elites.[28]

Machiavelli was far from an uncritical worshipper of populism. He understood that the people could come under the sway of confusing influences and that, on a bad day, their behaviour could be irrational and even destructive. His presumption in favour of the 'wisdom of the masses' was guided in part by the understanding that people's interests were far more beneficial to society than those of the oligarchy. In supporting an active role for the people in public life, Machiavelli understood the potentially creative dimension of participation. Unlike the contemporary opponents of populism, Machiavelli regarded the activation of the *demos* as the best guarantee for the flourishing of community life.

Whereas anti-populists have always interpreted the potential for the people to adopt unpredictable and volatile behaviour as a threat to social order, Machiavelli regarded such turbulence as a source of society's strength rather than a weakness. The potential for the turbulence of citizens serves as a counterbalance to the exercise of top-down, unresponsive, elite power.

What divides populism from liberalism, conservatism and identity politics is the issue of democracy

The disdain with which populism is regarded by supporters of mainstream liberal and conservative parties is often justified on the grounds that populist parties and their leaders are uncouth extremists whose very existence represents a threat to democracy. It is important to note that this sentiment is shared by conservative and liberal politicians alike. As Thomas Frank recalled: 'The Democracy Scare has been impressively pan-partisan. The liberal Center for American Progress came together in 2018 with its Beltway nemesis, the conservative American Enterprise Institute, to issue a report on "the threat of authoritarian populism" and to outline "the task facing America's political elites", which was to beat it back.'[29] Many Washington liberals and conservatives concluded that they had far more in common with each other than with the movement that led to Trump's 2016 electoral success.

The liberal account of populism counterposes its supposed rationalism to populist irrationalism. Liberal accounts of populism frequently hint that populists represent the moral equivalent of 1930s fascists and therefore should not be considered as legitimate political opponents, but as enemies.

Liberalism prefers the procedures associated with the rule of law to the practice of democratic decision making for the maintenance of stability and order. Since it perceives the *demos* as a potential source of volatility, liberal governance has opted to outsource decision making to unelected technocratic institutions and the courts. I have previously developed the concept of *illiberal liberalism* to capture this unease with democratic decision making,[30] which is ultimately based on a deep-seated suspicion of the people.

Unlike populists, liberals possess an instrumental attitude towards the principle of democracy. Despite its positive reforming impulses, classical liberalism always possessed an elitist dimension, often expressed through a quasi-aristocratic disdain for what it perceived as the corrupting influence of mass culture and society. Elitist disdain for public opinion continues to be communicated by many twenty-first-century liberals. Jason Brennan's assertion that 'asking everyone to vote is like asking everyone to litter'[31] is likely to be too extreme for most self-identifying liberals. However, a milder version of this view is all too prevalent in many liberal circles.

In effect, liberalism's formal idealization of democracy has always coexisted with mistrust about how people would use their political power. In response to this anxiety, the political classes adopted the twin-track strategy of insulating their institutions from direct popular pressure, and depoliticizing decision making through the use of expert, judicial and non-governmental organizations. In contrast, populism encourages a more direct form of political decision making. It also presumes in favour of expanding the domain of decision making and assigns the main role in this process to the electorate rather than to experts and other non-elected actors.

In practice, many liberal thinkers regard the rule of law as a first-order principle to which democracy must be subordinated.[32] This pragmatic orientation towards democracy often drives liberalism in an illiberal direction. Those who are prepared to challenge the project of curbing popular pressure are invariably perceived as liberalism's enemies.

Though conservatives often share populism's respect for tradition, the nation and the communities that bind together different generations, they still have some serious reservations about populism. Many conservatives are uncomfortable with any manifestation of mass politics. Populists – especially those with a plebeian orientation, such as the *gilets jaunes* movement in France or the 2024 European farmers' protests – rarely exhibit the deference to institutions that are characteristic of classical conservatism.

Though they tend to respect tradition, populists often question prevailing conventions. Unlike conservatives, populists are not simply animated by the goal of conserving traditional values and institutions but with challenging the prevailing cultural norms. That is why many conservatives regard populists as unpredictable and extreme. Their anxiety on this score has led many conservatives to embrace key features of the dominant narrative authored by anti-populists. Populist movements can indeed be volatile and willing to embrace tactics of direct action. However, as some recent examples like the farmers' protests indicate, such movements can play an essential role in defending a way of life or even a long-established tradition. At certain times, some conservatives are prepared to adopt aspects of the rhetoric of populism, but rarely support mobilizations supporting populists' objectives. Machiavelli's call for a ferocious populism certainly goes against the centrist instincts of many conservatives.

Identity activists positively hate populists. It is worth noting that, although they embrace almost every form of personal and cultural identity, identitarians make an exception when it comes to the identity of the nation. They are also deeply hostile to populist insistence on the maintenance of the traditional binary distinction between men and women, adults and children, and members and non-members of a community.

In turn, movements described as populist have gained strength from sections of society because of their unambiguous hostility to identity politics. Indeed, in contrast to liberals and even conservatives, populists have not been embarrassed about publicly challenging identity politics. They have been at the forefront of battles against the representatives of identity politics in today's culture wars and are therefore often the main target of the identitarian intellectual and cultural elites.

One striking difference between populism and its political rivals boils down to a contrasting orientation towards the *demos*. Machiavelli's contribution to grasping the relationship between the people and the elites retains its relevance to this day. Contrary to the anti-democratic prejudice that perceives the mass of society as a mob that threatens freedom, citizens constitute the most reliable defence against the attempt to encroach on hard-won liberties. Liberty, and the rule of law, are inextricably linked to democracy. Almost all the freedoms that matter to people were achieved through their willingness to fight for the realization of their democratic aspirations.

Freedoms were not granted by liberal oligarchs wedded to the idea of the rule of law, but were wrested from the powerful through centuries of democratic struggle.

Democracy is not just a medium for realizing the best results. If it is merely seen as a technocratic tool or a 'lesser evil', its potential for endowing public life with meaning and dynamism will go unrealized. Unfortunately, for many decades, democracy was relegated to the role of a medium of governance – and not surprisingly, many people have switched off from politics or adopted an anti-political cynical posture. In such circumstances, voting was often perceived as a pointless ritual; where and how one voted did not matter. Populist movements have challenged the technocratic-managerial control of public life. Through their activities, they have won millions of voters over to the conviction that there is an alternative to the way that society is managed.

Democracy is more than a set of procedures. It is an exercise in decision making, where citizens find ways to have their voices heard and where they can also hear the voices of others. Through its exercise, it fosters a climate that allows public life to flourish. In the public sphere, the individual voter interacts with others as a citizen. It is at this point that politics can bring out the active side of people so that through argument, debate, conflict and acts of solidarity, citizens are not simply 'voters' but active participants in public affairs.

The spirit of populism has created a climate that has fostered a mood of activism and defiance of the oligarchical tendencies in society. Through its defence of community, solidarity and voice, populism has succeeded in slowing down the moral disarmament of Western society. Its resistance to the corrosive influence of the technocratic-managerial classes shows that it is possible to develop an alternative to their fatalistic outlook. However, whether the spirit of populism is sufficient to transform this resistance into a coherent and durable movement remains to be seen. For now, populism is still in an early phase of movement building and has yet to evolve a coherent political programme with which it can help inspire people with a compelling vision of the future.

The spirit of populism and the zeitgeist it represents will not last forever. That is why the spirit that animates the forward movement of populist activism needs to develop a sturdy intellectual political outlook that can be institutionalized and can generate policies that are relevant for people's lives. Without the development of such an outlook, all the gains of the populist moment will become dissipated and the movement will be captured by the institutions that are committed to perpetuating the status quo

The politics of common sense

Though populist movements often lack the clarity necessary to provide democratic politics with a coherent orientation towards the future, they move society in the right direction. The spirit of populism soars above the usual discontent and frustration that many citizens feel about their circumstances. It reminds people that they are part of a wider community of people drawn together by a common legacy that bears the efforts of countless generations.

Nor does populism merely incite people to protest against the behaviour of their political masters. It encourages the politics of hope – 'that is, the hope that where established parties and elites have failed, ordinary folks, common sense and the politicians who give them a voice can find solutions'.[33]

Common sense is often looked down upon by self-styled sophisticates, who regard it as just a veiled term for prejudice. Yet the belief in the role of citizenship presumes that people are capable of possessing the ability to make sound judgements and sensible decisions. Common sense is not simply the attribute of an individual's accomplishment, but also the outcome of the distillation of sentiments and attitudes that prevail within a community.

As the *Oxford English Dictionary* reminds us, common sense can be defined as 'a generally held belief or opinion; a widely shared feeling or judgement'.[34] What is at issue here is not just a way of making sense of the world, but views that resonate widely because they are held in common. The commonality of this sensibility is sometimes dismissed as simply superficial folk knowledge. But the *common* in common sense is linked to a web of meaning that binds people together. That is probably why Trump referred to his re-election as 'the revolution of common sense' in his second inaugural address.[35]

Amongst academics, common sense is referred to as a form of 'lay epistemology'. Those who are sceptical of the efficacy of common sense argue that it is merely guided by 'direct experience, emotions and intuition'. However, it is more than simply an expression of a spontaneous, interpretative reaction to events. It embodies the accumulation of taken-for-granted knowledge of a community, building on the wisdom and experience of pre-existing generations of people. It is for that reason that opponents of populism dislike and denounce common sense as 'reactionary' and incoherent.[36]

Hannah Arendt understood the political significance of common sense. In her 'Understanding and politics', she wrote that common sense 'presupposes a common world into which we all fit, where we can live together because we possess one sense which controls and adjusts all strictly particular sense data to those of all others'.[37] Elsewhere she observed that common sense 'fits us into a community'.[38]

Populist common sense is often denounced on the grounds that it elevates lay epistemology at the expense of scientific and expert knowledge. It is the case that, in some instances, common sense is elevated to the point where it is assigned the status of serving as the principal source of truth. However, the populist affirmation of common sense easily co-exists with science and expertise and has no pretension to challenge the facts gained through scientific research. It merely claims the right to interpret the meaning of these facts for people's life world.

Arendt claimed that the possession of common sense was logically prior to and a precondition for 'true understanding'. Her thoughts on this matter are worth quoting at length.

> True understanding always returns to the judgements and prejudices which preceded and guided the strictly scientific inquiry. The sciences can only illuminate, but neither prove nor disprove, the uncritical preliminary understanding from which they start. If the scientist, misguided by the very labour of his inquiry, begins to pose as an expert in politics and despise the popular understandings from which he started, he loses immediately the Ariadne thread of common sense which alone will guide him securely through the labyrinth of his own results.[39]

Arendt warns of the risks posed to the flourishing of common sense by the technocratic impulses confronting twentieth-century totalitarian societies. She wrote of 'the breakdown of our common inherited wisdom . . . we are living in a topsy-turvy world, a world where we cannot find our way by abiding by the rules of what was once common sense'.[40]

The technocratic-managerial elites are often estranged from a community's common sense because of their detachment from it. That is why they don't understand that so many of their policies violate the common sense of millions of people. In contrast, populism champions an egalitarian form of common sense against the oligarchical disrespect for people's sensibilities.

Opponents of populism do not demonize common sense merely on the grounds that its insights are inferior to science, but also because it allegedly contains the most 'reactionary ideas'.[41] The Italian Marxist thinker Antonio Gramsci conceded that common sense contained 'nuggets of good sense', but he had no doubt that it was 'crudely neophobe and conservative'.[42] The misguided use of the term 'neophobe' – the fear of the new – misunderstands the significance of common sense. Common sense does not automatically presume in favour of the new, but fiercely upholds the existing system of meaning in the face of new interpretations of reality which, without common sense, can lead to the 'growth of meaninglessness'.[43]

If there is a phobia, it is communicated through hostility to populist common sense. 'What scares me most is the word "common sense"', wrote Lorenzo Robustelli, the director of *Eunews*.[44] Anxiety about the influence exercised by common sense is motivated by the fear that populist common sense makes more sense to millions of people than the outlook promoted by the technocratic-managerial elites. That is why, as long as it can communicate this sentiment, populism is assured of a powerful role in public life.

An insightful essay on this subject posits populism 'as an egalitarian impulse against oligarchic tendencies, centred on anti-elitism and the defence of a democratic common sense'.[45] This is an impulse that is principally defensive and, in many ways, serves pre-political ends. It is 'defensive-reactive' rather than ideologically oriented towards 'the establishment of a radically new social order'.[46] Its defensive impulse resonates with members of society who feel under siege. Its capacity to affirm what people take for granted is its strength. Whether it can move beyond its defensive posture and take the offensive depends on its ability to evolve programmatic initiatives that allow its democratic common sense to yield to new experience.

Following Arendt, who is said to have built 'a political theory rooted in common sense', I would suggest that the flourishing of this sensibility is essential for a healthy democracy.[47] As Sophia Rosenfeld observed in her *Common Sense: A Political History*:

In the more than 200 years since Paine's little pamphlet came off the Philadelphia presses, the idea of common sense has repeatedly jumpstarted the participation of ordinary citizens, that is, those with no specialized knowledge or expertise, in the business of making political judgments.[48]

Rosenfeld's reference to Thomas Paine's bestselling pamphlet *Common Sense* is apposite, since its populist message played an important role in mobilizing support for the American War of Independence.

As Rosenfeld notes, for Arendt 'common sense becomes both the groundwork and the goal of any successful democratic regime'. Arendt was by no means a self-declared advocate of populism, but her instincts were drawn towards valorizing the impulse towards the manifestation of democratic common sense. She believed that the experiences and interaction of people provided the resources that foster a climate where democracy could flourish and reproduce itself.

Now, more than at any other moment in the modern era, it is crucially important to uphold the value of common sense. Why? Because common sense is not only derided but faces a ferocious ideological onslaught. The knowledge that people have derived from their everyday experience is frequently called into question to the point that even the most banal problems of life are said to require expert intervention. People's lay knowledge is constantly dismissed as of little use for dealing with our supposedly ever-increasingly complex world. There is an ever-expanding number of mentors, parenting coaches, sex therapists and life coaches whose very existence calls into question the relevance of common sense. Even the common sense advice on parenting offered by grandmothers has been invalidated by expert knowledge.[49]

Most important of all, as I noted previously, the capacity of people to make mature political judgements is constantly called into question. From this perspective, people's common sense is not sufficient for democratic decision making. Populists' insistence on the appeal to common sense reinforces the influence of views that do not bear the stamp of approval of the technocratic-managerial elites. In this way, populism represents the answer to the dilution of citizenship and the weakening of pre-political bonds.

Concluding remarks on the spirit of populism

Although national populism is often represented as radical and even as revolutionary, its aims and achievements can come across as modest. It is important to reiterate that this movement is essentially a defensive phenomenon. It has sought to rescue, preserve and defend ways of life from the cultural attacks faced by communities. In the course of engaging in this conflict, it has succeeded in encouraging the emergence of a coherent set of values that challenge the hegemonic outlook of the ruling elites.

National populism is principally expressed through the medium of cultural politics rather than the classical theme of rich versus poor. As the Rassemblement Nationale in France showed, the movement is not indifferent to economic issues. But above all, national populism is focused on defending a way of life. In this respect its approach is very different to the focus on economic conflict adopted by left-wing populists, who obviously forgot to read their Gramsci and show little interest in the politics of culture.

National populism serves as a reminder that the people exist and cannot be taken for granted. Its supporters have become disillusioned with the traditional parties to the point of abandoning them altogether. The very existence of a vibrant populist voice serves as a reminder that democracy requires the active involvement of citizens. It serves the role of a guardian of democracy. Populism encourages a sense of agency and encourages its supporters to take control of their community and the restoration of people's voice.

Despite its impressive achievement on the plane of electoral and cultural politics, populism has yet to realize its potential. During the past two decades it has managed to carve out a role for itself as a distinct oppositional voice that can no longer be ignored by the ruling classes. No doubt it has benefitted from the decline of the legacy parties, but through its activity it has also contributed to their unravelling. Consequently, it has succeeded in establishing an influential position for itself within Western societies.

In most instances populist movements have had only a limited success in dominating the policy-making agenda. It has influenced policy making in the sphere of migration, multiculturalism, environmentalism and identity politics. But its work in the sphere of social and economic policy and the reform of existing forms of governance remain works in progress.

No doubt the spirit of populism will continue to fuel the forward momentum of this movement. But whether the sentiments that this movement represents can be turned into a stable political force depends on its capacity to learn from its experience. Though national populism has been around for over two decades, it is only now that it is being seriously tested. Unless populism can develop greater political clarity and develop an inspiring account of democratic citizenship, it will find it difficult to make progress. In the face of the considerable power of the political establishment, cultural elites and the mainstream media, populism can only advance if it develops a coherent alternative to the values of the prevailing political order.

One of the challenges that the populist movement needs to deal with is the unusually intense level of polarization of public life in the Western world. The West is deeply divided within itself, and it looks as if the cultural conflicts that fuel this polarization are likely to continue indefinitely. The conflict between populism and anti-populism appears to have acquired its own inner dynamic and inhibits the emergence of the kind of elementary consensus required for democratic decision making. Yet, what populism can offer is relevant to our era when the fragmentation of society is reinforced by cultural and ethnic divisions.

There is a lot at stake during the coming years, which is why the development of an enlightened, democratically informed version of populist politics is badly needed. Populist movements will have to become more professional if they are to transform their minority status and become the natural parties of the people. It will have to become professional but not bureaucratized. It will have to avoid the temptation of compromising its principles in exchange for short-term gains. At the same time, it needs to develop the kind of political sophistication necessary for becoming a party of government. All this will have to be done while preserving the spirit of populism and the energy and dynamism it affords. They will also have to create/attract an intelligentsia that can assist it to gain a degree of cultural authority. Populist movements have already made a significant cultural impact on the social media; now they have to find ways of establishing a presence in their nation's intellectual life.

It is when populist movements are in a position to gain governmental power that their capacity to remain a genuine party of the people will come under serious challenge. When the Italian Prime Minister Giorgia Meloni backtracked on her stance on immigration in 2023 and argued that 'Europe and Italy needed immigration', it became evident that the exigency of remaining in government forced her to compromise on principles.[50] In the same way, market forces put pressure on her government to disrupt her policy of raising taxes on banks.[51]

Unlike the Trump Administration, whose economic policies never pretended to be truly populist, Meloni's government set out to promote people-oriented policies. That is why the case of the Meloni government is so important because it indicates that there are formidable obstacles to the implementation of genuine populist policies. In the end Meloni, like Trump, had to pay heed to the demands of market forces.[52]

The setbacks suffered by parties who gained power on the wave of populist energy should not be interpreted fatalistically as the inevitable consequence of the political realities promoted by global capitalism. Without romanticizing the spirit of populism, it is important to note that it provides the kind of energy that democracy needs to thrive. Learning the lessons of past setbacks and failure can at the very least help ensure that populism has the potential to serve as a viable governmental force.

Recent events throughout the world have shown that populism possesses formidable creative disruptive energy. Now it must grow up and learn to project a positive political alternative that promotes the values of democracy and social solidarity. The crystallization of the populist impulse into a political movement that infuses the aspiration for solidarity with the ideals of popular sovereignty, consent and an uncompromising commitment to liberty is a cause well worth fighting for. Common sense dictates that democrats should unambiguously celebrate the spirit of populism.

Notes

Preface

1 For an account of this protest, see https://www.politico.eu/article/belgi um-farmer-protests-brussels-nitrogen-emissions/
2 https://www.populismstudies.org/the-nexus-between-activism-and-populism-amid-global-protests-and-digital-media/
3 See, for example, Bickerton, C.J. and Accetti, C.I. (2021) *Technopopulism: The New Logic of Democratic Politics*. Oxford: Oxford University Press.
4 On the flaggers movement, see https://www.spectator.co.uk/article/me et-the-man-putting-hundreds-of-england-flags-up-around-york/

Chapter 1: Introduction: A Spectre Haunting . . .

1 Ionescu, G. and Gellner, E. (eds) (1969) *Populism: Its Meanings and National Characteristics*. London: Weidenfeld and Nicolson, p. 1.
2 Tallon, E. (2019) '"A spectre is haunting europe": The rise of populism worldwide and its humanitarian implications'. NATO Association of Canada, 7 June, https://natoassociation.ca/a-spectre-is-haunting-eu rope-the-rise-of-populism-worldwide-and-its-humanitarian-implicati ons/
3 Hedman, E.L.E. (2001) 'The spectre of populism in Philippine politics and society: *artista, masa, Eraption!*'. *South East Asia Research*, 9(1), 5–44 and Albertazzi, D. and McDonnell, D. (eds) (2007) *Twenty-first Century Populism: The Spectre of Western European Democracy*. Berlin: Springer.
4 Reynié, D. (2016) 'The specter haunting Europe: "heritage populism" and France's National Front'. *Journal of Democracy*, 27(4), 47–57.

5 'Spectre', *Oxford English Dictionary*, https://www.oed.com/dictionary /spectre_n?tab=meaning_and_use#21672406

6 Stabenow, M. (2010) 'Anlaufstelle für Merkel und Sarkozy'. *Frankfurter Allgemeine Zeitung*, 9 April, https://www.faz.net/aktuell/politik/europ aeische-union/eu-ratspraesident-van-rompuy-anlaufstelle-fuer-merkel -und-sarkozy-1965888.html

7 O'Carroll, L. (2004) '"They want to destroy our Europe": von der Leyen condemns rise of populism'. *Guardian*, 7 March, https://www.thegu ardian.com/world/2024/mar/07/they-want-to-destroy-our-europe-von -der-leyen-condemns-rise-of-populism

8 European Commission (2004) 'Resisting authoritarian populism: Commission's Ethics Group issues new Statement on defending democracy and its values'. Directorate-General for Research and Innovation, 5 June, https://research-and-innovation.ec.europa.eu/news/all-resear ch-and-innovation-news/resisting-authoritarian-populism-commissio ns-ethics-group-issues-new-statement-defending-democracy-2024-06 -05_en

9 'Populism's threat to democracy in the EU', Horizon 2020, Cordis, https://cordis.europa.eu/article/id/434333-populism-s-threat-to -democracy-in-the-eu

10 https://ec.europa.eu/info/funding-tenders/opportunities/portal/screen /opportunities/projects-details/43353764/101175567

11 Mackert, J. (2018) 'Introduction'. In Fitzi, G., Mackert, J. and Turner, B. (eds) *Populism and the Crisis of Democracy*. London: Routledge, pp. 1–12.

12 Taguieff, P.A. (1997) 'Populism and political science: from conceptual illusions to real problems'. *Vingtieme Siecle. Revue dhistoire*, 56(4), 4–33, p. 5.

13 Goodwin, M. (2021) 'Populism by Michael Burleigh: a patronising book that sees voters as ignorant pawns manipulated by a shadowy elite'. *Daily Telegraph*, 28 February, https://www.telegraph.co.uk/books/non -fiction/populism-michael-burleigh-patronising-book-sees-voters-igno rant/

14 Molloy, D. (2018) 'What is populism, and what does the term actually mean?', BBC News, 6 March, https://www.bbc.co.uk/news/world-4330 1423

15 Krastev, I. (2007) 'The populist moment', *Eurozine*, 18 September, https://www.eurozine.com/the-populist-moment

16 Aslanidis, P. (2016), 'Is populism an ideology? A refutation and a new perspective', *Political Studies*, 64(1S), 88–104.

17 Mudde, C. (2004) 'The populist zeitgeist'. *Government and Opposition*, 39(4), 541–63.

18 Ibid.
19 Müller, J-W. (2016) *What Is Populism?* Philadelphia, PA: University of Pennsylvania Press, p. 20.
20 Mudde, C. (2017) 'Why nativism, not populism, should be declared word of the year'. *The Guardian*, 7 December, https://www.theguardian.com/commentisfree/2017/dec/07/cambridge-dictionary-nativism-populism-word-year
21 Müller, *What Is Populism?*, p. 1.
22 Erhardt, J. and Filsinger, M. (2025) 'A spectre of democracy: are populist citizens less supportive of democracy?'. *West European Politics*, 48(7), 1599–628, p. 1599.
23 Habermas, J. (2011) 'Europe's post-democracy era', *The Guardian*, 10 November.
24 https://www.freiheit.org/european-union/explaining-rise-authoritarian-populism-europe-five-take-aways-policymakers
25 See, for example, Guiso, L., Herrera, H., Morelli, M. and Sonno, T. (2024) 'Economic insecurity and the demand for populism in Europe'. *Economica*, 91(362), 588–620. The argument regarding the non-economic factors is put forward by Guido Tabellini in https://cepr.org/voxeu/columns/rise-populism.
26 See, for example, Piketty, T. and Saez, E. (2014) 'Inequality in the long run'. *Science*, 344(6186), 838–43.
27 *Timbro Authoritarian Index 2024*, https://www.epicenternetwork.eu/publications/timbro-authoritarian-populism-index-2024/
28 Borriello, A., Pranchère, J.-Y. and Vandamme, P.-É. (2024) 'Populism and democracy: a reassessment'. *Contemporary Politics*, 30(4), 416–36, p. 416.
29 Brubaker, R. (2018) 'Why populism?'. In Fitzi, G., Mackert, J. and Turner, B. (eds) *Populism and the Crisis of Democracy*. London: Routledge, pp. 27–46.
30 Revelli, M. (2019) *The New Populism*. London: Verso, p. 72.
31 See Furedi, F. (1989) *The Mau Mau War in Perspective*. Athens, OH: Ohio University Press.
32 Scruton, R. (2014) *How To Be a Conservative*. London: Bloomsbury, p. 135.
33 Germani, G. (2021) *Authoritarianism, National Populism and Fascism*. London: Routledge.
34 Goodwin, M. (2023) *Values, Voice and Virtue: the New British Politics*. London: Random House.
35 Roxborough, I. (1984) 'Unity and diversity in Latin American history'. *Journal of Latin American Studies*, 16(1), 1–26.

36 Borriello et al., 'Populism and democracy'.
37 Ibid., p. 416.
38 Canovan, M. (1999) 'Trust the people! Populism and the two faces of democracy'. *Political Studies*, 47(1), 2–16.
39 https://icds.ee/en/mudde-populism-is-based-on-morals/
40 https://www.thepublicdiscourse.com/2023/05/88965/
41 See Hochschild, A.R. (2019) 'Emotions and society'. *Emotions and Society*, 1(1), 9–13.
42 Hochschild, A.R. (2018) *Strangers in their Own Land: Anger and Mourning on the American Right*. New York: The New Press, p. 5.

Chapter 2: A Teleology of Evil

 1 Tourish, D. (2024) 'It is time to use the F word about Trump: fascism, populism and the rebirth of history'. *Leadership*, 20(1), 9–32, p. 9.
 2 Sherwood, H. (2017) 'Archbishop of Canterbury suggests Brexit "in fascist tradition"'. *The Guardian*, 13 February, https://www.theguardi an.com/uk-news/2017/feb/13/archbishop-suggests-brexit-fascist-tra dition
 3 Thornborrow, J., Ekstrom, M. and Patrona, M. (2021) 'Discursive constructions of populism in opinion-based journalism: a comparative European study'. *Discourse, Context & Media*, 44, 100542.
 4 Baker, P.C. (2019) '"We the people": the battle to define populism'. *The Guardian*, 10 January, https://www.theguardian.com/news/2019/jan /10/we-the-people-the-battle-to-define-populism
 5 Bachrach, P. (1967) *The Theory of Democratic Elitism: A Critique*. New York: Little Brown, p. 105.
 6 Ibid., p. 8.
 7 Singh, N.P. (1998) 'Culture/wars: recoding empire in an age of democracy'. *American Quarterly*, 50(3), 471–522, p. 483.
 8 Kazin, M. (1995) *The Populist Persuasion: An American History*. Ithaca, NY: Cornell University Press.
 9 Vann Woodward, C. (1976) 'The promise of populism'. *New York Review*, 28 October, https://www.nybooks.com/articles/1976/10/28/the -promise-of-populism/
10 Vann Woodward, C. (1981) 'Who are "The People"?'. *The New Republic*, 16 May.
11 Kaltwasser, C.R. (2018) 'How to define populism? Reflections on a contested concept and its (mis)use in the social sciences'. In Fitzi, G., Mackert, J. and Turner, B. (eds) *Populism and the Crisis of Democracy*. London: Routledge, pp. 62–78.

12 Mudde, C. and Kaltwasser, C.R. (2012) *Populism in Europe and the Americas*. Cambridge: Cambridge University Press.

13 Stavrakakis, Y. (2017) 'How did "populism" become a pejorative concept? And why is this important today? A genealogy of double hermeneutics'. POPULISMUS Working Papers No. 6.

14 Brubaker, R. (2018) 'Why populism?'. In Fitzi, G., Mackert, J. and Turner, B. (eds) *Populism and the Crisis of Democracy*. London: Routledge, pp. 27–46.

15 Taguieff, P.A. (1997) 'Populism and political science: from conceptual illusions to real problems'. *Vingtieme Siecle. Revue dhistoire*, 56(4), 4–33.

16 Ibid.

17 D'Eramo, M. (2013) 'Populism and the new oligarchy'. *New Left Review*, 82, 5–28, p. 6.

18 X account of the president of the European Council, 10 October 2016, https://x.com/eucopresident/status/785525603290275840?lang=ar

19 Lichfield, J. (2020) 'The next epidemic: resurgent populism'. *Politico*, 6 April, https://www.politico.eu/article/the-next-epidemic-resurgent -populism/

20 Cellini, M. and Archibugi, D. (2017) 'What causes the populist infection? How can it be cured?'. *OpenDemocracy*, 24 March, https://www .opendemocracy.net/en/can-europe-make-it/what-causes-populist-in fection-how-can-it-be-cure/

21 Pittella, G. (2016) 'Populism, racism and xenophobia have infected Europe'. *Euractiv*, 28 July, https://www.euractiv.com/section/global -europe/opinion/populism-racism-and-xenophobia-have-infected-eu rope/

22 Remeikis, A. (2019) 'Alastair Campbell on the "populist virus" and why Bill Shorten lost'. *Guardian*, 13 July, https://www.theguardian.com/ politics/2019/jul/14/alastair-campbell-on-the-populist-virus-and-why- bill-shorten-lost

23 Keane, J. (2017) 'The pathologies of populism'. *The Conversation*, 29 September, https://theconversation.com/the-pathologies-of-populi sm-82593

24 Leigh, A. (2024) *What's the Worst That Could Happen? Existential Risk and Extreme Politics*. Cambridge, MA: MIT Press.

25 See Furedi, F. (2018) *How Fear Works: Culture of Fear in the Twenty-first Century*. London: Bloomsbury, p. 98.

26 Bruno, V.A. (2018) 'The production of fear: European democracies in the age of populisms and technocracies'. *Social Europe*, 13 June, https://www .socialeurope.eu/the-production-of-fear-european-democracies-in-the -age-of-populisms-and-technocracies

27 Rothstein, B. (2018) 'Politics of fear versus politics of hope'. *Social Europe*, 12 June, https://www.socialeurope.eu/politics-of-fear-versus -politics-of-hope

28 Baker, '"We the people"'.

29 Frank, T. (2020) *The People, No: A Brief History of Anti-Populism*. New York: Metropolitan Books, p. 8.

30 Campbell, M. (2018) 'Italian election: Roman elite tremble over "ignorant beasts" at the gate'. *The Sunday Times*, 27 May, https://www.the times.com/uk/politics/article/roman-elite-tremble-over-ignorant-beas ts-at-the-gate-f2j3j6j07

31 FitzGerald, J. (2024) 'Biden tries to clarify "garbage" comment after uproar'. BBC News, 30 October, https://www.bbc.co.uk/news/articles /cdd09e4nl30o

32 Colliot-Thélène, C. (2018) 'Populism as a conceptual problem'. In Fitzi, G., Mackert, J. and Turner, B. (eds) *Populism and the Crisis of Democracy*. London: Routledge, p. 17.

33 This approach is exemplified by Howse, R. (2019) 'Epilogue: In defense of disruptive democracy – a critique of anti-populism'. *International Journal of Constitutional Law*, 17(2), 641–60.

34 Krastev, I. (2007) 'Is East-Central Europe backsliding? The strange death of the liberal consensus'. *Journal of Democracy*, 18(4), 56–64.

35 James, P. (2021) 'Defining populism and fascism relationally: exploring global convergences in unsettled times'. *ProtoSociology*, 37, 21–44.

36 D'Eramo, 'Populism and the new oligarchy'.

37 Paveau, M. (2012) 'Populisme: itinéraires discursifs d'un mot voyageur' [Populism: discursive itineraries of a traveling word]'. *Critique*, 16 March, 75–84.

38 Dorna, A. (2003) 'Faut-il avoir peur du populisme?', *Le Monde diplomatique*, November.

39 Biglieri, P. (2020) 'Hating the people! An anti-populist passion: the case of the Argentinean political alliance "Let's Change"'. *INTERFERE*, 1(1), 5–20.

40 Ibid.

41 Brown, W. (2021) 'Foreword'. In Biglieri, P., Cadahia, L. and Ciccariello-Maher, G., *Seven Essays on Populism*. Cambridge: Polity, p. vii. Unfortunately, Biglieri and Brown only perceive *demophobia* when it is directed at leftist movements. They assert that right-wing populists should be classified as fascists and authoritarian.

42 Arditi, B. (2024) *Is There Such a Thing as Populism?: 3 Provocations and 5 1/2 Proposals*. London: Taylor & Francis.

43 Ober, J. (2017) *Demopolis: Democracy Before Liberalism in Theory and Practice*. Cambridge: Cambridge University Press, p. 22.
44 See Cartledge, P. (2011) 'The democratic experiment'. BBC, 17 February, https://www.bbc.co.uk/history/ancient/greeks/greekdemocracy_01.shtml
45 McClelland, J.S. (1988) *The Crowd and the Mob: From Plato to Canetti*. London: Unwin Hyman, pp. 1–2.
46 Lippmann, W. (1922) *Public Opinion*. New York: Macmillan.
47 Cited in https://www.newstatesman.com/culture/books/2018/11/popul ism-book-review-ü-eatwell-goodwin-mudde-kaltwasser-mouffe
48 Cited in Fromm, E. (1965) *Escape from Freedom*. New York: Henry Holt and Company, p. 3.
49 Adorno, T.W. (1950) 'Democratic leadership and mass manipulation'. In Gouldner, A. (ed.) *Studies in Leadership: Leadership and Democratic Action*. New York: Harper & Brothers, p. 418.
50 https://bylinetimes.com/2022/11/15/its-the-stupidity-stupid-brexit -and-populism/
51 Sullivan, A. (2016) 'Democracies end when they are too democratic'. *New York* magazine, 1 May, https://nymag.com/intelligencer/2016/04 /america-tyranny-donald-trump.html
52 Goldhill, O. (2022) '2,400 years ago, Plato saw democracy would give rise to a tyrannical leader filled with "false and braggart words"'. *Quartz*, 20 July, https://qz.com/1293998/2400-years-ago-plato-saw-democracy -would-give-rise-to-a-tyrannical-leader-filled-with-false-and-braggart -words/
53 Hamdaoui, S. (2024) 'Anti-conspiracism as anti-populism under La République En Marche! (2020–2022)'. *Journal of Contemporary European Studies*, 33(2), 1–14.
54 Voutyras, S. (2024) 'Anti-populism, meritocracy and (technocratic) elit- ism'. In Stavrakakis, Y. and Katsambekis, G. (eds) *Research Handbook on Populism*. Cheltenham: Edward Elgar Publishing, pp. 35–47.

Chapter 3: Populism versus Anti-populism

1 Marchart, O. (2023) 'Liberal anti-populism as a case of demophobia'. In Payne, D., Stagnell, A. and Strandberg, G. (eds) *Populism and The People in Contemporary Critical Thought*. London: Bloomsbury Academic.
2 Stavrakakis, Y. (2015) 'Die Rückkehr des "Volkes": Populismus und Anti- Populismus im Schatten der europäischen Krise'. In Agridopoulos, A. and Papagiannopoulos, I. (eds) *Griechenland im europäischen Kontext: Krise und Krisendiskurse*. Heidelberg: Springer-Verlag, p. 110.
3 Streeck, W. (2017) 'The return of the repressed'. *New Left Review*, 104,

https://newleftreview.org/issues/ii104/articles/wolfgang-streeck-the-re turn-of-the-repressed

4 Demos (2022) 'How to respond to the populist challenge?'. 18 July, https://demos-h2020.eu/en/how-to-respond-to-the-populist-challenge

5 European Commission (2024) 'Resisting authoritarian populism: Commission's Ethics Group issues new Statement on defending democracy and its values'. 5 June, https://research-and-innovation.ec.europa .eu/news/all-research-and-innovation-news/resisting-authoritarian-po pulism-commissions-ethics-group-issues-new-statement-defending-de mocracy-2024-06-05_en

6 Agha, P. (2021) 'The politics of antipopulism'. CEU Democracy Institute, 19 March, https://democracyinstitute.ceu.edu/articles/politics-antipop ulism

7 De Cleen, B. and Voutyras, S. 'Anti-populist discourse in European politics and media'. Vrije Universiteit Brussel, https://researchportal.vub.be /en/projects/anti-populist-discourse-in-european-politics-and-media

8 Streeck, 'The return of the repressed'.

9 Schedler, A. (1997) 'Introduction: antipolitics – closing and colonizing the public sphere'. In Schedler, A. (ed.) *The End of Politics? Explorations into Modern Antipolitics.* Houndmills: Macmillan Press, pp. 1–20, p. 7.

10 Geuss, R. (2009) *Politics and the Imagination.* Princeton, NJ: Princeton University Press, p. 10.

11 Frank, T. (2020) 'The pessimistic style in American politics and its eternal war on reform'. *Harper's Magazine,* May, https://harpers.org/arch ive/2020/05/how-the-anti-populists-stopped-bernie-sanders/

12 Halliday, J. and Quinn, B. (2025) '"They really are all horrible": political anger marks Reform UK's Runcorn win'. *Guardian,* 2 May, https://www .theguardian.com/politics/2025/may/02/runcorn-byelection-voter-dis pleasure-disengagement-reform-uk

13 Chrisafis, A. (2018) 'Who are the gilets jaunes and what do they want?'. *Guardian,* 7 December, https://www.theguardian.com/world/2018/dec /03/who-are-the-gilets-jaunes-and-what-do-they-want

14 Lasch, C. (1996) *The Revolt of the Elites and the Betrayal of Democracy.* New York: W.W. Norton & Company.

15 See Kriesi, H. (2014) 'The populist challenge'. *West European Politics,* 37(2), 361–78.

16 Mair, P. (2000) 'Partyless democracy'. *New Left Review,* March/April, https://newleftreview.org/issues/ii2/articles/peter-mair-partyless-demo cracy.pdf

17 Mair, P. (2013) *Ruling the Void.* London: Verso.

18 Dalton, R.J. and Wattenberg, M.P. (eds) (2002) *Parties Without Partisans: Political Change in Advanced Industrial Democracies*. Oxford: Oxford University Press.

19 See Katz, R.S. and Mair, P. (2009) 'The cartel party thesis: a restatement'. *Perspectives on Politics*, 7(4), 753–66.

20 Dassonneville, R. and Hooghe, M. (2018) 'Indifference and alienation: diverging dimensions of electoral dealignment in Europe'. *Acta Politica*, 53(1), 1–23.

21 For a German case study, see Arzheimer, K. (2006) 'Dead men walking? Party identification in Germany, 1977–2002'. *Electoral Studies*, 25(4), 791–807.

22 Prime Minister's Office, 10 Downing Street (2025) 'PM remarks at Immigration White Paper press conference'. 12 May, https://www.gov.uk/government/speeches/pm-remarks-at-immigration-white-paper-press-conference-12-may-2025

23 https://www.bbc.com/news/articles/cj3rxrg2pnjo

24 Pfeifer, H. (2024) 'What can stop the rise of populism in Germany and elsewhere?'. DW.com, 26 October, https://www.dw.com/en/what-can-stop-the-rise-of-populism-in-germany-and-elsewhere/a-70585362

25 Heinö, A.J. (2024) *Timbro Authoritarian Populism Index 2024*. April, https://www.epicenternetwork.eu/wp-content/uploads/2024/04/Populism-Index-2024-Compressed.pdf

26 Canovan, M. (1999a) 'Trust the people! Populism and the two faces of democracy'. *Political Studies*, 47(1), 2–16.

27 Anderson, P. (2025) 'Regime change in the West?'. *London Review of Books*, 47(6).

28 Revelli, M. (2019) *The New Populism*. London: Verso, p. 48.

29 The Economist (2018) 'Brexit v Bernard-Henri Lévy'. *The Economist*, 7 June, https://www.economist.com/britain/2018/06/07/brexit-v-bernard-henri-levy

30 Cited in https://frankfuredi.substack.com/p/2016-2024-elite-resistance-replaced#_edn1

31 Rapoza, K. (2016) 'The populist revolt against "Davos Man"'. *Forbes*, 20 July, https://www.forbes.com/sites/kenrapoza/2016/07/20/the-populist-revolt-against-davos-man/?sh=73724aba1ca1

32 Kaletsky, A. (2016) 'Reversing Brexit'. *Project Syndicate*, 27 July, https://www.project-syndicate.org/commentary/reversing-brexit-referendum-by-anatole-kaletsky-2016-07

33 Zakaria, F. (2023) '2023 could be the year that exposes populism for the sham that it is'. *Washington Post*, 5 January, https://www.washingtonpost.com/opinions/2023/01/05/populists-2023-policies-poor-governance/

34 Adonis, A. (2023) 'We seem to have passed peak populism'. *Prospect*, 11 January, https://www.prospectmagazine.co.uk/politics/peak-populi sm-donald-trump-boris-johnson-jair-bolsonaro

35 Solace Global (2024) 'The populist wave and polarisation in Europe'. https://www.solaceglobal.com/report/populism-europe-2024/

36 Ivaldi, G. and Zankina, E. (2024) 'Euroviews. This year's European elections remain under the shadow of rising populism'. Euronews, 13 November, https://www.euronews.com/2024/11/13/this-years-euro pean-elections-remain-under-the-shadow-of-rising-populism

37 Taylor, P. (2019) 'Has Europe reached peak populism?'. *Politico*, 5 September, https://www.politico.eu/article/europe-reached-peak-po pulism-far-right-anti-european-government-election/

38 Strain, M.R. (2024) 'Populism never lasts'. *Project Syndicate*, 13 December, https://www.project-syndicate.org/commentary/trump -populism-politically-predictable-but-economically-unviable-by-mich ael-r-strain-2024-12

39 https://www.nytimes.com/2024/11/20/us/trump-womens-march-pro tests-activism.html

40 Howse, R. (2019) 'Epilogue: In defense of disruptive democracy – a critique of anti-populism'. *International Journal of Constitutional Law*, 17(2), 641–60.

41 For an interesting critique of ochlophobia, see McCormick, J P. (2019) 'The new ochlophobia? Populism, majority rule and prospects for democratic republicanism'. In Elazar, Y. and Rousselière, G. (eds) *Republican Democracy*. Cambridge: Cambridge University Press, pp. 122–42.

42 Voutyras, S. (2024) 'Anti-populism, meritocracy and (technocratic) elitism'. In Stavrakakis, Y. and Katsambekis, G. (eds) *Research Handbook on Populism*. Cheltenham: Edward Elgar Publishing, pp. 35–47.

43 Abrams, B. (2022) 'The rise of despotic majoritarianism'. *Democratic Theory*, 9(1), 73–86.

44 Stanley, J. (2018) *How Fascism Works: the Politics of Us and Them*. New York: Random House, chapter 10.

45 Finchelstein, F. (2020) *A Brief History of Fascist Lies*. Berkeley: University of California Press.

46 See Enright, J. (2025) 'The populism to fascism pipeline'. Medium, 7 January, https://medium.com/pigeons-peculiarities/the-populism-to -fascism-pipeline-ec50974f8f49

47 Stanley, J. (2021) 'America is now in fascism's legal phase'. *Guardian*, 22 December, https://www.theguardian.com/world/2021/dec/22/amer ica-fascism-legal-phase

48 Ibid.

49 Holl-Allen, G. (2025) 'McDonnell compares Farage to Hitler'. *The*

Telegraph, 9 September, https://www.telegraph.co.uk/news/2025/09/09/john-mcdonnell-compares-nigel-farage-to-hitler/
50 https://www.independent.co.uk/news/uk/politics/reform-conservatives-policy-echr-law-b2760532.html
51 https://www.theguardian.com/law/2025/may/30/attorney-general-richard-hermer-apologises-for-comparing-tories-and-reform-to-nazis

Chapter 4: The Quest for Home

1 Bellah, R.N., Madsen, R., Sullivan, W.M., Swidler, A. and Tipton, S.M. (1996) *Habits of the Heart: Individualism and Commitment in American Life*. Berkeley, CA: University of California, p. xxx.
2 https://partidochega.pt/index.php/manifesto/
3 Jay, M. (2018) 'A history of alienation'. Aeon, 14 March, https://aeon.co/essays/in-the-1950s-everybody-cool-was-a-little-alienated-what-changed
4 Ibid.
5 Nussbaum, M. (2002) *For Love of Country?* Boston, MA: Beacon Press, p. 7.
6 For a discussion of elite acquiescence to alienation, see Furedi, F. (2025) 'The normalisation of alienation and the embrace of cultural loss', https://frankfuredi.substack.com/p/the-normalisation-of-alienation-and
7 Cited in Bourne, R. (2019) 'Tony Blair is right – globalisation is a fact not a choice'. Cato Institute, 1 March, https://www.cato.org/commentary/tony-blair-right-globalisation-fact-not-choice
8 Wintour, P. (2017) 'Tony Blair launches pushback against "frightening populism"'. *Guardian*, 17 March, https://www.theguardian.com/politics/2017/mar/17/tony-blair-launches-pushback-against-frightening-populism
9 See Inglehart, R. (1977) *The Silent Revolution: Changing Values and Political Styles in Advanced Industrial Society*. Princeton, NJ: Princeton University Press.
10 Inglehart, R. and Norris, P. (2017) 'Trump and the populist authoritarian parties: the silent revolution in reverse'. *Perspectives on Politics*, 15(2), 443–54, p. 443.
11 Ignazi, P. (1995) 'The re-emergence of extreme right-wing parties in Europe' (Reihe Politikwissenschaft/Institut für Höhere Studien, Abt. Politikwissenschaft, 21). Vienna: Institut für Höhere Studien (IHS), p. 2. https://core.ac.uk/download/pdf/212119094.pdf
12 Ignazi,P. (1992) 'The silent counter-revolution'. *European Journal of Political Research*, 22(1), 3–34.
13 Cited, for example, in Gottfried, P.E. (2002) *Multiculturalism and the*

Politics of Guilt Toward a Secular Theocracy. Minneapolis: University of Minnesota Press.

14 Touraine, A. (2003) 'Meaningless politics'. *Constellations*, 10(3), 298–311, p. 310.

15 Ignazi, 'The re-emergence of extreme right-wing parties', p. 3.

16 Ibid., p. 5.

17 Furedi, F. (2013) *On Tolerance*. London: Bloomsbury Academic, p. 165.

18 Krastev, I. (2008) 'Two cheers for populism'. *Prospect*, January, https://www.prospectmagazine.co.uk/essays/52156/two-cheers-for-populism

19 Lasch, C. (2013) *The True and Only Heaven: Progress and Its Critics*. New York: Norton, p. 153.

20 Kazin, M. (1995) *The Populist Persuasion: An American History*. Ithaca, NY: Cornell University Press.

21 See Dasgupta, R. (2018) 'The demise of the nation state'. *Guardian*, 5 April, https://www.theguardian.com/news/2018/apr/05/demise-of-the-nation-state-rana-dasgupta

22 Pozen, A.S. (2022) 'The end of globalization? What Russia's war in Ukraine means for the world economy'. *Foreign Affairs*, 17 March, https://www.foreignaffairs.com/articles/world/2022-03-17/end-globalization

23 K.N.C. (2019) 'Globalisation is dead and we need to invent a new world order'. *The Economist*, 28 June, https://www.economist.com/open-future/2019/06/28/globalisation-is-dead-and-we-need-to-invent-a-new-world-order

24 Masters, B. (2022) 'BlackRock chief Larry Fink says Ukraine war marks end of globalisation'. *Financial Times*, 24 March, https://www.ft.com/content/0c9e3b72-8d8d-4129-afb5-655571a01025

25 Nussbaum, M. (2002) 'Patriotism and cosmopolitanism'. In Nussbaum, M., *For Love of Country?* Boston, MA: Beacon Press.

26 Fukuyama, F. (1992) *The End of History and the Last Man*. New York: The Free Press, p. 45.

27 Möhring, J. and Prins, G. (2013) *Sail On, O Ship of State*. London: Notting Hill Editions, p. 1.

28 Scruton, R. (2004) 'The Need for Nations'. The Roger Scruton Oikos, https://www.roger-scruton.com/articles/276-the-need-for-nations

29 Euractiv (2013) 'Juncker: Europe's nationalist demons are "only sleeping"'. *Euractiv*, 12 March, https://www.euractiv.com/section/politics/news/juncker-europe-s-nationalist-demons-are-only-sleeping/

30 Ellyatt, H. (2016) 'Europe faces "galloping populism", Juncker warns in State of the Union address'. CNBC, 14 September, https://www.cnbc

.com/2016/09/14/europe-faces-galloping-populism-juncker-warns-in
-state-of-the-union-address.html

31 Ferkiss, V.C. (1995) 'Ezra Pound and American fascism'. *The Journal of Politics*, 17(2), 173–97, p. 174.

32 Lipset, S.M. (1959) *Political Man*. London: Mercury Books, pp. 170–1.

33 BBC (2017) 'Pope Francis warns against rise in populism', BBC News, 22 January, https://www.bbc.co.uk/news/world-europe-38708485

34 See my discussion of this issue: Furedi, F. (2022) 'Stop calling Putin 'fascist''', *Compact*, 14 July, https://www.compactmag.com/article/stop -calling-putin-fascist/

35 Ibid.

36 Nussbaum, *For Love of Country?*, p. 7.

37 Ober, J. (2017) *Demopolis: Democracy Before Liberalism in Theory and Practice*. Cambridge: Cambridge University Press, pp. 168–9.

38 Canovan, M. (1996) *Nationhood and Political Theory*. Cheltenham: Edward Elgar, p. 1.

39 Scruton, R. (2014) *How To Be a Conservative*. London: Bloomsbury.

40 Maier, C.S. (2016) *Once within Borders: Territories of Power, Wealth, and Belonging since 1500*. Cambridge, MA: Harvard University Press, p. 290.

41 Ibid.

42 Cited in Cresswell, T. (2011) 'Elites are cosmopolitan, people are local?'. *Varve*, 9 July, https://tjcresswell.wordpress.com/2011/07/09/elites-are -cosmopolitan-people-are-local/

43 See Goodhart, D. (2017) *The Road to Somewhere; the New Tribes Shaping British Politics*. London: Penguin Books.

44 Sennett, R. (1994) 'The identity myth'. *The New York Times*, 30 January, https://www.nytimes.com/1994/01/30/opinion/the-identity-myth.html

45 Lasch, C. (1996) *The Revolt of the Elites and the Betrayal of Democracy*. New York: W.W. Norton & Company.

46 Beck, U. (2002) 'The cosmopolitan society and its enemies'. *Theory, Culture & Society*, 19(1–2), 17–44, p. 20.

47 https://www.oed.com/dictionary/nativism_n?tab=meaning_and_use#35 397108

48 This and the next three paragraph are based on my discussion of this theme in Furedi, F. (2020) *Why Borders Matter*. London: Routledge.

49 Scruton, *How To Be a Conservative*, p. 80.

50 Miller D. (2017) *Strangers in Our Midst: The Political Philosophy of Immigration*. Cambridge, MA: Harvard University Press, p. 27.

51 Yack, B. (2014) *Nationalism and the Moral Psychology of Community in Modern Political Life*. Chicago: University of Chicago Press, p. 37.

52 Stjerno, S. (2004) *Solidarity in Europe: the History of an Idea*. Cambridge: Cambridge University Press, p. 42.

53 Seligman, A. (2001) *The Idea of Civil Society*. New York: Knopf, p. 126.

54 Canovan, M. (1999b) 'Is there an Arendtian case for the nation state?'. *Contemporary Politics*, 5(2), 103–19, p. 108.

55 Hunter, J.D. (2024) *Democracy and Solidarity: On the Cultural Roots of America's Political Crisis*. New Haven, CT: Yale University Press.

56 Bellah et al., *Habits of the Heart*, p. xxx.

Chapter 5: Populism's Defence of the Pre-political Sphere

1 Scruton, R. (2014) *How To Be a Conservative*. London: Bloomsbury, p. 22.

2 Mudde, C. and Kaltwasser, C.R. (2013) 'Exclusionary vs. inclusionary populism: comparing contemporary Europe and Latin America'. *Government and Opposition*, 48(2), 147–74, p. 147.

3 See Kim, D. (2024) *Arendt's Solidarity*. Stanford, CA: Stanford University Press.

4 Gaffney, J. (2018) 'Solidarity in dark times: Arendt and Gadamer on the politics of appearance'. *Philosophy Compass*, 13(12), e12554.

5 Ibid.

6 See 'Solidarity in social and political philosophy'. In Zalta, E.N. and Nodelman, U. (2023) *Stanford Encyclopedia of Philosophy*, https://plato.stanford.edu/entries/solidarity/

7 Laitinen, A. (2022) 'Solidarity'. In *Oxford Research Encyclopedia of Politics*. Oxford: Oxford University Press, p. 1.

8 Yack, B. (2014) *Nationalism and the Moral Psychology of Community in Modern Political Life*. Chicago: University of Chicago Press, p. 36.

9 See the discussion in Bartninkas, V. (2014) 'The pre-political and the political in Aristotle's Politics'. *Problemos*, 85, 18–29.

10 Brubaugh, C. (2021) 'Hannah Arendt on anti-racism as a totalitarian ideology'. *Tablet*, 18 November, https://www.tabletmag.com/sections/news/articles/hannah-arendt-antiracism-little-rock

11 Arendt, H. (1959) 'Reflections on Little Rock'. *Dissent*, 6(1), 45–56, p.51.

12 Ibid.

13 It should be noted that until recent times, discrimination possessed positive linguistic qualities. Indeed, to be discriminating still conveys positive connotations.

14 Novais, R.A. and Christofoletti, R. (2025) *The Palgrave Handbook on Right-Wing Populism and Otherness in Global Perspective*. Cham, Switzerland: Palgrave Macmillan.

15 'Othering', Cambridge Dictionary, https://dictionary.cambridge.org/dic
tionary/english/othering#google_vignette
16 Kolko, G. (1968) *The Politics of War: The World and United States*. New
York: Vintage Books, p. 118.
17 Eco is cited in Müller, J.-W. (2013) *Contesting Democracy: Political Ideas
in Twentieth Century Europe*. New Haven, CT: Yale University Press,
p. 200.
18 Cited in Silver, H. (1994) 'Social exclusion and social solidarity: three
paradigms'. *International Labour Review*, 133(5), 531–78, p. 531.
19 Ibid.
20 Ibid., p. 536.
21 Barbash, F. (2016) 'Does America's first flag symbolize "exclusion and
hate," as this Mich. school superintendent said?'. *Washington Post*,
15 September, https://www.washingtonpost.com/news/morning-mix
/wp/2016/09/15/does-americas-first-flag-symbolize-exclusion-and-
hate-like-this-mich-school-superintendent-said/
22 'Exclusionary bullying behaviour', Anti-Bullying from the Diana Award,
https://www.antibullyingpro.com/support-and-advice-articles/exclu
sionary-bullying-behaviour
23 HM Courts and Tribunal Service, *Ms R Leher v Aspers (Stratford City)
Ltd and Others: 3200390/2019*, https://www.gov.uk/employment-tri
bunal-decisions/ms-r-leher-v-aspers-stratford-city-ltd-and-others-320
0390-slash-2019
24 Telegraph Reporters (2025) 'Nurse wins £41k payout after
being left out of tea round'. *Telegraph*, 26 February, https://
www.telegraph.co.uk/news/2025/02/26/nurse-wins-41k-payout-after-
being-left-out-of-tea-round/
25 Danaher, J. (2019) 'The politics of sexual exclusion: notes on Srinivasan's
"Does anyone have a right to sex?"'. Philosophical Disquisitions,
7 January, https://philosophicaldisquisitions.blogspot.com/2019/01/the
-politics-of-sexual-exclusion-notes.html
26 Danaher, J. (2020) 'A defence of sexual inclusion'. *Social Theory and
Practice*, 46(3), 467–96, p. 467.
27 Bartosch, J. (2021) 'Trans lobby group Stonewall brands lesbians "sexual
racists" for raising concerns about being pressured into having sex with
transgender women who still have male genitals'. *Mail on Sunday*,
20 November, https://www.dailymail.co.uk/news/article-10225111/
Stonewall-brands-lesbians-sexual-racists-raising-concerns-sex-transgen
der-women.html
28 Shah, S. (2022) 'Is workplace "banter" the enemy of inclusion?'. *People
Management*, 30 November, https://www.peoplemanagement.co.uk/ar
ticle/1806746/workplace-banter-enemy-inclusion

29 Royal Academy of Engineering, *Creating Inclusive Cultures: Language and Banter*, https://raeng.org.uk/media/bskiae3x/rae-tws-workshop2-language-banter.pdf

30 Habermas, J. (2011) 'Europe's post-democratic era'. *Guardian*, 10 November, https://www.theguardian.com/commentisfree/2011/nov/10/jurgen-habermas-europe-post-democratic

31 Müller, J.-W. (2017) *What is Populism?* Harmondsworth: Penguin Books, p. 26.

32 Prentoulis, M. (2020) 'Left populism as a political project'. In Eklundh, E. and Knott, A. (eds) *The Populist Manifesto: Understanding the Spectre of Populism*. London: Rowman & Littlefield, p. 102.

33 De Witte, M. (2020) 'Populism is a political problem that is putting democracy at risk, Stanford scholars say'. *Stanford Report*, 11 March, https://news.stanford.edu/stories/2020/03/populism-jeopardizes-democracies-around-world

34 Muro, D. (2017) 'Let the people rule. Definitions and theories of populism'. Barcelona Centre for International Affairs, April, https://www.cidob.org/en/publications/let-people-rule-definitions-and-theories-populism

35 Marneros, C. (2021) 'Against the populist ressentiment'. *Interdisciplinary Journal of Populism*, 2, 100–12.

36 Ibid.

37 Palonen, E. (2020) 'Ten theses on populism – and democracy'. In Eklundh, E. and Knott, A. (eds) *The Populist Manifesto*. London: Rowman & Littlefield, pp. 55–70, p. 59.

38 Knott, A. (2020) 'Populism: the politics of definition'. In Eklundh, E. and Knott, A. (eds) *The Populist Manifesto: Understanding the Spectre of Populism*. London: Rowman & Littlefield, p. 10.

39 Casullo, M.E. (2020) 'Populism and myth'. In Eklundh, E. and Knott, A. (eds) *The Populist Manifesto: Understanding the Spectre of Populism*. London: Rowman & Littlefield, p. 27.

40 Mouffe, C. (2018) *For a Left Populism*. London: Verso, p. 6.

41 Espejo, P.O. (2015) *The Time of Popular Sovereignty: Process and the Democratic State*. University Park, PA: Penn State Press, p. 41.

42 Benhabib, S. (2016) 'The new sovereigntism and transnational law: legal utopianism, democratic scepticism and statist realism'. *Global Constitutionalism*, 5(1), 109–44.

43 Benhabib, S. (2019) 'Brief reflections on populism (left or right)'. *Critique & Praxis*, 10 February, https://blogs.law.columbia.edu/praxis1313/seyla-benhabib-brief-reflections-on-populism-left-or-right/.

44 Ibid.

45 Himmelfarb, G. (2002) 'The illusions of cosmopolitanism'. In Nussbaum,

M., *For Love of Country?*, Boston, MA: Beacon Press, pp. 72–7, p. 77.

46 Mill is cited in Canovan, M. (2005) *The People*. London: Polity, p. 43.

47 See Goodhart, D. (2017) *The Road to Somewhere; the New Tribes Shaping British Politics*. London: Penguin Books, p. 21.

48 NPR (2007) 'Political scientist: does diversity really work?'. NPR, 15 August, https://www.npr.org/2007/08/15/12802663/political-scien tist-does-diversity-really-work

49 Putnam, R.D. (2000) *Bowling Alone: The Collapse and Revival of American Community*. New York: Simon and Schuster.

50 Gerbaudo, P. (2020) 'Populism and the politics of control'. In Eklundh, E. and Knott, A. (eds) *The Populist Manifesto: Understanding the Spectre of Populism*. London: Rowman & Littlefield, pp. 43–4.

51 Marneros, 'Against the populist ressentiment', p. 103.

52 Mouffe, *For a Left Populism*, p. 6.

53 Kelly, D. (2017) 'Populism and the history of popular sovereignty'. In Kaltwasser, C.R., Taggart, P.A., Espejo, P.O. and Ostiguy, P. (eds) *The Oxford Handbook of Populism*. Oxford: Oxford University Press, 511–34, p. 530.

54 Mudde, C. (2004) 'The populist zeitgeist'. *Government and Opposition*, 39(4), 541–63.

55 Baumeister, A. (2007) 'Diversity and unity: the problem with "constitutional patriotism"'. *European Journal of Political Theory*, 6(4), 483–503, p. 487.

56 See Abts, K. and Rummens, S. (2007) 'Populism versus democracy'. *Political Studies*, 55(2), 405–24.

57 Ibid.

58 Linsenmeier, K. (2016) 'The populist temptation – why populism is no option for green politics in Europe'. Heinrich-Böll-Stiftung, 27 September, https://eu.boell.org/en/2016/09/27/populist-temptation -why-populism-no-option-green-politics-europe

59 BBC (2000) 'Green card "may solve skills shortage"'. BBC News, 11 September, http://news.bbc.co.uk/1/hi/uk_politics/919891.stm

60 Simpson, C. (2024) 'The first Britons were Black, exhibition on diverse history claims', *Telegraph*, 27 January, https://www.telegraph.co.uk/ne ws/2024/01/27/the-first-britons-were-black-exhibition-on-diverse-his tory/

Chapter 6: A Response to the Condition of Cultural Insecurity

1 See Ahearne, J. (2017) 'Cultural insecurity and its discursive crystallisation in contemporary France'. *Modern & Contemporary France*, 25(3), 265–80.

2 Giddens, A. (1991) *Modernity and Self-Identity*. Cambridge: Polity.

3 Watson, H. and Furedi, F. (2009) 'Citizen journalism & public opinion'. Changing Perceptions of Security and Interventions (CPSI), https://www.cl.cam.ac.uk/events/shb/2010/watson.pdf

4 Inglehart, R. and Norris, P. (2017) 'Trump and the populist authoritarian parties: the silent revolution in reverse'. *Perspectives on Politics*, 15(2), 443–54.

5 Babst, A., Groß, M. and Lang, V. (2024) 'Rise of populism: identity threats as an explanation in relation with deprivation and cultural fear'. *Political Research Quarterly*, 77(3), 805–20.

6 Baumeister, R.F. (1986) *Identity: Cultural Change and the Struggle for Self*. Oxford: Oxford University Press, p. 142.

7 Kiefer, B. (2018) 'Honda Civic's typographic film champions breaking from the norm'. *Campaign*, 5 October, https://www.campaignlive.co.uk/article/honda-civics-typographic-film-champions-breaking-norm/1494998

8 Kemp, N. (2017) 'Consumers urge brands to push the boundaries of gender stereotyping'. *Campaign*, 25 July, https://www.campaignlive.co.uk/article/consumers-urge-brands-push-boundaries-gender-stereotyping/1440353

9 See the discussion in Lemert, C. (2011) 'A history of identity: the riddle at the heart of the mystery of life'. In Elliott, A. (ed.) *Routledge Handbook of Identity Studies*. London: Routledge, p. 18.

10 Marx, J.H. (1980) 'The ideological construction of post-modern identity models in contemporary cultural movements'. In Robertson, R. and Holzner, B. (eds) *Identity and Authority: Explorations in the Theory of Society*. Oxford: Basil Blackwell, p. 146.

11 Hobsbawm, E. (2020) *The Age of Extremes: 1914–1991*. London: Hachette UK, p. 327.

12 Cited in *The Nation*, 22 May 1989.

13 Inglehart, R. (1990) *Cultural Shift in Advanced Industrial Society*. Princeton, NJ: Princeton University Press.

14 Tyldesley, S. (2023) 'Dead, disgraced or deluded. Is this the end of populism?'. 13 June, https://www.secnewgate.co.uk/our-insights/dead-disgraced-or-deluded-end-populism

15 Strain, M.R. (2024) 'Populism never lasts'. *Project Syndicate*, 13 December, https://www.project-syndicate.org/commentary/trump-populism-politically-predictable-but-economically-unviable-by-michael-r-strain-2024-12

16 Cited in Spruyt, B., Keppens, G. and Van Droogenbroeck, F. (2016) 'Who supports populism and what attracts people to it?'. *Political Research Quarterly*, 69(2), 335–46.

17 Ibid., p. 336.
18 Babst et al., 'Rise of populism'.
19 Metten, A. and Bayerlein, M. (2023) 'The anxious voter: linking fears to right-wing populist voting'. *The Loop*, December, https://theloop.ecpr.eu/the-anxious-voter-linking-fears-to-right-wing-populist-voting/
20 Gerbaudo, P., De Falco, C.C., Giorgi, G., Keeling, S., Murolo, A. and Nunziata, F. (2023) 'Angry posts mobilize: emotional communication and online mobilization in the Facebook pages of Western European right-wing populist leaders'. *Social Media+ Society*, 9(1), https://doi.org/10.1177/20563051231163327.
21 Krastev, I. (2020) 'The end of European populists' fascination with America', Noema, 20 October, https://www.noemamag.com/the-end-of-european-populists-fascination-with-america/
22 For example, 'As Pippa Norris and Ronald Inglehart indicate, these policy trends can be related to a "cultural backlash" exploited by authoritarian-populist parties and leaders that explicitly reject global solidarity and other values that used to form part of the political consensus in European liberal democracies.' Pérez, A. (2020) 'Fortress Europe: an authoritarian-populist construct?'. Real Instituto Elcano, 30 October, https://www.realinstitutoelcano.org/en/analyses/fortress-europe-an-authoritarian-populist-construct/
23 Moffitt, B. (2015) 'How to perform crisis: a model for understanding the key role of crisis in contemporary populism'. *Government and Opposition*, 50(2), 189–217, p. 189.
24 Hinterleitner, M., Kammermeier, V. and Moffitt, B. (2023) 'How the populist radical right exploits crisis: comparing the role of proximity in the COVID-19 and refugee crises in Germany'. *West European Politics*, 47(7), 1503–28, p. 1503.
25 Fieschi, C. (2019) 'Why Europe's new populists tell so many lies – and do it so shamelessly'. *Guardian*, 30 September, https://www.theguardian.com/commentisfree/2019/sep/30/europe-populist-lie-shamelessly-salvini-johnson
26 Ibid.
27 Wodak, R. (2020) *The Politics of Fear: The Shameless Normalization of Far-right Discourse*. London: Sage Publications.
28 See an interesting account in Forkert, K. and Nahaboo, Z. (2025) 'The chronopolitics of the "left behind"': presentism, populism, and Global Britain', *Time & Society*, 34(1), 127–46.
29 Babst et al., 'Rise of populism'.
30 Meloni's statement is reproduced at https://www.youtube.com/shorts/FEovvFeyWis

31 https://anticapitalistmusings.com/2025/06/i-am-giorgia-and-you-are
   -not/
32 Hochschild, A.R. (2018) *Strangers in their Own Land: Anger and
   Mourning on the American Right*. New York: The New Press.
33 Pew Research Center (2015) 'The American family today'. 17 December,
   https://www.pewresearch.org/social-trends/2015/12/17/1-the-amer
   ican-family-today/
34 Norris, P. and Inglehart, R. (2019) *Cultural Backlash: Trump, Brexit,
   and Authoritarian Populism*. Cambridge: Cambridge University Press,
   chapter 4.
35 See Hochschild, A.R. (2019) 'Emotions and society'. *Emotions and
   Society*, 1(1), 9–13, p. 10.
36 Cox, M. (2018) 'Understanding the global rise of populism'. LSE Ideas,
   https://www.lse.ac.uk/ideas/Assets/Documents/updates/LSE-IDEAS
   -Understanding-Global-Rise-of-Populism.pdf
37 See Babst et al., 'Rise of populism'.
38 See Lüders, A., Mühlberger, C. and Jonas, E. (2020) 'Motivational and
   affective drivers of right-wing populism support: insights from an
   Austrian presidential election'. *Social Psychological Bulletin*, 15(3), 1–17,
   p. 1.
39 Stoneman, P. and Wright, J. (2022) 'The ties that bind: values and polarization'. The UK in the World Values Survey, 18 November, https://www
   .uk-values.org/news-comment?author=631b5fda4f5a9464849fc7ec
40 https://frankfuredi.substack.com/p/ukraine-and-the-moral-disarma
   ment
41 Cass, C. (2024) 'This is what elite failure looks like'. *The New York Times*,
   6 July, https://www.nytimes.com/2024/07/06/opinion/populism-power
   -elites-politics.html
42 See Axford, B. and Steger, M. (2020) 'Editorial: The globalization of populism'. *ProtoSociology*, 37, 5–17.
43 Reno, R. (2019) *Return of the Strong Gods*. Washington, DC: Regnery
   Gateway.
44 See Elçi, E. (2022) 'Politics of nostalgia and populism: evidence from
   Turkey'. *British Journal of Political Science*, 52(2), 697–714.
45 Lyons, N.S. (2025) 'Love of a nation'. *The Upheaval*, 13 March, https://
   theupheaval.substack.com/p/love-of-a-nation
46 Fitzgerald, J. (2018) *Close to Home*. Cambridge: Cambridge University
   Press, p. 31.
47 Bellè, E. (2024) 'Small homelands: populist radical right, territories and
   localism'. *The Loop*, 29 July, https://theloop.ecpr.eu/small-homelands
   -populist-radical-right-territories-and-localism/

48 Chou, M., Moffitt, B. and Busbridge, R. (2022) 'The localist turn in populism studies'. *Swiss Political Science Review*, 28(1), 129–41, p. 135.

49 Fitzgerald, *Close to Home*, p. 110.

50 Chou et al., 'The localist turn in populism studies'.

51 Ibid., p. 135.

52 Bellè, 'Small homelands'.

53 Chou et al., 'The localist turn in populism studies', p. 136.

54 Pilkington, E. (2008) 'Obama angers midwest voters with guns and religion remark'. *Guardian*, 14 April, https://www.theguardian.com/world/2008/apr/14/barackobama.uselections2008

55 See the discussion in Greisman, H.C. (1976) '"Disenchantment of the world": romanticism, aesthetics and sociological theory'. *The British Journal of Sociology*, 27(4), 495–507.

56 Canovan, M. (1999) 'Trust the people! Populism and the two faces of democracy'. *Political Studies*, 47(1), 2–16, p. 10.

57 Bauman, Z. (2013) *Community*. Cambridge: Polity, p. 9.

58 Ibid., p. 10.

Chapter 7: Championing Cultural Continuity

1 Kenny, M. (2017) 'Back to the populist future?: Understanding nostalgia in contemporary ideological discourse'. *Journal of Political Ideology*, 22(3), 256–73.

2 Tyson, C. (2024) 'You can't go home again: the uses of nostalgia'. *Hedgehog Review*, Spring, https://hedgehogreview.com/issues/missing-character/articles/you-cant-go-home-again

3 Arnold-Forster, A. (2024) 'That yearning feeling: why we need nostalgia'. *Guardian*, 28 April, https://www.theguardian.com/lifeandstyle/2024/apr/28/that-yearning-feeling-why-we-need-nostalgia

4 Ibid.

5 Lasch, C. (2021) 'Radical nostalgia'. *Harper's*, July, https://harpers.org/archive/2021/07/radical-nostalgia/

6 Kenny, 'Back to the populist future?'.

7 Hurst, A. (2024) 'I cast my first vote in France – just as the country fell for the far right's siren song of fake nostalgia'. *Guardian*, 10 June, https://www.theguardian.com/commentisfree/article/2024/jun/10/first-vote-france-far-right-nostalgia-european-elections

8 Gaston, S. (2018) 'The restoration of a "lost" Britain: how nostalgia becomes a dangerous political force'. LSE Blogs, 3 September, https://blogs.lse.ac.uk/brexit/2018/09/03/the-restoration-of-a-lost-britain-how-nostalgia-becomes-a-dangerous-political-force/

9 Westenburg, J.A. (2024) 'The nostalgia vote: why politicians are selling a return to an idealized past'. 9 October, https://medium.com/westen

berg/the-nostalgia-vote-why-politicians-are-selling-a-return-to-an-idea
lized-past-4e317fe822d8

10 Gaston, 'The restoration of a "lost" Britain'.

11 Davis, F. (1979) *Yearning for Yesterday: A Sociology of Nostalgia*. New York: The Free Press, p. 34.

12 Unger, I (1964). *Populism: Nostalgic or Progressive?* New York: Rand MacNally, p. 2.

13 For example, see Manucci, L. (2025) 'Authoritarian nostalgia and populist radical right parties'. ECPR, May, https://ecpr.eu/Events/Event/wor kshopdetails/15675

14 Müller, S. and Proksch, S.-O. (2024) 'Nostalgia in European party politics: a text-based measurement approach'. *British Journal of Political Science*, 54(3), 993–1005.

15 Ibid.

16 Nappey, G. (2025) 'Jean-Marie Le Pen, éternellement non'. *Le Temps*, 7 January, https://www.letemps.ch/opinions/editoriaux/jean-marie-le -pen-eternellement-non

17 Manucci, L. and Van Hauwaert, S.M. (2024) 'How authoritarian legacies and nostalgia underpin support for Chega in Portugal'. LSE Blogs, 8 March, https://blogs.lse.ac.uk/europpblog/2024/03/08/how-authorita rian-legacies-and-nostalgia-underpin-support-for-chega-in-portugal/

18 Smeekes, A. and Lubbers, M. (2024) 'Our gloomy future and glorious past: societal discontent, national nostalgia and support for populist radical-right parties in the Netherlands'. *Frontiers in Political Science*, 24 May, https://www.frontiersin.org/journals/political-science/articles /10.3389/fpos.2024.1390662/full

19 Schultheis, E. (2025) 'How Germany's far right is harnessing AI to win votes'. *Politico*, 20 February, https://www.politico.eu/article/germany -far-right-harness-artificial-intelligence-win-election/

20 McGreevy, N. (2022) 'Elizabeth II was an enduring emblem of the waning British Empire'. *Smithsonian Magazine*, 8 September, https:// www.smithsonianmag.com/history/elizabeth-ii-was-an-enduring-embl em-of-the-waning-british-empire-180979613/

21 Kunzru, H. (2022) 'My family fought the British Empire. I reject its myths'. *The New York Times*, 11 September, https://www.nytimes.com /2022/09/11/opinion/queen-hari-kunzru-imperial-delusions.html

22 Jasanoff, M. (2022) 'Mourn the Queen, not her Empire'. *The New York Times*, 8 September, https://www.nytimes.com/2022/09/08/opinion/ queen-empire-decolonization.html

23 Cited in Elçi, E. (2022) 'Politics of nostalgia and populism: evidence from Turkey'. *British Journal of Political Science*, 52(2), 697–714.

24 Betz, H.G. and Johnson, C. (2004) 'Against the current – stemming the

tide: the nostalgic ideology of the contemporary radical populist right'. *Journal of Political Ideologies*, 9(3), 311–27, p. 324.

25 Sullivan, A. (2017) 'The reactionary temptation'. *New York Magazine*, 1 May, http://nymag.com/daily/intelligencer/2017/04/andrew-sullivan-why-the-reactionary-right-must-be-taken-seriously.htm

26 Elçi, 'Politics of nostalgia and populism', p. 697.

27 Davis, *Yearning for Yesterday*, p. 100.

28 Casullo, M.E., cited in Jansma, J. (2025) 'Our culture is best! Populist engagement with culture in the construction of the populist myth'. *Journal of Intercultural Studies*, 46(1), 156–71.

29 Diehl, P. and Bargetz, B. (eds) (2023) *The Complexity of Populism: New Approaches and Methods*. London: Taylor & Francis.

30 Elçi, 'Politics of nostalgia and populism', p. 697.

31 Bauman, Z. (2017) *Retrotopia*. Cambridge: Polity, p. 5.

32 Maniaci, M. (2023) 'Conservatism is just weaponized nostalgia'. *Medium*, 18 October, https://medium.com/thing-a-day/conservatism-is-just-weaponized-nostalgia-430a78346ca9

33 Furedi, F. (2024) *The War Against the Past: Why The West Must Fight For Its History*. Cambridge: Polity.

34 See, for example, Ben-Ami, S.S. (2016) 'Populism, past and present', *Project Syndicate*, 10 August, https://www.project-syndicate.org/commentary/populism-economic-grievances-by-shlomo-ben-ami-2016-08

35 Mudde, C. (2016) 'Can we stop the politics of nostalgia that have dominated 2016?'. *Newsweek*, 15 December, https://www.newsweek.com/1950s-1930s-racism-us-europe-nostalgia-cas-mudde-531546

36 Solana, J. (2016) 'The EU has a dangerous case of nostalgia'. World Economic Forum, 27 April, https://www.weforum.org/stories/2016/04/javier-solana-the-eu-has-a-dangerous-case-of-nostalgia/

37 Trump, D.J. (2025) 'Restoring truth and sanity to American history'. White House, 27 March, https://www.whitehouse.gov/presidential-actions/2025/03/restoring-truth-and-sanity-to-american-history/

38 Davis, *Yearning for Yesterday*, p. 35.

39 Ibid., p. 31.

40 Baumeister, R.F. (1986) *Identity: Cultural Change and the Struggle for Self*. Oxford: Oxford University Press, p. 45.

41 Keniston, K. (1963) 'Social change and youth in America'. In Erikson, E.H. (ed.), *Youth: Change and Challenge*. New York: Basic Books, pp. 148–69.

42 Erikson, E.H. (1964) 'Identity and uprootedness in our time'. In *Insight and Responsibility: Lectures on the Ethical Implications of Psychoanalytic Insight*. London: Faber & Faber, p. 93.

43 Erikson, *Youth: Change and Challenge*, p. 138.

44 Davis, *Yearning for Yesterday*, p. vii.
45 Telegraph Reporters (2025) 'Why nostalgia can be good for your health'. *Telegraph*, 13 March, https://www.telegraph.co.uk/news/2025/03/13 /nostalgia-is-good-for-your-health-study-finds/
46 Routledge, C. (2025) 'Why Gen Z Is Resurrecting the 1990s'. *The New York Times*, 24 August, https://www.nytimes.com/2025/08/24/opinion /gen-z-technology-nostalgia.html

Chapter 8: Giving People a Voice: Giving Meaning to Democracy
 1 I discuss this exchange here: Furedi, F. (2015) 'Why the opinion polls got it so wrong'. *spiked*, 11 May, https://www.spiked-online.com/2015 /05/11/why-the-opinion-polls-got-it-so-wrong/
 2 BBC (2010) 'Gordon Brown "bigoted woman" comment caught on tape'. BBC News, 28 April, http://news.bbc.co.uk/1/hi/8649012.stm
 3 Woodcock, A. (2021) 'Labour conference: wrong to say that only women have a cervix, says Keir Starmer'. *Independent*, 26 September, https:// www.independent.co.uk/news/uk/politics/keir-starmer-trans-rights -duffield-b1927169.html
 4 Rothwell, J. (2016) 'Leading French philosopher: Marine Le Pen may win election as people have lost interest in whether politicians tell the truth'. *Telegraph*, 20 November, https://www.telegraph.co.uk/news/20 16/11/20/leading-french-philosopher-marine-le-pen-may-win-election -as-peo/
 5 Frank, T. (2020) *The People, No: A Brief History of Anti-Populism*. New York: Metropolitan Books, p. 13.
 6 Bolton, W. (2025) 'Mother banned from playground after complaining about trans identity lessons'. *Telegraph*, 13 April, https://www.telegraph .co.uk/news/2025/04/13/mum-banned-school-playground-trans-iden tity-row/
 7 Carroll, C. (2024) 'Irish voters overwhelmingly reject proposed changes to constitution'. *Guardian*, 9 March, https://www.theguardian.com/wo rld/2024/mar/09/vote-referendum-modernise-ireland-constitution-wo men-home
 8 Rancière, J. (2016) 'Europe: the return of the people, or of populism?'. Verso Books blogs, 24 October, https://www.versobooks.com/en-gb/ blogs/news/2896-europe-the-return-of-the-people-or-of-populism
 9 See, for example, 'The scientization of politics and public opinion'. In Habermas, J. (1971) *Toward a Rational Society: Student Protest, Science, and Politics*. Boston, MA: Beacon Press.
10 Saul, H. (2016) 'Richard Dawkins accuses David Cameron of "playing

Russian Roulette" with UK's future over EU referendum'. *Independent,*
1 June, https://www.independent.co.uk/news/people/richard-dawkins
-eu-referendum-brexit-david-cameron-a7059201.html

11 Ibid.

12 See the discussion in Furedi, F. (2018) *How Fear Works: Culture of Fear in the Twenty-first Century.* London: Bloomsbury, pp. 164–6.

13 Steerpike (2021) 'Fact check: what did Michael Gove actually say about "experts"?'. *Spectator,* 2 September, https://www.spectator.co.uk/article /fact-check-what-did-michael-gove-actually-say-about-experts/

14 Norris, P. and Inglehart, R. (2019) *Cultural Backlash: Trump, Brexit, and Authoritarian Populism.* Cambridge: Cambridge University Press, p. 5.

15 Motta, M. (2017) '"Had enough of experts?" Anti-intellectualism is linked to voters' support for movements that are skeptical of expertise'. LSE Blogs, 30 August, https://blogs.lse.ac.uk/usappblog/2017/08/30 /had-enough-of-experts-anti-intellectualism-is-linked-to-voters-sup port-for-movements-that-are-skeptical-of-expertise/

16 Mair, P. (2002) 'Populist democracy vs party democracy'. In Meny, Y. and Surel, Y. (eds) *Democracies and the Populist Challenge.* London: Palgrave Macmillan, pp. 81–98, p. 82.

17 Fiorina, M.P. (2019) 'The democratic distemper'. Hoover Institution, 14 May, https://www.hoover.org/research/democratic-distemper

18 Saviano, R. (2022) 'Giorgia Meloni is a danger to Italy and the rest of Europe'. *Guardian,* 24 September, https://www.theguardian.com/world /commentisfree/2022/sep/24/giorgia-meloni-is-a-danger-to-italy-and -the-rest-of-europe-far-right

19 Bonikowski, B. and Zhang, Y. (2023) 'Populism as dog-whistle politics: anti-elite discourse and sentiments toward minority groups'. *Social Forces,* 102(1), 180–201.

20 Holl-Allen, G. and Penna, D. (2025) 'Labour minister dismisses rape gangs as "dog whistle" issue'. *Telegraph,* 3 May, https://www.telegra ph.co.uk/politics/2025/05/03/labour-minister-dismisses-rape-gangs-as -dog-whistle-problem/

21 Beppler-Spahl, S. (2025) *Silencing Alternatives: Germany's War on Free Speech.* Brussels: MCC-Brussels.

22 Ibid., pp. 16–17.

23 Ibid., p. 22.

24 Zitelmann, R. (2024) 'Darf ich alles sagen? Viele Bürger fühlen sich unfrei – große Ausnahme sind Grünen-Fans'. *Focus,* 26 October, https://www.focus.de/politik/meinung/gastbeitrag-von-rainer-zitelma nn-umfrage-am-ehesten-denken-gruenen-waehler-dass-sie-frei-ihre -politische-meinung-sagen-koennen_id_260413907.html

25 See Noelle-Neumann, E. (1993) *The Spiral of Silence: Public Opinion –
    Our Social Skin*. Chicago: University of Chicago Press.
26 Neuwirth, K., Frederick, E. and Mayo, C. (2007) 'The spiral of silence and
    fear of isolation'. *Journal of Communication*, 57(3), 450–68.
27 Populace (2004) *Social Pressure Index: Private Opinion in America*.
    https://static1.squarespace.com/static/59153bc0e6f2e109b2a85cbc/t/67
    d0d70838fad962d3d58dfb/1741739814102/Social+Pressure+Index
28 Ibid., p. 5.
29 Gibson, J.L. and Sutherland, J.L. (2023) 'Keeping your mouth shut: spi-
    raling self-censorship in the United States'. *Political Science Quarterly*,
    138(3), 361–76, p. 361.
30 Ekins, E. (2020) 'Poll: 62% of Americans say they have political views
    they're afraid to share'. Cato Institute, 22 July, https://www.cato.org
    /survey-reports/poll-62-americans-say-they-have-political-views-they
    re-afraid-share#introduction
31 Populace, 'Populace Insights: Private Opinion in America 2025'. https://
    static1.squarespace.com/static/59153bc0e6f2e109b2a85cbc/t/6827531
    73ce4330d6ed785b0/1747407640404/Populace+Insights+-+Private+
    Opinion+in+America+2025.pdf
32 Robison, C. (2024) 'Commitment to democracy doesn't end at the ballot
    box'. FIRE, 4 November, https://www.thefire.org/news/commitment
    -democracy-doesnt-end-ballot-box
33 Franks, S. (2015) 'How could the polls have been so wrong?', UK Election
    Analysis, 16 May, https://www.electionanalysis.uk/uk-election-analysis
    -2015/section-2-voters/how-could-the-polls-have-been-so-wrong/
34 Wright, E.W. (2024) 'Young people, "woke" culture and self-censorship
    – How can we listen to what we aren't hearing?'. Strat7 Jigsaw, April,
    https://www.jigsaw-research.co.uk/blog/how-can-we-listen-to-what
    -we-arent-hearing/
35 Attenborough, F. (2024) 'Diversity training "forces workers to hide
    beliefs" for fear of losing job'. Free Speech Union, 1 April, https://fre
    espeechunion.org/diversity-training-forces-workers-to-hide-beliefs-for
    -fear-of-losing-job/
36 Loury, G.C. (1994) 'Self-censorship in public discourse: a theory of
    "political correctness" and related phenomena'. *Rationality and Society*,
    6(4), 428–61.
37 MacIntyre, A. (2024) *The Total State: How Liberal Democracies Become
    Tyrannies*. New York: Regnery, p. 68.
38 Ibid.
39 Moody, K. (2021) 'Stop calling women "females"'. *Daily Nexus*, 24 July,
    https://dailynexus.com/2021-07-24/stop-calling-women-females/

40 Clayton, T. and Nigatu, H. (2014) '6 reasons you should stop referring to women as "females" right now'. *Buzzfeed*, 8 October, https://www.bu zzfeed.com/tracyclayton/stop-calling-women-females

41 de Klerk, S. (2020) 'Why should you stop referring to women as "females"?'. LinkedIn, 26 November, https://www.linkedin.com/pulse /why-should-you-stop-referring-women-females-sacha-de-klerk/

42 Cited in https://www.euractiv.com/section/central-europe/opinion /hungary-s-turn-as-eu-president/

43 Habermas, J. (2011) 'Europe's post-democratic era'. *Guardian*, 10 November, https://www.theguardian.com/commentisfree/2011/nov /10/jurgen-habermas-europe-post-democratic

44 For a discussion of this revolt, see Slater, T. (2025) 'How flying the flag became a symbol of revolt'. *spiked*, 20 August, https://www.spiked-on line.com/2025/08/20/how-flying-the-flag-became-a-symbol-of-revolt/

45 Addley, E. (2025) '"Don't call this racist": row grows over motives behind England flag campaign'. *Guardian*, 20 August, https://www.theguardi an.com/uk-news/2025/aug/20/row-grows-over-motives-behind-engla nd-flag-campaign-far-right-racist

46 Hughes, P. (2025) 'St George's cross "intimidating", council says'. BBC News, 22 August, https://www.bbc.co.uk/news/articles/cy0q109g4nno

47 Clarke-Ezzidio, H. (2025) 'Flags and loathing in Birmingham'. *New Statesman*, 23 August, https://www.newstatesman.com/politics/society /2025/08/flags-and-loathing-in-birmingham

48 Third Way (2025) 'Was it something I said?'. 22 August, https://www. thirdway.org/memo/was-it-something-i-said

49 Millward, D. (2025) 'The "woke" language Democrats have been told to stop using'. *Telegraph*, 25 August, https://www.telegraph.co.uk/us/poli tics/2025/08/25/the-32-woke-words-democrats-told-stop-using/

50 Mutascu, M., Strango, C. and Turcu, C. (2025) 'Online social media and populism in Europe'. *European Journal of Political Economy*, 86, 102619.

51 Fukuyama, F. (2025) 'It's the Internet Stupid', https://www.persuasion .community/p/its-the-internet-stupid?utm_source=substack&utm _medium=email

Chapter 9: Conclusion: Taking Control

1 New Economics Foundation (2025) 'The big lesson progressives need to learn to counter right wing populism'. 20 January, https://neweconom ics.org/2025/01/the-big-lesson-progressives-need-to-learn-to-counter -right-wing-populism

2 Kaufmann, E. (2025) 'Time for populism to grow up'. *City Journal*,

27 February, https://www.city-journal.org/article/liberal-democracy-trump-populism-conservatives

3 Bild, 'Wahlkampf bizarr: Kölner Parteien sollen nicht über flüchtlinge reden'. 28 August, https://www.bild.de/politik/inland/wahlkampf-biza rr-koelner-parteien-sollen-nicht-ueber-fluechtlinge-reden-68b018bad4 92032667a5d6dd

4 Ibid.

5 Jones, S. (2025) 'Far-right Chega party becomes main opposition in Portugal's parliament'. *Guardian*, 28 May, https://www.theguardian.com/world/2025/may/28/far-right-chega-party-becomes-main-opposition-in-portugals-parliament

6 SEC Newgate EU (2024) 'How Portugal's far-right shift will influence the European political landscape'. 13 March, https://www.secnewgate.eu/how-portugals-far-right-shift-will-influence-the-european-political-landscape/

7 Santos, N., Serra-Silva, S. and Silva, T. (2025) 'The role of radical right parties in escalating parliamentary conflict: policy issues and party responses in Portugal'. *Frontiers in Political Science*, 7, https://www.frontiersin.org/journals/political-science/articles/10.3389/fpos.2025.1553921/full

8 Sandel, M. (2020) 'Disdain for the less educated is the last acceptable prejudice'. *The New York Times*, 2 September, https://www.nytimes.com/2020/09/02/opinion/education-prejudice.html

9 Schlott, R. (2024) 'It's not politics fueling the great American divide – it's elite contempt for working class: author'. *New York Post*, 29 March, https://nypost.com/2024/03/29/us-news/batya-ungar-sargon-calls-trump-the-working-class-voice-in-book/

10 Yang, L. (2019) 'People are criticizing Bill Maher for being "elitist" after he said people in Republican states are jealous of the "prosperity party" in Blue states'. *Business Insider*, 24 February, https://www.businessinsider.com/bill-maher-criticized-comments-americans-red-states-real-time-2019-2

11 See Bourdieu, P. (2010) *Distinction: A Social Critique of the Judgment of Taste*. London: Routledge, p. 49.

12 https://www.ipsos.com/sites/default/files/ct/news/documents/2024-02/Ipsos%20Populism%20Final%20February%202024%20AUSTRALIA.pdf

13 Blake, N. (2018) 'The dual legitimation crisis: elitism, populism, and political power'. *Public Discourse*, 24 April, http://www.thepublicdiscourse.com/2018/04/21326/

14 Editorial Board (2024) 'Democrats' huge mistake, revolt of the working

class and other commentary'. *New York Post*, 6 November, https://ny post.com/2024/11/06/opinion/democrats-huge-mistake-revolt-of-the -working-class-and-other-commentary/

15 Furedi, F. (2020) *Democracy Under Siege: Don't Let Them Lock It Down!*, Zer0 Books, p. 8.

16 Kaltwasser, C.R. (2014) 'The responses of populism to Dahl's democratic dilemmas'. *Political Studies*, 62(3), 470–87.

17 Goodhart, D. (2017) *The Road to Somewhere; the New Tribes Shaping British Politics*. London: Penguin Books, p. 43.

18 See https://x.com/alanvibe/status/1966805491981381990

19 Gerbaudo, P. (2020) 'Populism and the politics of control'. In Eklundh, E. and Knott, A. (eds) *The Populist Manifesto: Understanding the Spectre of Populism*. London: Rowman & Littlefield, pp. 39–54.

20 Runciman, D. (2025) 'Brexit's failures could foreshadow Trump's. Just not in the way you might think'. *New York Times Magazine*, 19 May, https://www.nytimes.com/2025/05/19/magazine/brexit-trump-populi sm.html

21 Richards, S. (2016) 'Take back control – the slogan the left should make its own'. *Guardian*, 19 December, https://www.theguardian.com/com mentisfree/2016/dec/19/take-back-control-slogan-left-power-right-sta te-intervention

22 Haughton, T., 'It's the slogan, stupid: The Brexit Referendum'. University of Birmingham, https://www.birmingham.ac.uk/research/perspective /eu-ref-haughton

23 See the discussion in Goldsmith, P. (2017) 'Why "take back control" trumped "project fear"'. UK in a Changing Europe, 23 November, https://ukandeu.ac.uk/why-take-back-control-trumped -project-fear/

24 Ibid.

25 McCormick, J.P. (2001) 'Machiavellian democracy: controlling elites with ferocious populism'. *American Political Science Review*, 95(2), 297–313.

26 Ibid., p. 298.

27 Machiavelli, N. (2009) *Discourses on Livy*. Chicago: University of Chicago Press, p. 116.

28 See Heiman, H. (1973) 'The building of a populist impulse'. Address to the Annual Faculty Lecture Series, University of North Dakota, https:// files.eric.ed.gov/fulltext/ED088114.pdf

29 Frank, T. (2020) 'The pessimistic style in American politics and its eternal war on reform'. *Harper's Magazine*, May.

30 Furedi, F. (2002) 'Illiberal liberalism: a genealogy'. Institute for European, Russian and Eurasian Studies (IERES), George Washington University,

16 December, https://www.illiberalism.org/illiberal-liberalism-a-genea logy/

31 Brennan, J. (2016) *Against Democracy*. Princeton, NJ: Princeton University Press.

32 Zakaria, F. (1997) 'The rise of illiberal democracy'. *Foreign Affairs*, 76(6), 22–43.

33 Spruyt, B., Keppens, G. and Van Droogenbroeck, F. (2016) 'Who supports populism and what attracts people to it?'. *Political Research Quarterly*, 69(2), 335–46, p. 336.

34 'Common sense', Oxford English Dictionary, https://www.oed.com/search/dictionary/?scope=HistoricalThesaurus&q=common+sense

35 Trump, D.J. (2025) 'The Inaugural Address'. White House, 20 January, https://www.whitehouse.gov/remarks/2025/01/the-inaugural-address/

36 Newth, G. and Scopelliti, A. (2023) 'Common sense, populism, and reactionary politics on Twitter: an analysis of populist far-right common-sense narratives between 2008 and 2022'. *Party Politics*, 31(2), 375–91.

37 Arendt, H. (1994) 'Understanding and politics'. In *Hannah Arendt: Essays in Understanding 1930–1954* (ed. J. Kohn). New York: Harcourt Brace, p. 318.

38 Arendt, H. (1982) *Lectures on Kant's Political Philosophy* (ed. R. Beiner). Chicago: University of Chicago Press, p. 70.

39 Arendt, 'Understanding and politics', p. 311.

40 Ibid., p. 314.

41 See Filippini, M. (2016) *Using Gramsci: A New Approach*. London: Pluto Press, p. 110.

42 Cited in Crehan, K. (2016) *Gramsci's Common Sense*. Durham, NC: Duke University Press, p. 48.

43 Arendt, 'Understanding and politics', pp. 316–17.

44 Robustelli, L. (2025) 'When the word "common sense" becomes scary'. *Eunews*, 22 January, https://www.eunews.it/en/2025/01/22/when-the-word-common-sense-becomes-scary/

45 Borriello et al., 'Populism and democracy', p. 416.

46 Ibid., p. 432.

47 Rosenfeld, S. (2011) *Common Sense: A Political History*. Cambridge, MA: Harvard University Press.

48 Ibid.

49 Tanskanen, A.O. (2013) 'The association between grandmaternal invest-ment and early years overweight in the UK'. *Evolutionary Psychology*, 11(2), 417–25.

50 CGTN (2023) '"Italy needs immigration" – Italian PM Meloni back-tracks on anti-immigration stance'. 25 July, https://newseu.cgtn.com

/news/2023-07-25/-Italy-needs-immigration-Italian-PM-Meloni-backt
racks-on-anti-immigration-stance-1lHVXvQjhoA/index.html

51 Sánchez, Á. (2023) 'Market forces pressure European leaders to reverse
course'. *El País*, 10 August, https://english.elpais.com/economy-and-bu
siness/2023-08-10/market-forces-pressure-european-leaders-to-rever
se-course.html

52 Pethokoukis, J. (2025) 'The failure of populist economics: then and now'.
AEI, 23 April, https://www.aei.org/economics/the-failure-of-populist
-economics-then-and-now/

References

Albertazzi, D. and McDonnell, D. (eds) (2007) *Twenty-first Century Populism: The Spectre of Western European Democracy*. Berlin: Springer.

Arditi, B. (2024) *Is There Such a Thing as Populism?: 3 Provocations and 5 1/2 Proposals*. London: Taylor & Francis.

Arendt, H. (1982) *Lectures on Kant's Political Philosophy* (ed. R. Beiner). Chicago: University of Chicago Press.

Arendt, H. (1994) 'Understanding and politics'. In *Hannah Arendt: Essays in Understanding 1930–1954* (ed. J. Kohn). New York: Harcourt Brace.

Bachrach, P. (1967) *The Theory of Democratic Elitism: A Critique*. New York: Little Brown.

Bauman, Z. (2013) *Community*. Cambridge: Polity.

Bauman, Z. (2017) *Retrotopia*. Cambridge: Polity.

Baumeister, R.F. (1986) *Identity: Cultural Change and the Struggle for Self*. Oxford: Oxford University Press.

Bellah, R.N., Madsen, R., Sullivan, W.M., Swidler, A. and Tipton, S.M. (1996) *Habits of the Heart: Individualism and Commitment in American Life*. Berkeley, CA: University of California.

Beppler-Spahl, S. (2025) *Silencing Alternatives: Germany's War on Free Speech*. Brussels: MCC-Brussels.

Bourdieu, P. (2010) *Distinction: A Social Critique of the Judgment of Taste*. London: Routledge.

Brennan, J. (2016) *Against Democracy*. Princeton, NJ: Princeton University Press.

Brown, W. (2021) 'Foreword'. In Biglieri, P., Cadahia, L. and Ciccariello-Maher, G., *Seven Essays on Populism*. Cambridge: Polity.

Canovan, M. (1996) *Nationhood and Political Theory*. Cheltenham: Edward Elgar.

Canovan, M. (2005) *The People*. London: Polity.

Casullo, M.E. (2020) 'Populism and myth'. In Eklundh, E. and Knott, A. (eds) *The Populist Manifesto: Understanding the Spectre of Populism*. London: Rowman & Littlefield, pp. 25–38.

Colliot-Thélène, C. (2018) 'Populism as a conceptual problem'. In Fitzi, G., Mackert, J. and Turner, B. (eds) *Populism and the Crisis of Democracy*. London: Routledge, pp. 17–26.

Crehan, K. (2016) *Gramsci's Common Sense*. Durham, NC: Duke University Press.

Dalton, R.J. and Wattenberg, M.P. (eds) (2002) *Parties Without Partisans: Political Change in Advanced Industrial Democracies*. Oxford: Oxford University Press.

Davis, F. (1979) *Yearning for Yesterday: A Sociology of Nostalgia*. New York: The Free Press.

Diehl, P. and Bargetz, B. (eds) (2023) *The Complexity of Populism: New Approaches and Methods*. London: Taylor & Francis.

Eklundth, E. and Knott, A. (2020) *The Populist Manifesto: Understanding the Spectre of Populism*. London: Rowman & Littlefield.

Erikson, E.H. (ed.) (1963) *Youth: Change and Challenge*. New York: Basic Books.

Erikson, E.H. (1964) 'Identity and uprootedness in our time'. In *Insight and Responsibility: Lectures on the Ethical Implications of Psychoanalytic Insight*. London: Faber & Faber.

Espejo, P.O. (2015) *The Time of Popular Sovereignty: Process and the Democratic State*. University Park, PA: Penn State Press.

Espejo, P.O. (2017) 'Populism and the idea of the people'. In Kaltwasser, C.R., Taggart, P.A., Espejo, P.O. and Ostiguy, P. (eds) *The Oxford Handbook of Populism*. Oxford: Oxford University Press, pp. 607–28.

Filippini, M. (2016) *Using Gramsci: A New Approach*. London: Pluto Press.

Fitzgerald, J. (2018) *Close to Home*. Cambridge: Cambridge University Press.

Fitzi, G., Mackert, J. and Turner, B. (eds) (2018) *Populism and the Crisis of Democracy*. London: Routledge.

Frank, T. (2020) *The People, No: A Brief History of Anti-Populism*. New York: Metropolitan Books.

Fromm, E. (1965) *Escape from Freedom*. New York: Henry Holt and Company.

Fukuyama, F. (1992) *The End of History and the Last Man*. New York: The Free Press.

Furedi, F. (1989) *The Mau Mau War in Perspective*. Athens, OH: Ohio University Press.

Furedi, F. (2013) *On Tolerance*. London: Bloomsbury Academic.

Furedi, F. (2018) *How Fear Works: Culture of Fear in the Twenty-first Century*. London: Bloomsbury.

Furedi, F. (2020) *Democracy Under Siege: Don't Let them Shut It Down*. London: Zer0 Books.

Furedi, F. (2024) *The War Against the Past: Why The West Must Fight For Its History*. Cambridge: Polity.

Gerbaudo, P. (2020) 'Populism and the politics of control'. In Eklundh, E. and Knott, A. (eds) *The Populist Manifesto*. London: Rowman & Littlefield, pp. 39–54.

Germani, G. (2021) *Authoritarianism, National Populism and Fascism*. London: Routledge.

Geuss, R. (2009) *Politics and the Imagination*. Princeton, NJ: Princeton University Press.

Giddens, A. (1991) *Modernity and Self-Identity*. Cambridge: Polity.

Goodhart, D. (2017) *The Road to Somewhere; the New Tribes Shaping British Politics*. London: Penguin Books.

Goodwin, M. (2023) *Values, Voice and Virtue: the New British Politics*. London: Random House.

Gouldner, A. (ed.) (1950) *Studies in Leadership: Leadership and Democratic Action*. New York: Harper & Brothers.

Himmelfarb, G. (2002) 'The illusions of cosmopolitanism'. In Nussbaum, M., *For Love of Country?*, Boston, MA: Beacon Press, pp. 72–7.

Hochschild, A.R. (2018) *Strangers in their Own Land: Anger and Mourning on the American Right*. New York: The New Press.

Hunter, J.D. (2024) *Democracy and Solidarity: On the Cultural Roots of America's Political Crisis*. New Haven, CT: Yale University Press.

Inglehart, R. (1977) *The Silent Revolution: Changing Values and Political Styles in Advanced Industrial Society*. Princeton, NJ: Princeton University Press.

Inglehart, R. (1990) *Cultural Shift in Advanced Industrial Society*. Princeton, NJ: Princeton University Press.

Ionescu, G. and Gellner, E. (eds) (1969) *Populism: Its Meanings and National Characteristics*. London: Weidenfeld and Nicolson.

Kaltwasser, C.R. (2018) 'How to define populism? Reflections on a contested concept and its (mis)use in the social sciences'. In Fitzi, G., Mackert, J. and Turner, B. (eds) *Populism and the Crisis of Democracy*. London: Routledge, pp. 62–78.

Kazin, M. (1995) *The Populist Persuasion: An American History*. Ithaca, NY: Cornell University Press.

Keniston, K. (1963) 'Social change and youth in America'. In Erikson, E.H. (ed.), *Youth: Change and Challenge*. New York: Basic Books.

Knott, A. (2020) 'Populism: the politics of definition'. In Eklundh, E. and Knott, A. (eds) *The Populist Manifesto*. London: Rowman & Littlefield, pp. 9–24.

Kolko, G. (1968) *The Politics of War: The World and United States*. New York: Vintage Books.

Lasch, C. (1996) *The Revolt of the Elites and the Betrayal of Democracy*. New York: W.W. Norton & Company.

Lasch, C. (2013) *The True and Only Heaven: Progress and Its Critics*. New York: Norton.

Lemert, C. (2011) 'A history of identity: the riddle at the heart of the mystery of life'. In Elliott, A. (ed.) *Routledge Handbook of Identity Studies*. London: Routledge.

Lippmann, W. (1922) *Public Opinion*. New York: Macmillan.

Lipset, S.M. (1959) *Political Man*. London: Mercury Books.

Machiavelli, N. (2009) *Discourses on Livy*. Chicago: University of Chicago Press.

MacIntyre, A. (2024) *The Total State: How Liberal Democracies Become Tyrannies*. New York: Regnery.

Mackert, J. (2018) 'Introduction'. In Fitzi, G., Mackert, J. and Turner, B. (eds) *Populism and the Crisis of Democracy*. London: Routledge, pp. 1–12.

Maier, C.S. (2016) *Once within Borders: Territories of Power, Wealth, and Belonging since 1500*. Cambridge, MA: Harvard University Press.

Mair, P. (2002) 'Populist democracy vs party democracy'. In Meny, Y. and Surel, Y. (eds) *Democracies and the Populist Challenge*, London: Palgrave Macmillan, pp. 81–98.

Mair, P. (2013) *Ruling the Void*. London: Verso.

Marchart, O. (2023) 'Liberal anti-populism as a case of demophobia'. In Payne, D., Stagnell, A. and Strandberg, G. (eds) *Populism and The People in Contemporary Critical Thought*. London: Bloomsbury Academic.

Marx, J.H. (1980) 'The ideological construction of post-modern identity models in contemporary cultural movements'. In Robertson, R. and Holzner, B. (eds) *Identity and Authority: Explorations in the Theory of Society*. Oxford: Basil Blackwell.

McCormick, J P. (2019) 'The new ochlophobia? Populism, majority rule and prospects for democratic republicanism'. In Elazar, Y. and Rousselière, G. (eds) *Republican Democracy*. Cambridge: Cambridge University Press, pp. 122–42.

Miller D. (2017) *Strangers in Our Midst: The Political Philosophy of Immigration*. Cambridge, MA: Harvard University Press.

Möhring, J. and Prins, G. (2013) *Sail On, O Ship of State*. London: Notting Hill Editions.

Mouffe, C. (2018) *For a Left Populism*. London: Verso.

Mudde, C. and Kaltwasser, C.R. (2012) *Populism in Europe and the Americas*. Cambridge: Cambridge University Press.

Müller, J.-W. (2013) *Contesting Democracy: Political Ideas in Twentieth Century Europe*. New Haven, CT: Yale University Press.

Müller, J-W. (2016) *What Is Populism?* Philadelphia, PA: University of Pennsylvania Press.

Müller, J.-W. (2017) *What is Populism?* Harmondsworth: Penguin Books.

Noelle-Neumann, E. (1993) *The Spiral of Silence: Public Opinion – Our Social Skin*. Chicago: University of Chicago Press.

Norris, P. and Inglehart, R. (2019) *Cultural Backlash: Trump, Brexit, and Authoritarian Populism*. Cambridge: Cambridge University Press.

Nussbaum, M. (2002) 'Patriotism and cosmopolitanism'. In Nussbaum, M., *For Love of Country?* Boston, MA: Beacon Press.

Ober, J. (2017) *Demopolis: Democracy Before Liberalism in Theory and Practice*. Cambridge: Cambridge University Press.

Palonen, E. (2020) 'Ten theses on populism – and democracy'. In Eklundh, E. and Knott, A. (eds) *The Populist Manifesto*. London: Rowman & Littlefield, pp. 55–70.

Prentoulis, M. (2020) 'Left populism as a political project'. In Eklundh, E. and Knott, A. (eds) *The Populist Manifesto*. London: Rowman & Littlefield, pp. 95–106.

Putnam, R.D. (2000) *Bowling Alone: The Collapse and Revival of American Community*. New York: Simon and Schuster.

Reno, R. (2019) *Return of the Strong Gods*. Washington, DC: Regnery Gateway.

Revelli, M. (2019) *The New Populism*. London: Verso.

Rosenfeld, S. (2011) *Common Sense: A Political History*. Cambridge, MA: Harvard University Press.

Schedler, A. (1997) 'Introduction: antipolitics – closing and colonizing the public sphere'. In Schedler, A. (ed.) *The End of Politics? Explorations into Modern Antipolitics*. Houndmills: Macmillan Press, pp. 1–20.

Scruton, R. (2014) *How To Be a Conservative*. London: Bloomsbury.

Seligman, A. (2001) *The Idea of Civil Society*. New York: Knopf.

Stanley, J. (2018) *How Fascism Works: the Politics of Us and Them*. New York: Random House.

Stavrakakis, Y. (2015) 'Die Rückkehr des "Volkes": Populismus und Anti-Populismus im Schatten der europäischen Krise'. In Agridopoulos, A. and Papagiannopoulos, I. (eds) *Griechenland im europäischen Kontext: Krise und Krisendiskurse*. Heidelberg: Springer-Verlag.

Unger, I (1964). *Populism: Nostalgic or Progressive?* New York: Rand MacNally.

Voutyras, S. (2024) 'Anti-populism, meritocracy and (technocratic) elitism'. In Stavrakakis, Y. and Katsambekis, G. (eds) *Research Handbook on Populism*. Cheltenham: Edward Elgar Publishing, pp. 35–47.

Wodak, R. (2020) *The Politics of Fear: The Shameless Normalization of Far-right Discourse*. London: Sage Publications.

Yack, B. (2014) *Nationalism and the Moral Psychology of Community in Modern Political Life*. Chicago: University of Chicago Press.

Index